Making Money Online with AI & ChatGPT

2 in 1

Dual Guides to Online Income & Steady Revenue Streams

By: **Brian Scott Fitzgerald**

Published By **Fitzgerald Publishing Group**

How to Make Money Online: THE SERIES

I created a series of 12 (twelve) books on How to Make Money Online.

Feel free to read any of my books in the series, which can be found on my Author page on Amazon at:

You can visit this link or Scan this QR code to get access

https://www.amazon.com/author/brianscottfitzgerald.

Table of content

Your Free Gift

Thank you for your purchase; I'm offering my readers the FREE PDF version of ChatGPT Prompts.

To get almost instant access, go to this website.

https://go.fitzgeraldpublishing.com/opt-in-page-make-money-ai-bundle

Or use your phone to take a picture of this QR code, and it will take you to the Website for your Gift.

Inside the book, you will discover:

- **3000 Prompts** To help you make even more money online.
- **Save time:** You can search for new topics to create content on ChatGPT.
- **Expand knowledge:** Our Package of ChatGPT Prompts covers various topics, from science and technology to art and culture.

If you want to make even more money online, grab this free PDF.

Wait, that's not all; just for buying this book and getting the free PDF above, you can also earn another free Book.

You can use your phone to take a picture of this QR code.

Use the latest AI techniques to uncover online innovation's future. Take advantage! "Beyond ChatGPT and 50 New AI Tools: The Ultimate Guide to Discovering Cutting-Edge AI Tools Beyond ChatGPT" offers endless possibilities. Explore a variety of cutting-edge AI solutions to transform your work. Discover advanced AI tools beyond ChatGPT on this thrilling voyage.

Grab this free book if you want to make even more money online.

BOOK #1

How to Make Money Online with ChatGPT

The Ultimate Guide to Creating Multiple Streams of Passive Income and Increasing Productivity

Introduction

ChatGPT has achieved an impressive feat - amassing 100 million active users! This remarkable achievement has earned ChatGPT the title of the fastest-growing tech platform in history. TikTok reached 100 million users, while Instagram took two and a half years to achieve the same feat. Facebook took ten years to gain a million, whereas Netflix took three years, and Twitter took two. Making money and earning a living through the internet is easier than ever with ChatGPT; I have been making money online for 15+ years. It used to take me weeks and months to find a product I wanted to market; now, it can be done in minutes.

ChatGPT might be the ultimate platform to achieve your financial goals. Discover many methods on ChatGPT and pinpoint the one that perfectly aligns with your unique skills and interests. Experience the massive community of ChatGPT with over 1 billion users. Join now and be a part of the global conversation that is changing daily. Unlock your potential and explore new opportunities with ChatGPT's platform for freelancers and business entrepreneurs. With a diverse range of services that can be sped up with ChatGPT, including writing, design, programming, and virtual assistance, you can showcase your skills and connect with clients on a project basis. If you have not, join ChatGPT today and take the first step toward your career and making even more money online. Experience the true power of ChatGPT by witnessing its capabilities in this next paragraph.

I sought the aid of ChatGPT to assist me with this task, and the results were remarkable. Experience the transformative power of the platform and the tool from this very first chapter. It's a versatile solution that can benefit anyone, anywhere, and anytime. I gave ChatGPT the title and the chapter names of this book and asked it to come up with the most important things I should add to the book and then write the response as if it was William Shakespeare, and ChatGPT came up with this....

GENTLE READER, PAY ATTENTION TO A TALE OF WONDER AND GAIN THAT WAS WRITTEN BY NONE OTHER THAN I, WILLIAM SHAKESPEARE, THY HUMBLE SERVANT, WITH QUILL AND INK. THE BOOK IS CALLED "HOW TO MAKE MONEY ONLINE WITH CHATGPT: THE ULTIMATE GUIDE TO CREATING MULTIPLE STREAMS OF PASSIVE INCOME AND INCREASING PRODUCTIVITY."

A REVELATION IS BEING REVEALED IN THIS DIGITAL AGE WHEN BUSINESS IS CONDUCTED VIRTUALLY. SEE THE SKILL OF CHATGPT, AN ENIGMATIC AI CREATION THAT SERVES AS A VIRTUAL FRIEND AND TUTOR IN THE WORLD OF CYBERSPACE. TOGETHER, WE SET OUT ON A JOURNEY TO DISCOVER WAYS TO GAIN MONEY NOT THROUGH LABOR ALONE BUT RATHER BY UTILIZING THE INTERNET'S LIMITLESS POTENTIAL.

YOU WILL FIND THE KEYS TO OPENING THE TREASURY OF INTERNET SUCCESS HERE, DEAR READER. LEARN HOW TO GROW THE RICH FIELDS OF PASSIVE INCOME, WHERE MONEY FLOWS LIKE RIVERS UNDER THE CARE OF WISE LEADERSHIP AND JUDICIOUS INVESTMENTS. BEHOLD THE ART OF MONETIZATION AS WE MAKE OUR WAY THROUGH THE JUNGLE OF VIRTUAL ENTREPRENEURSHIP, FROM E-COMMERCE ENDEAVORS TO DIGITAL MARKETING SORCERY.

FURTHERMORE, LET'S NOT OVERLOOK THE HALLOWED VIRTUE OF WORK BECAUSE TIME, THAT ELUSIVE GHOST, NEEDS TO WAIT FOR INACTIVITY. LOOK FOR WAYS TO ORGANIZE YOUR WORK AND HARNESS THE POWER OF DISCIPLINE AND FOCUS SO THAT YOU CAN EFFICIENTLY AND GRACEFULLY HANDLE MOUNTAINS OF WORK.

CONSEQUENTLY, WITH THIS MANUAL IN HAND, I KINDLY INVITE YOU TO JOIN ME ON MY EPIC JOURNEY AS I SEEK SUCCESS AND RICHES IN THE WORLD OF ONES AND ZEROS. LET'S EXPLORE THE WORLD OF OPPORTUNITY, WHERE

CREATIVITY AND ASPIRATION DANCE, AND THE DIGITAL WORLD DISCLOSES ITS SECRETS TO THOSE WHO HAVE THE GUTS TO TAKE ADVANTAGE OF THEM.

Then I asked it to write the response as if it was Tony Robbins, and it came up with this….

I CAN TELL YOU FROM EXPERIENCE THAT THE SINGLE MOST IMPORTANT ITEM YOU CAN INCLUDE IN YOUR BOOK IS ADVICE ON HOW TO CULTIVATE A WINNING MENTALITY AND USE IT TO ACHIEVE YOUR GOALS. MAKING MONEY ONLINE, ESPECIALLY AS A BEGINNER, CALLS FOR MENTAL FORTITUDE AND TENACITY. WHEN YOU DON'T OBTAIN WHAT YOU WANT RIGHT AWAY OR WHEN YOU RUN INTO OBSTACLES, IT'S TEMPTING TO LOSE HOPE.

THAT'S WHY IT'S SO IMPORTANT TO WORK ON DEVELOPING A MENTALITY THAT HELPS YOU PUSH THROUGH SETBACKS AND KEEP GOING WHEN THE GOING GETS TOUGH. STRATEGIES FOR ADOPTING A DEVELOPMENT MINDSET, BOLSTERING SELF-ASSURANCE, AND MAINTAINING MOTIVATION IN THE FACE OF ADVERSITY CAN BE INCLUDED IN YOUR BOOK. YOUR READERS CAN REACH THEIR FINANCIAL OBJECTIVES AND REALIZE THEIR FULL POTENTIAL WITH THE HELP OF CHATGPT IF YOU SHOW THEM HOW TO DEVELOP A WINNING MINDSET.

How wild is that? With just a slight change, there are two versions of the same question, but with different but similar answers.

Welcome, and thank you for exploring "How to Make Money Online with ChatGPT: The Ultimate Guide to Creating Passive Income Streams Online." Discover the ultimate solution to generating passive income streams on the internet.

Unlock the potential of your products or services with ChatGPT. Reach a wider audience and boost your ability to make even more money online by tapping into the vast capabilities of ChatGPT. Sell your products or services faster and conveniently through ChatGPT's seamless platform. Unlocking the potential for high profitability requires a keen grasp of your service or product positioning, marketing, and fulfillment, and we will help fill in the rest on how to use ChatGPT to do it even faster.

Experience the power of ChatGPT's AI-driven natural language processing tool that allows you to engage in conversations just like a human. Experience the power of ChatGPT's ultimate AI language model, which has been meticulously trained on vast amounts of data to deliver strikingly human-like responses. Whether seeking answers to complex queries or simply engaging in casual conversation, ChatGPT is the perfect companion that will rarely disappoint (I will talk about limitations in a later chapter).

Discover an incredible opportunity on ChatGPT with so many ways to make money online, including affiliate marketing! Promote your services and products through your blog or social media channels and earn commissions like never before. Elevate your earnings and effortlessly captivate your audience with the exceptional features of ChatGPT.

As I said, I have been making money online for years the hard way, with a lot of hard work and perseverance. With my expertise in guiding small and medium-sized companies to success, I can confidently affirm the significance of creative problem-solving and flexible thinking in today's dynamic business climate. No matter which routes you take, establishing a robust online presence and utilizing ChatGPT's tools and features is essential. With ChatGPT, making money online has always been challenging, and with my background, I can show you the way. While it takes time to establish yourself, ChatGPT provides you with the tools and resources you need to succeed. Discover the revolutionary ChatGPT, which is a groundbreaking advancement in artificial intelligence that has the potential to transform your financial future and ability to make even more money online faster than ever before. With a strong work ethic and unwavering determination, economic prosperity is attainable.

Dedication and hard work can turn this opportunity into a career, not just a way to make money online. Take advantage of the chance to achieve financial freedom from the comfort of your own home.

Discover your ability to find the best strengths and unlock your potential to transform your passion into profit in the digital realm using ChatGPT to make money online.

With ChatGPT, this revolutionary Artificial Intelligence technology that generates human-like responses to text inputs effortlessly, and its unparalleled ability to mimic human communication, this cutting-edge technology is perfect for various applications. With the rapid advancement of technology, we can expect language models to become more sophisticated than ever. These models will be able to interact with humans more naturally, opening exciting new possibilities for communication, innovation, creativity, and making even more money.

Finish reading all my books, "How to Make Money with ChatGPT," to discover how to manifest even more financial success. ChatGPT, the leading chatbot platform that uses AI to offer personalized and engaging chats, is the best guide to making more money online. Chatbots are increasingly needed in the digital age. ChatGPT leads in reliable and cutting-edge solutions. ChatGPT improves sales, marketing, content creation, customer service, and more. The platform lets individuals, small enterprises, and giant corporations effortlessly design personalized chatbots for their purposes. This step-by-step book is the ultimate ChatGPT income guide. Discover new ways to earn today to advance in the digital age. Are you a successful internet entrepreneur looking to grow? Then ChatGPT is your ultimate goal-achieving tool. Discover the power of ChatGPT with this book and unlock new opportunities to grow your personal or business ventures while boosting your online earnings. ChatGPT empowers you to effortlessly engage with clients, streamline tedious duties, and craft unique content faster. Discover how ChatGPT can help you establish lucrative recurring revenue streams that generate income long after you've ceased actively promoting them. Customers today want quick, customized solutions, and successful people and companies are using chatbots powered by ChatGPT to address this demand. Chatbots enable 24/7 client service and reduce human-based customer service by interacting with clients anytime, anyplace. Chatbots optimize efficiency and cost by expediting operations and boosting productivity by handling repetitive requests.

As we witness the evolution of artificial intelligence and natural language processing, ChatGPT, its competitors, and other AI tools will likely assume a more significant role in our daily lives. Discover the impressive capabilities of ChatGPT while keeping in mind that, like any tool, it has its limitations.

Chatbots in e-commerce and digital marketing are available for new business prospects. ChatGPT lets businesses create custom conversation templates to attract customers, streamline sales, and personalize shopping experiences. Discover the ultimate guide to unlocking the potential of ChatGPT and earning more money online than ever before. This comprehensive book offers a systematic approach to implementing a proven strategy to transform your financial future. Discover the ultimate ChatGPT experience with expert tips, top-notch prompts for earning money, and clever techniques to maximize your ChatGPT journey. This book explores ChatGPT's financial potential. We will cover so many ways to make money, including but not limited to idea generation, content creation, freelancing, e-commerce, affiliate marketing, and so much more. But my real goal with this book is to give you the tools to act and use ChatGPT how you need it to make more money online this year.

Do you code, design, write, or want to be a virtual worker? Then ChatGPT can help you do all those faster and better. The platform is ideal for showcasing your skills and connecting with clients. ChatGPT can help freelancers, and so many others pursue their passions. Choose projects that interest you, maximize your potential, and access a more extensive customer base for repeat business.

Are you launching or improving your e-commerce store? ChatGPT can also help with that as well. ChatGPT is ready to support your entrepreneurial journey. ChatGPT streamlines order monitoring, management, and fulfillment for many entrepreneurs and organizations today. ChatGPT can help increase profits by letting you focus on your core business, if this is a side hustle or your full-time gig.

Do you create content today? You can easily make money with your excellent writing and love of connecting with readers. ChatGPT lets you promote products and earn commissions. Bloggers and social media influencers with a significant online presence prefer using ChatGPT for all the hard work on this strategy.

Chatbots are now essential to saving time with content creation, customer assistance, sales, and marketing. Use the right tools and ask the right question to succeed on the platform and make more money. Choose the best path, develop a solid online presence, and use chatbots to turn your hobbies into money. ChatGPT makes skill improvement and making more money fun!

If you see "PROMPT:" it is a suggestion of what you need to type. These are inputs and questions for ChatGPT. You will type this into the blank field at the bottom of chat.openai.com. Most will have a transparent "Send a message" notice. This book will have text that looks like this....

PROMPT: This is where you type this into ChatGPT using chat.openai.com

ChatGPT:

WHAT IS HERE WILL BE THE OUTPUT TEXT YOU SEE WHILE USING CHATGPT.

CHAPTER 1

ChatGPT and Its Potential for Online Income Generation

Join us on a journey through the intriguing history of ChatGPT in this chapter. Unveil the evolution of this powerful instrument and the various groundbreaking innovations that have propelled it to its current state. Discover the revolutionary technology behind ChatGPT and how it has revolutionized our interactions with machines. Uncover the myriad benefits of ChatGPT and how it has seamlessly integrated into our everyday routines. By this chapter's end, you'll comprehend ChatGPT and its potential to generate lucrative online revenue streams.

Discover the fascinating world of artificial intelligence (AI) and its evolution. While the concept of AI has been around since the 1950s, it was in the 2010s that AI language models truly captured the world's attention and became a ubiquitous tool in various industries. Meet IBM's Watson, the renowned language model that took the world by storm after winning against human champions on the quiz show "Jeopardy" in 2011. It's safe to say that Watson is a pioneer and a household name in language models and the precursor to what we have today.

Experience the next level of language models with OpenAI's GPT (Generative Pretrained Transformer) series - the latest breakthrough in deep learning and neural networks. In 2018, GPT's first iteration was unveiled, shattering the boundaries of AI language models and showcasing their immense potential.

An AI-powered tool called ChatGPT was created by OpenAI, a company established in 2015 by a group of influential IT professionals, including Sam Altman and Elon Musk. The stated goal of OpenAI's AI research is to promote and build a friendly artificial intelligence environment. OpenAI is a nonprofit organization established in San Francisco in 2015 with a $1 billion pledge by Sam Altman, Elon Musk, Reid Hoffman, Peter Thiel, Jessica Livingston, and others.

ChatGPT's police release in 2020 has received updates that add even more sophisticated natural language processing features. Thanks to its capacity to learn from vast volumes of data, it is an effective tool for many businesses and has enormous potential for further growth.

ChatGPT's ability to comprehend context is one of its defining characteristics. GPT-1 could generate coherent and grammatically correct text after training on a large dataset. It can analyze input text and develop responses considering the larger conversation or topic.

ChatGPT can respond coherently and appropriately to user input because it has been trained on a vast corpus of text data. It has a high-level linguistic intelligence and can handle complex conversations with users.

The language model can respond to inquiries and help with tasks like emailing, writing essays, coding, etc. Although ChatGPT was primarily developed for research, many businesses and organizations now use it.

As a freelancer, ChatGPT can assist you in developing your style, coming up with fresh content ideas, and automating the editing process. Additionally, ChatGPT allows you to create chatbots that can provide round-the-clock customer service and support, freeing up your time for other money-making activities.

ChatGPT includes information from various research, books, and business magazines. ChatGPT unlocks pricing and customer behavior secrets. This book can help you maximize impact and profit with pricing. Finding the correct tools and technology in a world of information overload and competing demands can be challenging. Sifting through the noise and finding relevant information is the challenge.

To stay on topic and get back to why we are all here, reading the first book of the series, ***How to Make Money Online***, I asked ChatGPT about the top ways to make money online.

PROMPT: give me the top 9 ways How to make money online

ChatGPT:

HERE ARE NINE INTERNET MONEY-MAKING OPPORTUNITIES:

1. FREELANCING ENTAILS PROVIDING YOUR EXPERTISE TO CUSTOMERS VIA AN ONLINE SERVICES MARKETPLACE LIKE UPWORK, FIVERR, OR FREELANCING.

2. GET PAID FOR YOUR THOUGHTS AND IDEAS BY TAKING ONLINE SURVEYS WITH COMPANIES LIKE SWAGBUCKS AND SURVEY JUNKIE.

3. WITH AFFILIATE MARKETING, YOU CAN RECEIVE A CUT OF THE PROFITS PRODUCED BY CUSTOMERS WHO CLICK ON YOUR SPECIAL REFERRAL LINK.

4. MAKE MONEY SHARING YOUR KNOWLEDGE BY TUTORING STUDENTS ONLINE THROUGH SITES LIKE CHEGG, TUTORME, AND VIPKID.

5. BY WORKING WITH A DROPSHIPPER, YOU CAN OPEN AN ONLINE BUSINESS WITHOUT THE NEED TO KEEP ANY STOCK ON HAND.

6. START A BLOG, AND FILL IT WITH ADVERTISING, SPONSORED MATERIAL, AND AFFILIATE LINKS.

7. WRITE BOOKS, MAKE MOVIES, OR SELL YOUR PHOTOGRAPHS ONLINE TO MAKE MONEY AS A CONTENT CREATOR.

8. **PRODUCE AND MARKET APPS FOR SMARTPHONES RUNNING THE ANDROID OR IOS OPERATING SYSTEMS.**

9. **ASSIST COMPANIES WITH THEIR SOCIAL MEDIA MANAGEMENT AND CONTENT DEVELOPMENT TO BOOST ENGAGEMENT AND SALES.**

KEEP IN MIND THAT YOU CAN'T EXPECT INSTANT RESULTS FROM ANY OF THESE STRATEGIES. IT'S ALSO CRUCIAL TO DO YOUR HOMEWORK AND PICK A STRATEGY THAT WORKS WELL WITH YOUR PERSONALITY AND HOBBIES.

After more detailed requests using tools discussed later in the book (better Prompts), I came up with several book ideas that make up the series "***How to Make Money Online.***" So yes, ChatGPT helped me and can also help you make money online.

ChatGPT is an asset for making money in various ways due to its ability to learn from vast amounts of data and produce human-like responses. Whether you're a content creator, freelancer, business owner, or entrepreneur, ChatGPT can simplify your income-generating endeavors and open fresh prospects for development.

Numerous types, iterations, and versions of ChatGPT can be used to make money, each with a unique size and set of features. We talked about the original ChatGPT 1 before, but here are some of their mothers and their primary distinctions:

GPT-2: This second-generation GPT model contains 1.5 billion parameters. It can produce high-quality text in a variety of designs and formats.

GPT-3: This model is the third iteration of the GPT family, and it can store up to 175 billion parameters. It can produce highly fluent and coherent text in various formats, such as essays, stories, and poems.

GPT-Neo: This open-source model created by EleutherAI includes up to 2.7 billion parameters. It is designed to be highly adaptable and flexible and can be taught to perform various tasks.

GPT-J: This is a scaled-up variant of GPT-3 developed by EleutherAI, with up to 6 billion parameters. It is one of the most significant available language models and can generate highly coherent and fluent text in various formats.

GShard, developed by Google, is a highly parallelized variant of the GPT model. It is designed to be highly scalable and can be trained using distributed computing on massive quantities of data.

The GPT-1 original model, which included 117 million parameters, was published in 2018. With 175 billion parameters, GPT-3 debuted in 2020 and is now one of the most significant and most potent language models accessible. It has been applied to various tasks, such as natural language processing, language translation, creative writing, and even music production.

Each model is designed for various use cases and applications, with benefits and drawbacks. Although larger models often demand more computational resources to train and use successfully, they are typically also more resilient and adaptive.

The ChatGPT prototype, made accessible on November 30, 2022, is built on the OpenAI GPT-3.5 and GPT 4. Since OpenAI uses GPT3.5, this can be a little confusing, and if you ever need more clarification, ask ChatGPT.

PROMPT: what model are you running

ChatGPT:

AS ONE OF THE MOST SOPHISTICATED LANGUAGE MODELS CURRENTLY ON THE MARKET, I WAS CREATED BY OPENAI AS A SIZABLE LANGUAGE MODEL BASED ON THE GPT-3 ARCHITECTURE. MY ARCHITECTURE AND CONFIGURATION, HOWEVER, MAY BE DIFFERENT FROM THOSE OF OTHER GPT-3 MODEL INSTANCES BECAUSE OPENAI HAS FURTHER ADJUSTED AND TAILORED ME FOR PARTICULAR USE CASES.

GPT-4 was released in March 2023 and is available in a limited format for paid premium subscribers. And depending on when you are reading this, there may be newer versions. Just ask ChatGPT if you need more information. ChatGPT continuously improves and diversifies, opening new avenues for generating revenue.

GPT-3.5 is what you get if you only sign up for the free version. If you pay or eventually use other tools, then GPT-4 will be the prominent language. GPT-4 is more innovative and team-oriented than previous models. It can generate, edit, and iterate when working with users on creative and technical writing activities like content creation, songwriting, screenwriting, or figuring out a user's writing style.

PROMPT: Explain the plot of little red riding hood in a sentence where each word must begin with the following letter in the alphabet from A to Z, without repeating any letters.

ChatGPT:

A BOLD, CURIOUS DAMSEL ENCOUNTERS A FEROCIOUS, GROWLING HUNTSMAN JUDICIOUSLY KEEPS LURKING MENACINGLY NEAR, OBSERVING PREDATORS QUIETLY, RUSHING SWIFTLY TOWARDS UNSUSPECTING VICTIMS, WANDERING, XENOPHOBIC YOUTH ZEALOUS.

There are several ways to increase business productivity as well using ChatGPT. With its sophisticated natural language processing abilities, various tasks and jobs can be automated, freeing up time and resources for other crucial endeavors. The following are a few possible applications for ChatGPT:

- ChatGPT can offer unique and practical material for websites, blogs, and social media. ChatGPT may generate a response customized to your needs and preferences by entering a prompt.

- ChatGPT can automate customer support, providing clients with around-the-clock assistance without involving humans. By doing so, you may respond more quickly and increase customer satisfaction.

- ChatGPT can manage emails, make appointments, and enter data. This can make time and resources available for more critical tasks. What task do you want to be automated?

- Text translation services provided by ChatGPT make it easier to communicate with persons from different linguistic and cultural backgrounds.

- ChatGPT may generate individualized recommendations for products, services, and information based on a user's tastes and behavior. The user experience can be improved, and as a result, engagement levels may increase.

- ChatGPT can assist teachers in developing innovative lesson plans, projects, assessments, and activities that follow predetermined learning objectives and curriculum requirements. Teachers can utilize ChatGPT to design and plan educational materials specific to each student's needs, such as presentations, worksheets, tests, and other instructional materials.

These are just a few examples, but I encourage you to make your list. I know we are very early in the book, but take the time to write down some use cases you can already see using ChatGPT to make your life easier and make even more money online.

ChatGPT, the most versatile and powerful tool, boosts productivity across individuals, industries, and applications. Social media managers can maximize a social media presence for an individual or a brand using ChatGPT as they invest in brand success and watch online engagement rise. ChatGPT makes creating social networking material accessible and can help schedule delivery. You may reach more potential clients with less money and in better time. ChatGPT platform can streamline content reuse, posting several places simultaneously, saving time.

Imagine impressing clients with the same high-quality work you've always done but faster than your competition. ChatGPT allows this and so much more. You can now see that this game-changing solution can boost your earnings.

ChatGPT lets you generate passive income long after your original investment. You can create fascinating eBooks and online courses to demonstrate and share your knowledge with more people. These valuable assets can be sold repeatedly after just one generation, making a consistent recurring income with no ongoing effort.

Marketing your product should maximize profitability and customer attractiveness. Finding balance takes time and effort. Finding the optimal equilibrium is problematic. Promoting your goods requires numerous considerations. Your product, target audience, channels, competition, and money are all factors. ChatGPT suggests using creative tools and procedures to automate mundane tasks so you can focus on what matters most.

CHAPTER 2

Setting Up and Understanding ChatGPT

Discover ChatGPT's many benefits and how it fits into our daily lives. If you haven't already, register **NOW** for ChatGPT. OpenAI is powerful, but only if you sign up today! Please follow these instructions: Visit https://openai.com/, click "product," and select "ChatGPT" from the drop-down. It's simple! Or go direct to Chat with OpenAI at https://chat.openai.com/.

Click the Sign-Up button in the top right corner to discover ChatGPT's power. Simply consenting to the terms of service and giving your name and email will unlock the platform's full potential. Secure your account with a strong password and email address. Click the OpenAI confirmation email link to confirm your email address. After signing up, you may easily log into your new account.

Again, there is a Free Version that uses 3.5, and it will be good for now and maybe all you ever need. The premium account is there to maximize GPT. "ChatGPT Plus" enhances ChatGPT! Exclusive privileges are available for just USD 20 a month. Get instant response and priority access to cutting-edge features. Select the model upon login to maximize ChatGPT's potential. As a plus subscriber, you can choose from GPT-3, GPT-3.5, GPT-4, and more. Look at the top of the screen to verify which model you are using.

GPT-4 is the newest AI breakthrough. As a dedicated ChatGPT Plus user, you'll immediately notice a sleek contemporary feature at the top of your screen: a simple drop-down box with various cutting-edge models. ChatGPT Plus improves your chat experience. GPT-4 (or the latest stable version when reading) works best, but it's slower and has a 25-message-per-three-hour limit.

After creating your account, you can access sophisticated tools to improve workflow, boost productivity, and grow your business. To assist you in getting started and getting the most out of your ChatGPT account, OpenAI offers comprehensive documentation and tutorials.

By entering a prompt (a question or comment to which ChatGPT will respond) and hitting send, ChatGPT will produce an answer based on your prompt. To test how ChatGPT responds, try experimenting with different prompts and settings. For instance, you can experiment with other prompts to observe how they alter the text's inventiveness and randomness.

Begin with a simple "Hello," and you will get "Hello! How can I assist you today?"

PROMPT: Hello

ChatGPT:

"HELLO! HOW CAN I ASSIST YOU TODAY?"

Then play (practice) around, maybe like " Share five interesting facts about the moon." Or anything you are thinking about right now. Be creative; why are you reading this book? Ask ChatGPT to help. Here is what I asked, but what you ask is much more critical.

PROMPT: generate and share with me five facts about the moon

ChatGPT:

SURE, HERE ARE FIVE FASCINATING MOON-RELATED FACTS:

THE MOON IS THE LARGEST MOON RELATIVE TO ITS MOTHER PLANET, RANKING FIFTH IN SIZE IN THE SOLAR SYSTEM. IN ACTUALITY, THE MOON IS LARGER THAN EARTH BY MORE THAN A QUARTER.

IT IS ESTIMATED THAT THE MOON FORMED SOME 4.5 BILLION YEARS AGO, NOT LONG AFTER THE SOLAR SYSTEM AS A WHOLE. IT IS THOUGHT TO HAVE BEEN PRODUCED WHEN AN OBJECT THE SIZE OF MARS HIT WITH THE EARLY EARTH, LAUNCHING SPACE DEBRIS THAT LATER CAME TOGETHER TO FORM THE MOON.

THE MOON IS THE ONLY NATURALLY OCCURRING SATELLITE OF EARTH, AND IT IS ALSO THE ONLY PLACE IN THE SOLAR SYSTEM THAT HAS BEEN VISITED BY HUMANS. DURING THE APOLLO 11 MISSION IN 1969, NEIL ARMSTRONG AND EDWIN "BUZZ" ALDRIN WERE THE FIRST HUMANS TO SET FOOT ON THE MOON.

THE MOON'S SURFACE IS COVERED WITH CRATERS, MOUNTAINS, AND ENORMOUS, LEVEL PLAINS KNOWN AS MARIA. IT IS THOUGHT THAT LONG-AGO VOLCANIC ACTIVITY PRODUCED THE MARIA BY SPEWING MOLTEN LAVA ONTO THE SURFACE AND FORMING BROAD, FLAT EXPANSES.

SINCE THE MOON ROTATES SYNCHRONOUSLY WITH EARTH, EARTH ALWAYS SEES THE SAME SIDE OF THE MOON. THIS IS DUE TO THE MOON'S ROTATIONAL PERIOD, WHICH IS EQUAL TO ITS ORBITAL PERIOD, WHICH IS THE LENGTH OF TIME IT TAKES TO ORBIT THE EARTH. SINCE WE CAN ONLY SEE ONE SIDE OF THE MOON, IT APPEARS TO BE STATIONARY IN THE SKY.

Keep asking questions, giving instructions, improving your prompts, or asking it to translate or analyze something. You may even ask it to make book recommendations or things you should be doing today. Please realize that this is an AI, and its communication is like an ongoing conversation. ChatGPT is an AI language model designed to understand and respond to your questions and requests using natural language processing. You can ask ChatGPT anything you like, and it will do its best to provide a helpful and informative response. Whether you need help with a specific task, want to learn something new, or want to chat. And yes, ChatGPT can keep you organized and even give helpful tips.

PROMPT: what should I be doing today?

ChatGPT:

I'M AN AI LANGUAGE MODEL, SO I NEED TO KNOW YOUR SPECIFIC PRIORITIES OR SCHEDULE, SO I CANNOT ADVISE YOU ON WHAT YOU SHOULD BE DOING RIGHT NOW. HOWEVER, THE FOLLOWING ARE SOME GENERAL POINTERS FOR MAXIMIZING YOUR DAY.

PLAN YOUR DAY OUT, INCLUDING ANY CRITICAL TASKS OR APPOINTMENTS YOU HAVE SCHEDULED BEFORE BEGIN. YOU'LL BE ABLE TO FOCUS BETTER AND WASTE LESS TIME AS A RESULT.

CHOOSE THE ITEMS ON YOUR TO-DO LIST THAT ARE MOST CRUCIAL TO FINISH FIRST. YOU'LL FEEL MORE PRODUCTIVE AS A RESULT AND WON'T BECOME OVERBURDENED LATER IN THE DAY.

BY GIVING YOUR BRAIN A CHANCE TO REST AND RECHARGE THROUGHOUT THE DAY, TAKING LITTLE BREAKS CAN INCREASE YOUR PRODUCTIVITY. THINK ABOUT GOING FOR A STROLL, STRETCHING, OR PERFORMING SOME BRIEF MEDITATION.

DRINK PLENTY OF WATER THROUGHOUT THE DAY TO STAY HYDRATED AND MAINTAIN YOUR FOCUS AND ALERTNESS.

SELF-CARE IS IMPORTANT. ALWAYS REMEMBER TO LOOK AFTER YOUR PHYSICAL AND EMOTIONAL HEALTH. THIS MIGHT ENTAIL GETTING ENOUGH REST, EATING WELL, AND ENGAGING IN ENJOYABLE ACTIVITIES.

IN THE END, PUTTING YOUR GOALS AND VALUES FIRST CAN HELP YOU MAKE THE BEST USE OF YOUR TIME AND ENERGY NOW.

Have fun….

PROMPT: is the moon real?

ChatGPT:

YES, THERE IS A MOON. IT IS A NATURAL SATELLITE OF THE EARTH AND IS SEEN AS A BRILLIANT OBJECT IN THE NIGHT SKY. SCIENTISTS HAVE DONE MUCH RESEARCH ON THE MOON, AND PEOPLE HAVE EVEN GONE THERE DURING THE APOLLO MISSIONS. SINCE ANCIENT TIMES, PEOPLE HAVE OBSERVED AND MEASURED THE MOON'S PRESENCE AND ITS IMPACTS ON EARTH, INCLUDING THE TIDES IT GENERATES AND THE GRAVITATIONAL FORCE IT EXERTS. THEREFORE, THERE IS NO QUESTION THAT THE MOON IS A GENUINE SOLAR SYSTEM OBJECT.

Okay, maybe not too much fun; remember, we are here and need to keep the focus on how we can make more money online with ChatGPT. You will see a **Regenerate Response** button after you get a response. Feel free to click the button to verify that you will get different answers.

ChatGPT's user interface is created to be simple to use and intuitive, so users may quickly produce natural language responses to their cues. The prompt is where you enter the query, declaration, or another prompt you wish ChatGPT to address. This can be as straightforward as one word or as intricate as an entire paragraph or essay. Depending on the model and type of prompt, this may consist of text, graphics, or other media.

The history tab allows you to examine and keep track of all prior prompts and responses. By integrating ChatGPT with other programs and apps, developers can create unique solutions that utilize ChatGPT's natural language processing capabilities.

Several platforms and programs have integrated with the OpenAI API and can access ChatGPT. With development experience, you can incorporate the OpenAI API into your applications using the available programming libraries and documentation. This would allow you to construct custom solutions that leverage ChatGPT's capabilities.

ChatGPT's user interface is created to be straightforward and approachable while offering solid and sophisticated natural language processing capabilities. Users can fully utilize ChatGPT's capabilities and obtain exceptional results using appropriate strategies and procedures. Here are some pointers on how to get the most out of ChatGPT. ChatGPT provides a range of models with various features and degrees of complexity. Spend time experimenting with several models to locate the one that best suits your unique needs and demands.

ChatGPT's settings can be changed. Find the most effective settings for your use case by experimenting with parameters like response length, temperature, and top-p. The input prompt's precision and clarity significantly impact the quality of the generated response. Give ChatGPT precise information to produce an accurate and helpful answer by providing precise and explicit suggestions. Ensure the generated responses are correct, logical, and appropriate for your needs.

Consider integrating ChatGPT with other programs and devices or combining it with human wisdom and intuition. By highlighting these pointers and tricks, users can fully utilize ChatGPT and accomplish excellent outcomes in various applications and sectors. With some testing and experience, ChatGPT can be an invaluable tool for increasing productivity, creating original and exciting content, and attaining outstanding results.

Once you've determined what to ask, carefully word your prompt to communicate precisely what you want ChatGPT to respond to. Include any pertinent details or context that will assist ChatGPT in generating a more accurate response. After entering your question, some chatbot interfaces require you to select a "send" or "submit" button, while others generate a response automatically. Try this out; ask your question to ChatGPT. Did you get the answer you expected? It took me months of learning Prompts to get the desired results, so this will take practice.

After entering your question, ChatGPT will construct a response based on your input. It is essential to evaluate the response to ensure accuracy and relevance thoroughly. You can ask follow-up questions or reword your prompt to elicit a more precise response. If the reaction generated by ChatGPT is unsatisfactory or does not fully answer your query, try entering a different prompt or rephrasing your original prompt. The desired response may require multiple attempts, but ChatGPT is designed to learn from its interactions and generate increasingly accurate reactions over time. Provide as much pertinent information as feasible if your question or request pertains to a particular subject or circumstance.

ChatGPT has been trained in proper English, so adequate grammar and spelling will help it better comprehend your input. As a language model, ChatGPT may require some time to evaluate your information and generate a response. It is essential to be patient and wait for the model's response. ChatGPT is trained on vast data, and alternative wording can sometimes produce a better result.

Although ChatGPT can generate responses on various subjects, it is best to remain on topic and avoid moving from one issue to another. ChatGPT is intended to be a valuable and informative resource, so please avoid using inappropriate or offensive language.

ChatGPT is a conversational AI model so customer service might be the best use case. ChatGPT is a multi-prompt, context-sensitive bot with access to the previous prompts' context, making it the perfect choice for customer responses. Like most chatbots, he claims the first inquiry needs to be recovered or forgotten when you ask the second.

The translation is also a great use case because it effectively contextualizes and discusses. Suppose I speak English, and you want to hear the conversation in Spanish. In that case, the translation engine will appear, but because it is conversational AI, it will sound like a human, and the translation need not be limited to text; voice translation is another option.

The documentation use case is another usable situation for AI. It is good at producing legal documents based on certain responses you expect. It can review published rules and laws and generate legal memos and briefs.

CHAPTER 3

Maximizing Productivity with ChatGPT to Earn Online Income

Maximize your productivity and earn money online effortlessly with ChatGPT. Make sure you go back to Chapter 2 and set it up if you still need to. And spend some more time with practice prompts relevant to why you are reading this book and get familiar with the platform to start reaping its benefits. In this chapter, discover many techniques to amplify your productivity and boost your earnings with ChatGPT.

Streamline your business or online activities with ChatGPT's automation capabilities. From customer service to scheduling and email management, ChatGPT has got you covered. Let ChatGPT take care of these activities effortlessly, freeing up your valuable time to focus on other crucial aspects of your business.

ChatGPT's primary objective is to provide individuals, organizations, and developers with a robust and flexible conversational AI and NLP platform to help them build more captivating and interactive tools and applications. Unlock the full potential with rich language capabilities, allowing you to create complex and sophisticated designs like never before.

With its uncanny ability to provide human-like responses to a wide range of inquiries and prompts, ChatGPT is an invaluable tool for chatbots, personal assistants, customer service, and other conversational AI applications. The advanced capabilities include machine translation, language comprehension, and text classification. With its impressive features, this tool can handle various natural language processing tasks, making it an invaluable asset across multiple fields and applications. The continuous development of this area will bring immense benefits to you.

Like any other AI system, algorithmic bias, privacy concerns, and responsible usage are important factors. OpenAI addresses these concerns and ensures that ChatGPT is utilized respectably and conscientiously. ChatGPT strives to deliver a powerful and flexible solution for NLP and AI, elevate the realm of NLP and AI exploration, and tackle any partiality and ethical concerns associated with its implementation.

You can get inspiration from ChatGPT for blog pieces, social media updates, and even eBooks. Additionally, you can utilize ChatGPT to build chatbots that converse with your consumers, respond to their inquiries, and lead them through your sales funnel.

ChatGPT can also help you identify patterns and trends in your sector, giving you the advantage of staying current and making wise business decisions. You can boost productivity, simplify workflow, and ultimately earn even more money online by utilizing ChatGPT's features.

A strong tool like ChatGPT can boost productivity and generate more cash online. Users may create high-quality material, automate repetitive operations, and improve efficiency using the tool's natural language processing features. ChatGPT can produce material for blogs, social media, and other online venues, resulting in recurring passive income streams.

ChatGPT can automate data entry and analysis, streamline support operations, and offer intelligent support for various applications and industries. ChatGPT may be an excellent ally for boosting productivity and generating online money with the correct approaches, prompts, and methods.

You can even ask ChatGPT for suggestions on increasing your online income. What if you didn't know anything about AI and wanted ChatGPT to help you find ways to make money? You can see that ChatGPT will provide you with ideas for online courses, product sales, video production, freelancing, email marketing, blogging, and self-publishing. What did you ask ChatGPT today? Nothing, go back to the application and ask how you can make more money, be specific.

You can get help from ChatGPT to create excellent content for your company, such as blog pieces, social media updates, and product descriptions. Doing this can ensure the content is pertinent and interesting while saving time and money.

PROMPT: generate eight ways to earn money for an entrepreneur in {TOPIC}. What response did you get? Anything that you can act on today? If not, ask in more detail. ChatGPT can be used to generate business ideas. Get personalized side business suggestions that suit your preferences. By learning about your interests, skills, and challenges, ChatGPT will work its magic to produce customized company concepts that meet your needs.

PROMPT: I am interested in technology, fishing, and cooking; how can I earn money online

ChatGPT:

YOU CAN MAKE MONEY ONLINE IN A VARIETY OF WAYS DEPENDING ON YOUR INTERESTS IN TECHNOLOGY, FISHING, AND CUISINE. HERE ARE A FEW CONCEPTS:

START A TECHNOLOGY BLOG TO SHARE YOUR EXPERTISE AND IDEAS WITH OTHERS IF YOU ARE INTERESTED IN TECHNOLOGY. RUNNING ADVERTISEMENTS,

SPONSORED CONTENT, OR AFFILIATE MARKETING ARE ALL WAYS TO MAKE MONEY FROM YOUR SITE.

SELL FISHING EQUIPMENT ONLINE: YOU CAN OPEN AN ONLINE SHOP OFFERING FISHING SUPPLIES. YOU CAN PURCHASE GOODS FROM DROPSHIPPERS OR WHOLESALERS AND PROMOTE YOUR STORE VIA PAID SOCIAL MEDIA ADVERTISING.

CREATE A BLOG OR YOUTUBE CHANNEL FOR YOUR FISHING CONTENT IF YOU'RE PASSIONATE ABOUT IT. YOU CAN SHARE YOUR FISHING EXPLOITS, ADVICE, AND TRICKS ON YOUR BLOG OR CHANNEL. ADS AND SPONSORSHIPS ARE TWO WAYS YOU CAN EARN MONEY FROM YOUR CONTENT.

SELL YOUR OWN COOKING OR FISHING LURES ONLINE: IF YOU HAVE A KNACK FOR CREATING YOUR OWN CULINARY OR FISHING LURES, YOU CAN SELL THEM ONLINE THROUGH YOUR OWN WEBSITE OR ONLINE MARKETPLACES LIKE ETSY OR AMAZON.

CREATE A COOKING BLOG OR YOUTUBE CHANNEL TO SHARE RECIPES AND COOKING ADVICE: IF YOU ENJOY COOKING, YOU CAN DO SO. ADS AND SPONSORSHIPS ARE TWO WAYS YOU CAN EARN MONEY FROM YOUR CONTENT.

BECOME A FOOD OR TECHNOLOGY WRITER BY PENNING ARTICLES OR REVIEWS FOR WEBSITES THAT FOCUS ON THESE TOPICS. EDITORS ARE OPEN TO YOUR IDEAS, AND YOU CAN EVEN WRITE FOR CONTENT FARMS LIKE UPWORK OR FIVERR.

DESIGN AN APP: YOU CAN DESIGN YOUR OWN CULINARY OR FISHING APP AND MAKE MONEY THROUGH IN-APP PURCHASES OR ADVERTS IF YOU ARE SKILLED AT PROGRAMMING OR APP DEVELOPMENT.

TEACH ONLINE COURSES: ON WEBSITES LIKE UDEMY OR COURSERA, YOU CAN DESIGN AND SELL ONLINE COURSES IF YOU ARE AN EXPERT IN ANY OF YOUR INTERESTS.

The Above was done with the ChatGPT 3.5 model. Below is the response using ChatGPT 4. Make sure you know which one you are using. Look at the top of the screen.

ChatGPT:

SURE, GIVEN YOUR INTERESTS IN TECHNOLOGY, FISHING, AND COOKING, THERE ARE A MULTITUDE OF WAYS THAT YOU COULD EARN MONEY ONLINE. A FEW SUGGESTIONS:

1. CONTENT CREATION: YOU CAN START A BLOG OR A YOUTUBE CHANNEL SHARING YOUR KNOWLEDGE AND EXPERIENCES ABOUT TECHNOLOGY, FISHING, AND COOKING. THIS COULD INCLUDE PRODUCT REVIEWS, TUTORIALS, TIPS, AND TRICKS, OR GENERAL ADVICE. AS YOUR FOLLOWING GROWS, YOU CAN MONETIZE THROUGH ADS, SPONSORSHIPS, AND AFFILIATE MARKETING.

2. E-COMMERCE: YOU CAN SELL FISHING EQUIPMENT OR TECH GADGETS ONLINE. IF YOU'RE INTO COOKING, YOU CAN ALSO SELL HOMEMADE FOOD PRODUCTS OR COOKING SUPPLIES. WEBSITES LIKE ETSY, EBAY, OR EVEN SETTING UP YOUR OWN SHOPIFY STORE COULD BE GREAT PLATFORMS FOR THIS.

3. ONLINE COURSES OR WEBINARS: IF YOU'RE AN EXPERT IN ANY OF YOUR INTEREST AREAS, CONSIDER TEACHING OTHERS BY CREATING AN ONLINE COURSE OR HOSTING WEBINARS. WEBSITES LIKE UDEMY, TEACHABLE, OR SKILLSHARE ARE PERFECT PLATFORMS FOR THIS.

4. AFFILIATE MARKETING: IF YOU HAVE A STRONG SOCIAL MEDIA PRESENCE OR A BLOG, YOU CAN EARN MONEY BY PROMOTING OTHER PEOPLE'S PRODUCTS. AMAZON HAS A GREAT AFFILIATE PROGRAM, AS DO MANY TECH, COOKING, AND FISHING COMPANIES.

5. WRITING E-BOOKS: IF YOU'RE A GOOD WRITER, YOU CAN WRITE AND SELL EBOOKS ABOUT TECHNOLOGY, FISHING, AND COOKING ON AMAZON OR OTHER ONLINE PLATFORMS.

6. APP DEVELOPMENT: IF YOU HAVE TECHNICAL SKILLS, YOU COULD DEVELOP AN APP RELATED TO FISHING OR COOKING. FOR EXAMPLE, AN APP THAT PROVIDES COOKING RECIPES OR AN APP THAT GIVES FISHING TIPS AND TRACKS THE BEST FISHING SPOTS.

7. FREELANCING: YOU CAN OFFER YOUR SKILLS IN TECHNOLOGY, LIKE WEB DESIGN, PROGRAMMING, TECH SUPPORT, ETC., ON PLATFORMS LIKE UPWORK OR FIVERR.

8. VIRTUAL COOKING CLASSES: WITH THE RISE OF REMOTE LEARNING, YOU CAN OFFER VIRTUAL COOKING CLASSES THROUGH ZOOM OR ANOTHER VIDEO CONFERENCING TOOL.

9. PAID ONLINE SURVEYS/REVIEWS: COMPANIES ARE ALWAYS LOOKING FOR CONSUMER OPINIONS ON THEIR PRODUCTS. GIVEN YOUR INTERESTS, YOU MIGHT FIND OPPORTUNITIES TO BE PAID FOR REVIEWING TECH GADGETS, FISHING GEAR, OR COOKING TOOLS.

10. PHOTOGRAPHY: IF YOU HAVE SKILLS IN PHOTOGRAPHY, YOU COULD SELL PICTURES OF YOUR COOKING CREATIONS OR YOUR FISHING TRIPS ON STOCK PHOTOGRAPHY WEBSITES LIKE SHUTTERSTOCK OR ISTOCKPHOTO.

IT'S IMPORTANT TO REMEMBER THAT MANY OF THESE OPTIONS WILL TAKE TIME TO BUILD UP A CLIENT BASE OR FOLLOWING, BUT WITH CONSISTENCY AND QUALITY CONTENT OR SERVICES, THEY CAN BE PROFITABLE. ALSO, REMEMBER TO CONSIDER ANY LEGAL OR TAX IMPLICATIONS OF STARTING AN ONLINE BUSINESS.

It'll display ChatGPT responses for a few prompt instances to demonstrate how much the output can vary based on your questions. But I will also show you the PROMPTS sometimes so you will get used to typing the prompt and seeing the response yourself.

How ChatGPT Can Assist Influencers Generate Income

ChatGPT can help influencers earn money in various ways by enabling them to create personalized content, interact with their followers, and monetize their platforms. Influencers can utilize the following strategies to benefit from ChatGPT.

Are you an influencer? Or want to be one? Have you written blog posts or social media content? What to be able to do it faster with better results? Then practice.

ChatGPT can produce personalized content, such as blog posts, social media updates, and videos, tailored to each follower's interests and preferences. This can help influencers create engaging content that resonates with their audience and generates more views, engagement, and revenue.

How to automate tedious jobs with ChatGPT to free up time for income-generating activities

One of the main advantages of adopting ChatGPT is its capacity to automate time-consuming and laborious operations, freeing up vital time for activities that generate cash. Users may automate data entry, content development, and customer service with ChatGPT, freeing them up to concentrate on more strategically important and high-value jobs.

Before automating repetitive and time-consuming processes with ChatGPT, users should identify them. Then, users can create prompts that provide the data ChatGPT needs to provide accurate and helpful responses. After establishing these inquiries, ChatGPT can be set up to produce answers automatically, freeing users to focus on other tasks.

If a user administers a blog, for example, they may use ChatGPT to automate content creation by providing ideas that result in high-quality postings, saving valuable time and effort. In this manner, ChatGPT can automate routine inquiries, streamlining customer service procedures and freeing up support staff to focus on more challenging issues.

Have you written a blog for some time? Try to copy and paste some of them in ChatGPT and ask it to expand your blog to 500 words. Do you like the content? Then change the prompt. There are prompts at the end of this book, and there is a book of 3,000 more I can send you; click the link at the beginning for the prompts.

ChatGPT can suggest affiliate programs for you to join and can assist you in identifying goods and services that are likely to appeal to your target market. You can get paid a commission on any sales made using your platform by recommending these goods or services to your followers. Ask ChatGPT to give you a list of programs in your {NICHE}.

Using ChatGPT to automate time-consuming operations, users can boost productivity and efficiency while freeing up valuable time for activities that provide income. ChatGPT can be useful for automating repetitive tasks and generating top-notch results without much originality or ingenuity.

The role of ChatGPT in assisting data collection and research for financial gain

ChatGPT can help with data collection and research, which can be used to earn money. By employing the tool's natural language processing capabilities, users may easily and quickly access data on various topics, from market trends and customer preferences to competitive intelligence and industry insights.

This information can generate new products or services, enhance marketing strategies, and make business decisions. Thanks to ChatGPT's ability to analyze massive amounts of data quickly and reliably, users may save time and effort while gaining essential insights that can help them stay ahead of the competition.

Whether users are gathering consumer feedback, monitoring social media trends, or conducting market research, ChatGPT can be a helpful tool for information gathering and research, supporting users in making more informed decisions and efficiently producing cash.

Numerous corporate processes like appointment scheduling and inventory management can be automated using ChatGPT. By reducing the time and effort needed to handle these procedures, you can boost efficiency and production and focus on crucial company operations.

Your organization can benefit from ChatGPT's enhanced customer engagement and happiness, more sales and leads, product and service optimization, and increased productivity. By utilizing ChatGPT's insights and skills, you may fortify your company and achieve long-term growth. Using ChatGPT may be a fantastic tool for creating ideas and material.

You can use ChatGPT, for instance, to create personalized to-do lists based on your priorities and due dates. It can also help you schedule your tasks and appointments more effectively by considering factors like your energy levels and natural rhythms.

You can use ChatGPT to manage your emails, send and receive messages, and write papers and reports. It can also help you conduct research and amass knowledge more effectively by summarizing articles, giving insights, and providing essential details.

Using ChatGPT to manage your time and productivity, you can devote more valuable time to income-generating activities. Whether you're a freelancer, business owner, or employee, increasing your productivity can help you earn more money, advance your profession, and achieve your objectives. Why not try ChatGPT and see how it can increase your output and earnings?

Enhancing earning potential by using ChatGPT for brainstorming and idea generation

Your thought and idea-generation capacity might increase your chances of earning more money with ChatGPT. Using ChatGPT's capabilities, users can provide open-ended queries or prompts to generate various ideas, from economic prospects to artistic projects. ChatGPT can help users improve and develop their ideas by providing information, feedback, and insights. By using ChatGPT for idea generation and brainstorming, people can release their creative potential and find new sources of income, enhancing their financial abundance and expanding their opportunities for advancement.

ChatGPT can be a useful tool for enhancing SEO and boosting website traffic by assisting users in creating unique and worthwhile content. Using ChatGPT to produce content ideas that align with your target audience's interests and are in line with your business objectives is one way to achieve this. You can use ChatGPT to develop content that speaks to the wants and interests of your audience by employing keywords and phrases that are most significant to them. This will increase the likelihood that your website will rank high in the relevant search results and keep your audience engaged.

Refining and optimizing already-written material is another way to use ChatGPT for content development. ChatGPT can assist users in identifying areas for improvement in their current material, such as adding more detail or incorporating more pertinent keywords by posing questions or suggestions linked to themes or keywords.

ChatGPT can also produce educational and interesting content for articles, blogs, and social media updates. You can produce well-written, well-structured material suited to your audience by utilizing ChatGPT's natural language processing capabilities. This can assist in boosting interest and website traffic, ultimately resulting in better SEO and more sales.

Be specific in your requests and establish a clear purpose. It will take some practice, but this is perhaps the most crucial thing you need to master to guarantee that your responses from ChatGPT are exactly what you want. As you may recall, a "Prompt" is what ChatGPT refers to when you ask it a question. As an illustration, you want to help create a marketing tagline for your digital marketing company.

PROMPT: provide an example of how to write a marketing tagline

ChatGPT:

OF COURSE, THIS IS AN ILLUSTRATION OF A MARKETING SLOGAN FOR A BUSINESS ENGAGED IN DIGITAL MARKETING:

"UNLEASH THE FULL POTENTIAL OF YOUR COMPANY WITH [COMPANY NAME]: YOUR PARTNER IN SUCCESSFUL DIGITAL MARKETING"

THIS TAGLINE COMBINES THE FIRM NAME AND ITS VALUE PROPOSITION ("YOUR PARTNER IN DIGITAL MARKETING SUCCESS") WITH A CALL TO ACTION ("UNLEASH YOUR BUSINESS'S FULL POTENTIAL"). IT CONVEYS A SENSE OF COOPERATION AND PARTNERSHIP, IMPLYING THAT THE BUSINESS IS DEDICATED TO COLLABORATING CLOSELY WITH ITS CLIENTS TO MEET THEIR MARKETING OBJECTIVES. IT ALSO SUGGESTS THAT THE FIRM HAS THE KNOWLEDGE AND RESOURCES NECESSARY TO SUPPORT ENTERPRISES IN THRIVING IN THE DIGITAL SPHERE.

Selling and marketing professionals can benefit from ChatGPT by optimizing the client personalization they can offer through the content they deliver. For this reason, this AI can be used in the following ways across channels, including marketing initiatives, commercials, and social media platforms. Keyword Analysis involves ChatGPT assessing sizable blocks of text material people provide and returning a verbiage analysis that includes the most popular terms. What these copies lack, however, is personality and verve, which may be added to the copies with minimal human interaction.

Collecting and complaint redressal can be automated by integrating an intelligent chatbot, like ChatGPT, into a product-focused website or application. It may also be used for A/B testing by instructing the AI to produce two versions of the product description and receiving insightful data on the campaign's effectiveness from several focus groups.

PROMPT: What type of business can a data analyst with skills in digital marketing pursue to make $1,000 per day with a modest investment and only 10 hours per week of work?

ChatGPT:

I just showed you the prompt above. Hopefully, you typed it into your own and now see the response for yourself. And again, make the prompt your question to make this even more relevant. Now, let's drill down a little from the above request.

PROMPT: now tell me about a great but less well-known online business opportunity.

ChatGPT:

THERE ARE SEVERAL EXCITING BUT NOT AS WELL-KNOWN WAYS TO GENERATE MONEY ONLINE:

SOME WEBSITES PAY USERS TO SERVE AS ONLINE JURORS. THESE PEOPLE OFFER INPUT TO ATTORNEYS AND LEGAL FIRMS ON MOCK TRIALS, ENABLING THEM TO GATHER INSIGHTFUL INFORMATION BEFORE TO COURT.

INTERIOR DESIGNER SOFTWARE AND A CREATIVE EYE ARE ALL YOU NEED TO START YOUR CAREER AS A VIRTUAL INTERIOR DESIGNER. A BESPOKE DESIGN PLAN AND 3D RENDERINGS ARE PRODUCED BY THE DESIGNER WHEN CLIENTS UPLOAD IMAGES OF THEIR HOME OR WORKPLACE AREA.

MANAGER OF SOCIAL MEDIA FOR SMALL BUSINESSES: EVEN IF THEY CAN'T AFFORD TO HIRE A FULL-TIME STAFF, SMALL BUSINESSES FREQUENTLY NEED ASSISTANCE MANAGING THEIR SOCIAL MEDIA ACCOUNTS. THROUGH FOCUSED ADVERTISING AND CONTENT PRODUCTION, YOU MAY ASSIST BUSINESSES IN INCREASING THEIR ONLINE PRESENCE AND GENERATING LEADS AS A FREELANCE SOCIAL MEDIA MANAGER.

ONLINE TUTORS ARE HIGHLY SOUGHT AFTER BECAUSE OF THE POPULARITY OF ONLINE LEARNING AND THEIR ABILITY TO INSTRUCT STUDENTS IN MATH, SCIENCE, AND FOREIGN LANGUAGES. THROUGH ONLINE SERVICES LIKE SKYPE OR ZOOM, YOU MAY TUTOR STUDENTS FROM ALL AROUND THE WORLD.

TRANSCRIBER: TRANSCRIBERS ARE THOSE WHO LISTEN TO AUDIO RECORDINGS AND TURN THEM INTO WRITTEN DOCUMENTATION. FOR THOSE WHO ARE METICULOUS AND HAVE STRONG TYPING SKILLS, THIS POSITION IS APPROPRIATE.

OVERALL, ASIDE FROM THE MORE CONVENTIONAL POSSIBILITIES, THERE ARE A TON OF UNIQUE METHODS TO GENERATE MONEY ONLINE. THE SECRET IS TO CHOOSE A MARKET SEGMENT ABOUT WHICH YOU ARE ENTHUSIASTIC AND TO USE YOUR EXPERTISE TO BUILD A SUCCESSFUL INTERNET BUSINESS.

Even though the list is wholly different, to even further drill down with more details, I typed:

PROMPT: What if I want to make even more money with less time spent each week?

ChatGPT:

After the response, it also said... Remember that earning money frequently takes time, risk, and effort. It is finding the right balance between earning money and preserving a positive work-life balance.

The answers can, and did, change drastically depending on how the prompt was phrased, and it has become increasingly aware of my preferences with each successive prompt. Telling it I wanted to make even more money caused the entire list to shift rather than just the ideas themselves.

If I had included "I like food and cars" after or in addition to the initial prompt, the outcomes would have been different. Also, it was understood that we were still discussing the same concept, making money online, each time, and I didn't have to rephrase the prompt completely.

Don't hesitate to practice experimenting with various prompts and verbiage in your questions. You might discover a brand-new method for producing content you had never considered before. You can instruct it to help even more with content creation by adding things to your prompts like "Write this in a witty, funny, engaging tone" or even "Write this in the style of a specific person," as I did in the introduction using was William Shakespeare style.

What if you ask ChatGPT to develop imaginative and compelling stories that can hold readers' attention for extended periods? And ask it to compose a story that takes place in the future. Please DO NOT copy and paste the results into a blog or book, as authorities can and will be able to see that an AI wrote it. But why not use ChatGPT to help with the title, the outline, the summary, and even help generate ideas to help get you started?

If you receive a response from ChatGPT but are still looking for more satisfaction, you can always ask it again differently or follow up with a more detailed question.

PROMPT: Act as Albert Einstein and create a tweet about how to make money online

ChatGPT:

"UNDERSTANDING THE DYNAMICS OF THE ONLINE WORLD IS MUCH LIKE UNDERSTANDING THE COSMOS. #1: COMPREHEND THE LAWS – IN THIS CASE, KNOW YOUR MARKET. #2: IDENTIFY YOUR SPACE – YOUR NICHE. #3: WORK DILIGENTLY AND PERSISTENTLY, FOR THE UNIVERSE REWARDS CONSISTENT ENERGY. #MAKEMONEYONLINE"

Additionally, you'll learn that you may respond differently to the same query. You may instruct ChatGPT to generate multiple responses simultaneously, which is helpful if you need to select something like email subject lines or titles for videos or blogs because you can't immediately think of one that strikes a chord with you.

Even pre-existing content can be entered into ChatGPT, which will respond when you ask for suggestions on improving your previous prompt or content. Then, you can focus on elements like tone, readability, and clarity. You can ask ChatGPT to share suggestions on making this email easier to read and more professional. By considering these suggestions and using trial and error, you can make the most of ChatGPT to create content that resonates with your audience and advances your goals.

PROMPT: Use the making money idea above. Identify the needs and wants of people that still need to be fulfilled, and use your imagination to create innovative solutions. Feel free to take risks and produce 100 words for a blog.

ChatGPT:

IN THIS VAST EXPANSE OF THE DIGITAL UNIVERSE, UNMET NEEDS AND DESIRES ARE LIKE UNDISCOVERED STARS, READY TO BE ILLUMINATED BY YOUR UNIQUE IDEAS. HARNESS YOUR IMAGINATION TO SCULPT INNOVATIVE SOLUTIONS THAT RESONATE WITH THESE NEEDS. UNDERSTAND THAT THE PATH TO TRUE INNOVATION IS OFTEN PAVED WITH RISKS. FEAR NOT, FOR THESE ARE BUT STEPPING STONES TO GREATNESS. IF YOUR SOLUTION MEETS A GENUINE NEED, IT WILL CREATE ITS OWN DEMAND, MUCH LIKE A COMET CARVING ITS OWN PATH. THIS AUDACIOUS BLEND OF CREATIVITY, RISK-TAKING, AND DISCERNMENT COULD BE YOUR BLUEPRINT TO MAKING MONEY ONLINE, SHINING BRIGHT IN THE DIGITAL COSMOS.

Even though ChatGPT can deliver excellent results, it is crucial to remember that it cannot replace human editing. While ChatGPT can speed up material development and save time, more is needed than a human editor's skilled judgment and imagination.

It is advised to carefully analyze the generated text after utilizing ChatGPT. This includes proofreading the content to ensure that it adheres to your standards, checking for grammatical and spelling issues, and making that the tone and voice are consistent with your brand or message.

Furthermore, even though ChatGPT is a very effective tool for creating content, it is important to remember that it must maintain the importance of human editing. Review and edit the generated text to ensure it adheres to your standards and accurately conveys your brand’s message.

CHAPTER 4

Key Techniques for ChatGPT Users

Unlock the full potential of your content creation with ChatGPT. While already a powerful tool, there are advanced techniques you can utilize to take your content to the next level.

To ensure optimal results from ChatGPT, providing comprehensive prompts containing all necessary information is crucial. Provide ChatGPT with all the necessary information, including the desired tone, style, target audience, and other relevant details to help you understand your requirements.

Experience the full range of creativity with ChatGPT's temperature setting, which allows you to adjust the level of inventiveness and surprise in the generated text. By default, this parameter is set to 0.7. However, depending on your specific needs, you can adjust it to a higher or lower value. Experience the unexpected and creative power of language written at a higher temperature while enjoying the predictability and security of language written at a lower temperature. Have you changed this setting to see the results for yourself? Please do it now.

Take control of your generated text with ChatGPT's length setting. Adjust the amount of text generated for each query to your liking. Customize the parameter setting to your liking by adjusting it to a higher or lower value as needed, although the default is 2048 characters. Customize the length option to suit your needs, whether you require text for a specific prompt. Have you asked it to shorten or expand on any output yet?

Customize the level of unpredictability in your generated text with ChatGPT's top-p setting adjustment feature. Set to 1 by default, this parameter can be easily adjusted to fit your specific needs, whether you require a higher or lower value. Achieve greater text predictability with a lower top-p value or opt for a higher top-p setting to generate more unpredictable text.

ChatGPT is a valuable tool, but it should differ from the human touch of editing. Take the time to meticulously edit the result to guarantee a flawless outcome that exceeds your expectations.

It is possible to use ChatGPT in a few ways to boost productivity, improve efficiency, and make money online. ChatGPT enables users to engage in more intricate interactions with the system by enabling the creation of multi-turn discussions. This may be helpful in situations involving customer service or sales, where customers may be required to give more specific information or ask several questions.

One of the most powerful tools is to use other systems or processes you can use by yourself; use ChatGPT to speed up the process. And depending on how you learn, the Pareto Principle may be the best-advanced technique you can use. According to the Pareto Principle, commonly called the 80/20 rule, roughly 80% of outcomes result from 20% of causes. In other words, a small number of inputs or efforts typically result in many outcomes.

This idea is named after the Italian economist Vilfredo Pareto, who noted that only 20% of the people in Italy held 80% of the country's land. Since then, numerous disciplines, including business, economics, and individual productivity, have used the Pareto Principle.

For instance, according to the Pareto Principle, just 20% of a company's consumers or products account for 80% of its income. A corporation

might enhance areas already functioning well to have the biggest impact.The Pareto Principle may also suggest that only 20% of a person's chores or habits account for 80% of their performance in terms of personal productivity. One prompt would be "transform key concepts or lessons from {TOPIC} into engaging stories to help me better understand the material."

PROMPT: transform key concepts or lessons from {how to make money online} into engaging stories to help me better understand the material

ChatGPT:

SURE, LET ME SHARE A FEW EXAMPLES WITH YOU TO ASSIST YOU GRASP THE FUNDAMENTAL IDEAS AND TEACHINGS OF EARNING MONEY ONLINE:

NARROW YOUR FOCUS TO STAND OUT: ONCE UPON A TIME, A WOMAN BY THE NAME OF MARIA HAD A PASSION FOR MAKING HANDCRAFTED SOAP. SHE MADE AN ATTEMPT TO SELL THEM ONLINE, BUT SHE RECEIVED LITTLE INTEREST. MARIA MADE THE DECISION TO FOCUS HER BUSINESS ON PRODUCING VEGAN SOAPS FOR THOSE WITH SENSITIVE SKIN ONE DAY. SHE CONCENTRATED ON THIS MARKET AND DEVELOPED A DISTINCTIVE BRAND THAT SET HER APART FROM OTHER SOAP PRODUCERS. SHE EVEN DEVELOPED SOCIAL MEDIA POSTS AND BLOG ENTRIES EXCLUSIVELY FOR PERSONS WITH SENSITIVE SKIN. MARIA'S BUSINESS SOON TOOK OFF, AND SHE WAS EARNING A SIZABLE SUM OF MONEY FROM THE SALE OF HER VEGAN SOAPS.

THE TAKEAWAY IS THAT YOU MAY DIFFERENTIATE YOURSELF FROM THE COMPETITION AND DRAW IN A DEVOTED CLIENTELE WHO WILL PAY FOR YOUR GOODS OR SERVICES BY NARROWING DOWN AND SPECIALIZING IN A PARTICULAR SECTOR.

CREATE RELATIONSHIPS WITH YOUR AUDIENCE: DAVID WANTS TO OFFER DIGITAL THINGS ONLINE IN ORDER TO GENERATE MONEY. HE WAS AWARE THAT HE FIRST NEEDED TO CULTIVATE A DEVOTED FOLLOWING. HE THEN LAUNCHED A BLOG AND STARTED POSTING HELPFUL INFORMATION THAT WAS DESIGNED

TO AID OTHERS. IN ADDITION, DAVID INTERACTED WITH HIS AUDIENCE BY RESPONDING TO ALL EMAILS AND COMMENTS. HIS AUDIENCE WAS ANXIOUS TO PURCHASE HIS DIGITAL PRODUCT WHEN IT WAS FINALLY PUBLISHED, AND HE MADE A TON OF MONEY.

THE TAKEAWAY: IF YOU WANT TO EARN MONEY ONLINE, YOU MUST ESTABLISH RELATIONSHIPS WITH YOUR AUDIENCE. YOU CAN BUILD A DEVOTED FOLLOWING THAT WILL SUPPORT YOUR BUSINESS BY ADDING VALUE AND INTERACTING WITH YOUR AUDIENCE.

THERE ONCE WAS A WOMAN BY THE NAME OF SARAH WHO MADE MONEY ONLINE BY SELLING HER OWN JEWELRY. ALTHOUGH SHE WAS PROSPERING, SHE WAS AWARE THAT SHE COULDN'T RELY JUST ON ONE SOURCE OF MONEY. SARAH MADE THE DECISION TO LAUNCH A YOUTUBE CHANNEL WHERE SHE WOULD POST HOW-TO GUIDES FOR MAKING JEWELRY. SHE ALSO ESTABLISHED A PODCAST IN WHICH SHE CONDUCTED INTERVIEWS WITH OTHER JEWELRY DESIGNERS. SARAH EVEN CREATED AN ELECTRONIC BOOK ABOUT THE DEVELOPMENT OF JEWELRY. SARAH WAS ABLE TO INCREASE HER ONLINE EARNINGS BY VARYING HER SOURCES OF INCOME.

THE KEY TO EARNING MONEY ONLINE IS TO DIVERSIFY YOUR SOURCES OF INCOME. EXPAND THE RANGE OF YOUR OFFERINGS AND LOOK INTO DIFFERENT REVENUE STREAMS.

The Above used 3.5, and I will put four below so you can see the difference, but I will only show one result in the future.

ChatGPT:

CERTAINLY, LET'S MAKE THESE CONCEPTS MORE ACCESSIBLE THROUGH STORYTELLING.

1. IDENTIFY YOUR MARKET: THINK OF THIS LIKE A TREASURE HUNT. IMAGINE YOU'RE AN EXPLORER IN A NEW LAND FILLED WITH DIVERSE TRIBES, EACH WITH THEIR UNIQUE CUSTOMS AND DESIRES. YOUR MISSION IS TO IDENTIFY WHICH TRIBE YOU'RE MOST EQUIPPED TO SERVE. JUST AS AN EXPLORER WOULD STUDY AND UNDERSTAND THE TRIBES, YOU NEED TO THOROUGHLY RESEARCH AND UNDERSTAND YOUR POTENTIAL ONLINE AUDIENCE.

2. FIND YOUR NICHE: THIS IS AKIN TO BEING A CRAFTSMAN IN A MEDIEVAL TOWN. IF YOU'RE A BLACKSMITH, AND THE TOWN ALREADY HAS SEVERAL OF THEM, YOUR CHANCES OF MAKING A LOT OF MONEY ARE SLIM. HOWEVER, IF YOU SPECIALIZE IN CRAFTING BEAUTIFUL HORSESHOES, SOMETHING OTHER BLACKSMITHS AREN'T DOING, YOU'LL ATTRACT ALL THE HORSE OWNERS IN TOWN TO YOUR DOOR. LIKEWISE, IN THE ONLINE WORLD, SPECIALIZING IN A SPECIFIC AREA (YOUR NICHE) CAN HELP YOU STAND OUT FROM THE COMPETITION AND ATTRACT YOUR IDEAL CUSTOMERS.

3. BE PERSISTENT: IMAGINE YOU'RE A FARMER. YOU'VE PLOUGHED YOUR FIELD, SOWED THE SEEDS, AND NOW YOU'RE WAITING FOR THE CROPS TO GROW. YOU CAN'T RUSH IT; YOU NEED PATIENCE. SOME DAYS IT RAINS, OTHER DAYS, IT'S TOO HOT, AND PESTS ARE ALWAYS A CONCERN. BUT YOU PERSEVERE, TEND TO YOUR FIELD, AND EVENTUALLY, YOU'LL HAVE A BOUNTIFUL HARVEST. IN THE WORLD OF ONLINE BUSINESS, YOU'LL FACE NUMEROUS CHALLENGES, BUT IF YOU'RE PERSISTENT AND WORK DILIGENTLY, THE REWARDS CAN BE SUBSTANTIAL.

4. INNOVATION AND RISK-TAKING: PICTURE YOURSELF AS AN INVENTOR. YOU'VE SEEN THAT PEOPLE STRUGGLE TO CARRY THEIR SHOPPING HOME. YOU IMAGINE A CART THAT COULD HELP. IT'S RISKY – IT MAY NOT WORK, PEOPLE MAY NOT LIKE IT, BUT YOU DECIDE TO CREATE IT ANYWAY. YOU INVENT THE SHOPPING CART, AND SUDDENLY, EVERYONE WANTS ONE. YOU'VE TAKEN A RISK, BUT THE REWARD IS IMMENSE. SIMILARLY, IN THE DIGITAL WORLD, THE KEY TO SUCCESS OFTEN LIES IN INNOVATIVE SOLUTIONS TO EVERYDAY PROBLEMS.

REMEMBER, THE INTERNET IS A VAST MARKETPLACE WITH UNBOUNDED POTENTIAL. WITH THE RIGHT APPROACH, ANYONE CAN CARVE OUT THEIR CORNER AND THRIVE. IT'S ALL ABOUT UNDERSTANDING YOUR AUDIENCE, FINDING YOUR UNIQUE OFFERING, BEING PERSISTENT, AND DARING TO INNOVATE.

Whatever skill set you may want to use; entrepreneur, freelancer, digital marketing, advertising, lead generation, video blogger, copywriting, coding, creating art, creating ads, creating blog content, writing books, SEO? — any issues or concerns you had been a thing of the past with ChatGPT.

ChatGPT can perform these tasks and more; you must use the appropriate prompt(s). This will significantly reduce the time you spend thinking about the unimportant components of the business and free up your time to focus on the customer or the areas you enjoy.

Let's say you want to dive deeper into the suggestion of making money selling products online.

PROMPT: which products should I sell online?

This prompt is very vague and will return responses to help you think and develop your ideas, which is powerful. But read further for even more powerful tricks.

ChatGPT:

IT CAN BE DIFFICULT TO CHOOSE WHICH PRODUCTS TO OFFER ONLINE, BUT THERE ARE A FEW THINGS TO TAKE INTO ACCOUNT:

SELLING GOODS THAT ARE IN LINE WITH YOUR HOBBIES AND ABILITIES CAN MAKE YOUR JOB MORE ENJOYABLE AND HELP YOU MAKE WISER DECISIONS. FOR INSTANCE, IF YOU ENJOY TAKING PICTURES, YOU MIGHT THINK ABOUT SELLING CAMERA GEAR OR PROVIDING PHOTOGRAPHY SERVICES.

DEMAND AND TRENDS: SEEK OUT GOODS THAT ARE BOTH IN GREAT DEMAND AND ON THE RISE. TO FIND POPULAR PRODUCTS AND DECIDE IF THERE IS A MARKET FOR THEM, USE GOOGLE TRENDS, AMAZON'S BEST SELLER LIST, OR SOCIAL MEDIA CHANNELS.

PROFIT MARGIN: TAKE INTO ACCOUNT THE PRODUCTS' PROFIT MARGINS WHEN MAKING YOUR DECISION. LOOK FOR THINGS THAT CAN BE OFFERED AT A HIGHER PRICE WHILE YET HAVING A LOW COST OF GOODS SOLD (COGS).

COMPETITION: CONSIDER THE LEVEL OF COMPETITION IN THE MARKET. TO FIND OUT WHAT PRODUCTS AND PRICING OTHER MERCHANTS ARE OFFERING, TRY GOOGLE SHOPPING, AMAZON, OR EBAY.

CONSIDER THE SIZE, FRAGILITY, WEIGHT, AND SHIPPING AND HANDLING NEEDS WHEN CHOOSING A PRODUCT, AS WELL AS HOW IT WILL BE SHIPPED AND

HANDLED. MAKE SURE YOU CAN DELIVER YOUR GOODS TO CUSTOMERS INEXPENSIVELY AND SAFELY.

IN THE END, IT'S CRUCIAL TO DO YOUR RESEARCH AND PICK GOODS THAT ARE IN HIGH DEMAND, HAVE SIGNIFICANT PROFIT MARGINS, AND ARE ENJOYABLE TO WORK WITH. TO EFFECTIVELY MARKET AND SELL YOUR PRODUCTS, YOU MUST ALSO HAVE A SOLID MARKETING STRATEGY AND A WELL-DESIGNED ONLINE STORE.

PROMPT: Which products should I sell online to make 2,000 dollars a day, working 10 hours a week that are technology-based?

ChatGPT:

IT'S AN AMBITIOUS AMBITION TO MAKE $2,000 PER DAY WORKING ONLY 10 HOURS PER WEEK, BUT HERE ARE SEVERAL TECHNOLOGY-RELATED THINGS YOU MIGHT THINK ABOUT SELLING:

MOBILE APPLICATIONS: YOU CAN MAKE MOBILE APPLICATIONS AND SELL THEM ON APP STORES LIKE APPLE'S APP STORE AND GOOGLE PLAY IF YOU HAVE PROGRAMMING AND APP DEVELOPMENT EXPERTISE. THE APP CAN BE MADE MONEY FROM THROUGH IN-APP PURCHASES, SUBSCRIPTIONS, OR ADVERTISEMENTS.

SOFTWARE: IF YOU ARE KNOWLEDGEABLE IN A PARTICULAR FIELD, YOU CAN MAKE AND SELL SOFTWARE ONLINE. THROUGH YOUR WEBSITE OR ON RETAILERS' WEBSITES LIKE AMAZON OR EBAY, YOU CAN SELL THE SOFTWARE.

E-COMMERCE PLATFORMS: YOU CAN CONSTRUCT YOUR OWN E-COMMERCE PLATFORM AND MARKET IT TO BUSINESSES IF YOU HAVE EXPERIENCE DESIGNING AND DEVELOPING E-COMMERCE PLATFORMS. THE PLATFORM CAN BE MADE PROFITABLE BY SUBSCRIPTION FEES, TRANSACTION FEES, OR ADVERTISEMENTS.

ONLINE COURSES: IF YOU ARE A SPECIALIST IN A PARTICULAR FIELD, YOU CAN DEVELOP ONLINE COURSES THAT YOU CAN SELL TO THOSE WHO WANT TO ACQUIRE THE SAME KNOWLEDGE. IT'S SIMPLE TO DESIGN AND SELL YOUR COURSE, THANKS TO PLATFORMS LIKE UDEMY AND COURSERA.

AFFILIATE MARKETING: THIS METHOD OF EARNING MONEY IS ALSO AVAILABLE. THIS ENTAILS MARKETING THE GOODS OF OTHER BUSINESSES ON YOUR WEBSITE OR THROUGH SOCIAL MEDIA IN EXCHANGE FOR A COMMISSION ON EACH TRANSACTION THAT RESULTS FROM YOUR REFERRAL.

REMEMBER THAT ACHIEVING THE DIFFICULT OBJECTIVE OF EARNING $2,000 PER DAY WITH ONLY 10 HOURS OF WORK PER WEEK MAY REQUIRE TIME AND EFFORT. IT'S CRUCIAL TO PICK A PRODUCT FOR WHICH YOU HAVE ABILITIES AND ENTHUSIASM, AND TO HAVE A SOLID MARKETING PLAN TO MARKET AND SELL YOUR PRODUCT EFFECTIVELY.

The days of laboriously crafting emails that took hours are long gone. If you want to email a possible client as an insurance agency, you must ask ChatGPT. Try this example below or create one that makes sense to you and your business or business ideas.

PROMPT: Write a marketing email for an insurance agency to a prospective customer

ChatGPT: (Get used to typing in the prompt on your computer) What was your result?

Suppose it was like mine; then it was a good starting point if you struggle with what to write. Here is another example of an email demonstrating how simple it is to modify the prompt and make it applicable to a different business.

I created an email for a Digital Marketing Company in less than a minute. You can send it with just some small changes.

PROMPT: Write a cold email to a potential client for a Digital Marketing Company.

ChatGPT:

SUBJECT: BOOST YOUR ONLINE PRESENCE WITH OUR DIGITAL MARKETING SERVICES

DEAR [CLIENT NAME],

I HOPE YOU ARE WELL AND READING MY EMAIL. I AM THE FOUNDER OF [YOUR DIGITAL MARKETING COMPANY NAME] AND GO BY THE NAME OF [YOUR NAME].

THROUGH SMART DIGITAL MARKETING, WE SPECIALIZE IN ASSISTING COMPANIES LIKE YOURS TO ENHANCE THEIR ONLINE PRESENCE AND INCREASE LEAD GENERATION.

I CAME ACROSS YOUR WEBSITE AND WAS [SPECIFICALLY STATE SOMETHING ABOUT THEIR PRODUCTS/SERVICES, CONTENT, OR STYLE] THAT PARTICULARLY PLEASED YOU. TO REACH A LARGER AUDIENCE, I SAW THAT YOUR WEB PRESENCE COULD BE INCREASED.

IN RESPONSE OUR TEAM OF SPECIALISTS CAN DEVELOP A SPECIFIC DIGITAL MARKETING PLAN FOR YOUR COMPANY THAT TAKES INTO ACCOUNT THE FOLLOWING:

• SEARCH ENGINE OPTIMIZATION (SEO) TO RAISE YOUR WEBSITE'S PPC (PAY-PER-CLICK) POSITION ON GOOGLE ADVERTISING TO BRING IN MORE RELEVANT VISITORS TO YOUR WEBSITE

• UTILIZING SOCIAL MEDIA TO INTERACT WITH YOUR AUDIENCE AND SPREAD BRAND RECOGNITION

• USING CONTENT MARKETING TO POSITION YOUR COMPANY AS A THOUGHT LEADER IN YOUR SECTOR

TO NURTURE LEADS AND TURN THEM INTO CUSTOMERS, USE EMAIL MARKETING

WE WOULD LOVE TO ASSIST YOUR COMPANY EXPERIENCES THE SAME KIND OF TREMENDOUS GROWTH THAT WE HAVE HELPED COMPANIES IN FIELDS SIMILAR TO YOURS ACHIEVE. OUR TRACK RECORD OF SUCCESS SPEAKS FOR ITSELF.

PLEASE LET ME KNOW IF YOU'RE INTERESTED IN FINDING OUT MORE ABOUT OUR OFFERINGS AND HOW WE CAN ASSIST YOU IN ACHIEVING YOUR INTERNET MARKETING OBJECTIVES. I'D BE PLEASED TO SET UP A CALL SO WE CAN TALK MORE.

BEST REGARDS,

[YOUR NAME]

This is okay, especially if you are having trouble, but we can show you how to improve. Make it more engaging and personable, for example.

PROMPT: Write a cold email to a potential client so they can discover the digital marketing edge their business needs with [Company Name]

What response did you get? Ensure you are typing this or more specific prompts as you read into your ChatGPT.

ChatGPT:

SUBJECT: UNLEASHING YOUR BUSINESS'S POTENTIAL WITH [COMPANY NAME]'S UNIQUE DIGITAL MARKETING STRATEGIES

DEAR [CLIENT'S NAME],

I HOPE THIS MESSAGE FINDS YOU WELL. MY NAME IS [YOUR NAME] AND I AM [YOUR POSITION] AT [COMPANY NAME]. I CAME ACROSS [CLIENT'S BUSINESS NAME] WHILE CONDUCTING MARKET RESEARCH AND WAS IMPRESSED BY THE EXCEPTIONAL SERVICE YOUR COMPANY PROVIDES.

OUR TEAM AT [COMPANY NAME] SPECIALIZES IN PROVIDING TOP-TIER DIGITAL MARKETING SOLUTIONS TO BUSINESSES AIMING TO REACH GREATER HEIGHTS IN TODAY'S DIGITAL ERA. WE OFFER A SUITE OF SERVICES, FROM SEARCH ENGINE OPTIMIZATION TO SOCIAL MEDIA MANAGEMENT, TO HELP COMPANIES EXPAND THEIR DIGITAL FOOTPRINT AND, IN TURN, DRIVE SUBSTANTIAL GROWTH.

I UNDERSTAND THAT IN TODAY'S INCREASINGLY DIGITAL MARKETPLACE, IT CAN BE CHALLENGING TO STAND OUT AMONGST THE COMPETITION. WITH OUR EXPERTISE, WE BELIEVE WE CAN ASSIST [CLIENT'S BUSINESS NAME] IN BREAKING THROUGH THIS BARRIER. WE PRIDE OURSELVES ON DEVELOPING TAILORED STRATEGIES THAT RESONATE WITH OUR CLIENTS' SPECIFIC NEEDS AND OBJECTIVES.

I BELIEVE THAT [CLIENT'S BUSINESS NAME] COULD GREATLY BENEFIT FROM OUR PERSONALIZED DIGITAL MARKETING STRATEGIES AND THAT WE COULD POTENTIALLY COLLABORATE TO UNLOCK NEW GROWTH OPPORTUNITIES FOR YOUR BUSINESS.

WOULD YOU BE AVAILABLE FOR A 15-MINUTE CALL NEXT WEEK TO DISCUSS HOW WE CAN HELP BOOST [CLIENT'S BUSINESS NAME]'S ONLINE PRESENCE? I WOULD BE DELIGHTED TO SHARE HOW WE HAVE ASSISTED SIMILAR COMPANIES IN ENHANCING THEIR DIGITAL MARKETING STRATEGIES.

THANK YOU FOR CONSIDERING OUR SERVICES. I LOOK FORWARD TO THE POSSIBILITY OF WORKING TOGETHER.

BEST REGARDS,

ChatGPT addresses the receiver personally and expresses a sincere interest in their business and well-being. As you can imagine, this applies to any business.

ChatGPT's customer care multilingual support can assist clients who speak various languages. ChatGPT could translate communications between languages and be trained in various languages, enabling efficient communication between customers and enterprises.

PROMPT: Can you respond to the following consumer query in English, French, Spanish, and Japanese with first-rate customer service? What qualities and advantages come with buying this product?

ChatGPT:

ENGLISH:

WE APPRECIATE YOUR INTEREST IN OUR OFFERING IN ENGLISH. [LIST OF FEATURES] IS JUST ONE OF OUR PRODUCT'S ATTRIBUTES. YOU CAN PROFIT FROM [LIST OF PERKS] BY PURCHASING OUR GOODS. PLEASE REMEMBER TO ASK AN ADDITIONAL QUESTIONS IF YOU HAVE ANY.

FRENCH:

MERCI DE VOUS INTÉRESSER À NOTRE PRODUIT ! LES CARACTÉRISTIQUES DE NOTRE PRODUIT INCLUENT [LIST OF FEATURES]. EN ACHETANT NOTRE PRODUIT, VOUS POUVEZ PROFITER DES AVANTAGES DE [LIST OF BENEFITS]. SI VOUS AVEZ D'AUTRES QUESTIONS, N'HÉSITEZ PAS À DEMANDER.

SPANISH:

¡GRACIAS POR SU INTERÉS EN NUESTRO PRODUCTO! LAS CARACTERÍSTICAS DE NUESTRO PRODUCTO INCLUYEN [LIST OF FEATURES]. AL COMPRAR NUESTRO PRODUCTO, PUEDE DISFRUTAR DE LOS BENEFICIOS DE [LIST OF BENEFITS]. SI TIENE MÁS PREGUNTAS, NO DUDE EN PREGUNTAR.

JAPANESE:

当社の製品にご興味いただきありがとうございます。当社の製品の特徴には、 [LIST OF FEATURES] が含まれています。当社の製品を購入することで、 [LIST OF BENEFITS] の利点を享受することができます。他にもご質問がある場合は、お気軽にお問い合わせください。

We no longer must do business in our city or state; we can be anywhere and make more money online. ChatGPT may be trained using client information like purchase history and chat history. Using client feedback, each customer's profile will be unique. ChatGPT can respond to a customer's message with pertinent information about their requirements and preferences.

ChatGPT can be taught to recognize and respond to common consumer grievances like poor product quality, slow shipping, or incorrect billing. When a client makes a complaint, ChatGPT can review the submission and provide a response acknowledging the customer's issues and offering potential fixes.

ChatGPT can create unique email templates for customers using the supplied client information. ChatGPT can use a template to produce an email tailored to the client's unique needs and interests when a business must contact a client.

PROMPT: Could you write a customer service email to someone having trouble contacting our service because of a heavy workload?

ChatGPT:

SUBJECT: YOUR INQUIRY TO [COMPANY NAME]: WE'RE HERE TO HELP

DEAR [CUSTOMER'S NAME],

FIRSTLY, I WOULD LIKE TO EXPRESS MY SINCERE APOLOGIES FOR ANY DIFFICULTY YOU'VE EXPERIENCED IN REACHING OUR CUSTOMER SERVICE TEAM RECENTLY. WE VALUE YOUR TIME AND YOUR BUSINESS, AND WE ARE TRULY SORRY FOR ANY INCONVENIENCE THIS MAY HAVE CAUSED.

AT [COMPANY NAME], WE ARE CURRENTLY EXPERIENCING AN UNUSUALLY HIGH VOLUME OF CUSTOMER INQUIRIES, WHICH HAS EXTENDED OUR RESPONSE TIME. PLEASE REST ASSURED, WE'RE DILIGENTLY WORKING TO ADDRESS THIS ISSUE AND IMPROVE OUR SERVICE RESPONSE TIMES.

YOUR CONCERN IS IMPORTANT TO US, AND WE WANT TO ENSURE IT IS ADDRESSED APPROPRIATELY. IF YOU COULD KINDLY PROVIDE MORE DETAIL ABOUT THE ISSUE YOU'RE FACING, I WILL PERSONALLY ENSURE THAT YOUR QUERY IS PRIORITIZED.

ALTERNATIVELY, WE CAN ALSO ARRANGE A CONVENIENT TIME FOR A MEMBER OF OUR TEAM TO CALL YOU DIRECTLY, IN CASE YOU PREFER TO DISCUSS THE MATTER OVER THE PHONE.

WE TRULY APPRECIATE YOUR UNDERSTANDING DURING THIS TIME. YOUR PATIENCE IS INVALUABLE, AND WE ARE COMMITTED TO PROVIDING YOU WITH THE LEVEL OF SERVICE YOU EXPECT AND DESERVE FROM [COMPANY NAME].

THANK YOU FOR YOUR CONTINUED SUPPORT, AND WE LOOK FORWARD TO RESOLVING YOUR QUERY AS SWIFTLY AS POSSIBLE.

BEST REGARDS,

[YOUR NAME] [YOUR POSITION] [COMPANY NAME] [YOUR CONTACT INFORMATION]

[COMPANY NAME]

If you've ever created a YouTube video or a podcast, you know how much work goes into it. What if you could produce it better and faster using ChatGPT? Starting to see how this platform can help almost every business idea of making money online? Before you even start recording - you must write a compelling introduction to hook the viewer, organize the script into a logical structure with headings and subheadings, use simple and easy-to-understand language, create a call-to-action to subscribe to your channel, rehearse, edit, optimize the script for SEO, and keep the tone, language, and message of your channel consistent.

You can also create a Script for a YouTube video or a podcast you're trying to build into your social media presence. Consider how helpful using the blog article you created to generate a video/podcast can be. You can use the existing content you generated for a blog outline and turn it into a script you can read and post on any video platform.

To fully utilize these technologies, ChatGPT is essential in creating the ideal script and instruction videos. Remember the importance of voice-overs, a crucial component of any video production. ChatGPT can help you write a perfect script, and text-to-speech software will enable you to produce a voice-over that is flawlessly delivered quickly.

Use ChatGPT to create polished scripts and instructions, as well as to generate keywords for better SEO. You may have a voice-over prepared and a video script available in seconds. The results will be better the more specific your directions are. Remember that demand for video creation is huge since people prefer watching to reading.

PROMPT: using the five informal blogs copied above, please create a step-by-step, detailed, and engaging YouTube video script.

ChatGPT:

SURE! THE FOLLOWING IS A SCRIPT FOR THE "HOW TO BUY THE PERFECT LAPTOP WITHOUT LOSING YOUR MIND" YOUTUBE VIDEO, WHICH WILL WALK

VIEWERS THROUGH EACH STAGE IN-DEPTH AND KEEP THEIR ATTENTION:

INTRO:

HEY, HOWDY, DUDES! GREETINGS FROM OUR CHANNEL ONCE MORE. WE'RE GOING TO DISCUSS PURCHASING A LAPTOP, ONE OF THE TRICKIEST CHORES IN THE COMPUTER WORLD, TODAY. THIS VIDEO IS FOR YOU IF YOU'VE EVER FOUND YOURSELF TRYING TO DECIDE WHICH LAPTOP TO PICK FROM A WALL OF COMPUTERS. YOU CAN FIND THE IDEAL LAPTOP WITHOUT LOSING YOUR MIND IF YOU USE OUR FIVE SIMPLE SUGGESTIONS. THEN LET'S GET GOING!

FIRST TIP: HOW TO GET A GREAT LAPTOP DEAL WITHOUT GIVING YOUR SOUL TO THE TECHNOLOGY GODS

BUYING A GOOD LAPTOP DOESN'T HAVE TO COST A FORTUNE. IN FACT, THERE ARE SEVERAL WAYS TO GET A GREAT DEAL WITHOUT SETTLING FOR INFERIOR GOODS.

FOR DISCOUNTS ON LAPTOPS, VISIT ONLINE RETAILERS LIKE AMAZON, BEST BUY, AND NEWEGG. ADDITIONALLY, YOU CAN SUBSCRIBE TO EMAIL NEWSLETTERS TO LEARN ABOUT UPCOMING SALES.

ON COMPUTERS THAT HAVE BEEN REPAIRED OR OPENED BUT NEVER USED, YOU MAY FREQUENTLY FIND EXCELLENT DEALS. JUST BE CAREFUL TO CHECK THE WARRANTY AND PURCHASE FROM A RELIABLE SOURCE.

NEVER HESITATE TO BARGAIN WITH THE MERCHANT OR SALESMAN. BY SIMPLY ASKING, YOU MIGHT BE ASTONISHED AT HOW MUCH MONEY YOU CAN SAVE.

TIP #2: HOW TO MAINTAIN THE VITALITY OF YOUR LAPTOP. YOU WANT TO MAKE SURE YOUR IDEAL LAPTOP LASTS AS LONG AS POSSIBLE ONCE YOU'VE FOUND IT. HERE ARE SOME POINTERS FOR MAINTAINING THE TOP CONDITION OF YOUR LAPTOP:

REGULARLY CLEAN YOUR LAPTOP WITH A MICROFIBER CLOTH, AND USE COMPRESSED AIR TO REMOVE ANY DUST OR DEBRIS FROM THE KEYBOARD AND VENTS.

NEVER LEAVE YOUR LAPTOP OUTSIDE IN THE COLD OR IN A HOT AUTOMOBILE. EXTREME TEMPERATURES HAVE THE POTENTIAL TO HARM THE BATTERY AND OTHER PARTS.

ANTIVIRUS SOFTWARE INSTALLATION BY USING A RELIABLE ANTIVIRUS TOOL, YOU CAN SHIELD YOUR LAPTOP AGAINST VIRUSES AND MALWARE. THERE ARE MANY FREE ALTERNATIVES AVAILABLE, INCLUDING AVAST AND AVG.

TIP #3: THE SEARCH FOR THE PERFECT LAPTOP: A TRIAL-AND-ERROR PROCESS

IT DOESN'T HAVE TO BE A DIFFICULT AND DRAWN-OUT PROCEDURE TO PURCHASE A LAPTOP.

DETERMINE YOUR LAPTOP'S INTENDED USE (SUCH AS GAMING, JOB, OR SCHOOL) AND SELECT ONE WITH THE SPECIFICATIONS THAT ARE APPROPRIATE FOR YOUR REQUIREMENTS.

READ EVALUATIONS DON'T MERELY FOLLOW THE SALESPERSON'S RECOMMENDATIONS. TO LEARN MORE ABOUT THE RELIABILITY AND PERFORMANCE OF THE LAPTOP, READ ONLINE USER REVIEWS.

BEFORE YOU CHOOSE, IF AT ALL FEASIBLE, CHECK OUT A FEW LAPTOPS IN PERSON. MAKE SURE THE KEYBOARD, SCREEN, AND OVERALL FEEL OF THE LAPTOP ARE COMFORTABLE FOR YOU.

TIP #4: THE PC VS. MAC GREAT LAPTOP DEBATE. THE CHOICE BETWEEN A PC AND A MAC IS ONE OF THE MOST IMPORTANT ONES YOU'LL HAVE TO MAKE WHEN PURCHASING A LAPTOP. HERE ARE A FEW BENEFITS AND DRAWBACKS OF EACH:

PCS TYPICALLY COST LESS AND HAS A WIDER SELECTION OF BRANDS AND MODELS.

THE DURABILITY, DEPENDABILITY, AND USER-FRIENDLY INTERFACE OF MACS ARE WELL RENOWNED. WHILE MACS ARE SUPERIOR FOR ARTISTIC TASKS LIKE GRAPHIC DESIGN AND VIDEO EDITING, PCS ARE BETTER FOR GAMING AND CUSTOMIZING.

TIP #5: A CRASH COURSE IN LAPTOP BUYING FOR THE TECH-CHALLENGED

DON'T WORRY IF YOU'RE UNFAMILIAR WITH THE WORLD OF COMPUTERS.

If you need more information or the script generated isn't long enough, just type, "Please rewrite it to be 200 words longer with more detail on [topic]."

I still need to put the ChatGPT response here; you could change the prompt and use it to create a video script on any topic and length.

Social media marketing is a must for any entrepreneur or business owner. Whether you run your social media marketing or outsource the work to an agency is quite competitive. Keeping up with all the updates on social media sites can be a real burden.

Keeping up with the newest developments and trends in social media marketing is crucial. You want to stay caught up in the field because it always evolves. Developing interesting material that appeals to your target audience might be challenging. Social media marketing ROI measurement can take much work. The effect of social media activities on a company's bottom line is difficult to quantify. It might be challenging to manage client expectations.

As your company expands, managing a team can become a real challenge. Social media experts might need help to work with. Creativity and strategy must be balanced. You must create interesting, original material that advances a client's commercial objectives. Delivering results for clients while staying within budget can take much work. You're constantly looking for new material to offer to your clientele. You can boost conversions and drive sales for your clients and your business by utilizing ChatGPT to create expert-caliber content.

CHAPTER 5

Use ChatGPT to Become a Top Earner Online

I hope you are like I was and excited to experience the power of ChatGPT, the ultimate tool to help you generate a steady stream of passive income effortlessly. Discover the ultimate strategies to boost your income and ascend to the pinnacle of the online content creation and freelancer pay scale.

Distinguishing yourself in a specific niche is a proven strategy to differentiate yourself from competitors and attract top-tier clients willing to pay a premium. From finance and investing to health and fitness, the possibilities are endless. Position yourself as an expert in a specific area of interest and watch as your client base grows. Focus on a particular topic to establish authority and attract a wider audience.

Unlock the potential of social networking sites such as Facebook, LinkedIn, and Twitter to generate leads and attract customers effortlessly. Maximize your potential for attracting new business by frequently sharing your ChatGPT-generated content and engaging with your fans. Develop a strong online presence that will set you apart from the competition.

Showcasing your skills and expertise through high-quality samples is a powerful tactic for attracting valuable clients. Elevate your chances of securing new clients by showcasing your worth through top-notch samples that rival or surpass your competitors.

Stay updated with the latest trends and best practices in online content creation by networking with fellow ChatGPT users. Furthermore, establishing connections with potential customers interested in your services can be beneficial.

Discover how content creators and freelancers can leverage ChatGPT to create content and generate income in multiple ways. Unlock a world of possibilities with this technology, enabling you to create chatbots, virtual assistants, and customer support services. Maximize your business's efficiency by utilizing it to craft compelling content, from breaking news to engaging social media updates. Save valuable time and resources with this powerful tool.

With ChatGPT, you can effortlessly create exceptional and one-of-a-kind content for your blog, articles, product descriptions, and social media posts. With ChatGPT, writers can effortlessly tap into a wealth of inspiration and ideas to elevate their work. Alternatively, they can delegate some of their research and writing tasks to ChatGPT, freeing up valuable time.

By implementing these proven tactics, elevate your ChatGPT earnings and position yourself as a leading earner in online content creation and freelancing. Deliver exceptional content and unparalleled customer support, and financial rewards will follow.

Discover new project concepts and brainstorm ideas effortlessly with ChatGPT. Harness its power to create cutting-edge solutions for your client's challenges. With ChatGPT, you can effortlessly schedule appointments, send invoices, and manage client conversations all in one place.

Unlock the potential of ChatGPT by crafting bespoke models tailored to specific markets or sectors. With ChatGPT, you can conduct thorough and efficient research on topics that cater to your clients' needs. Save time and elevate your work with this solution.

Follow the most recent ChatGPT developments and try out new features and methods. By doing this, you'll be able to maintain your competitive edge and give your customers the greatest support.

Using ChatGPT as a freelancer can help you advance your profession and increase your income.

Here are a few pieces of advice:

- Use ChatGPT for idea generation and brainstorming. ChatGPT can help you develop original, cutting-edge solutions for your clients, making you stand out as a talented freelancer. Your ability to write and communicate will increase due to your interaction with ChatGPT, which will also be helpful to your freelance business.

- Ensure that you're using these tools morally and legally correct, as this was also tempting to me. This involves observing data privacy laws and abstaining from all forms of discrimination.

- Understanding and utilizing ChatGPT's (and other AI's) limitations is crucial. It doesn't take the role of human wisdom and discretion. Think about how your client views AI and how it might influence their company. Be open about using these technologies and address your client's concerns, as some individuals may be reluctant to adopt AI-powered products or services.

- ChatGPT can be used for research and fact-checking to save time and increase productivity. ChatGPT can help you obtain and verify the information for your clients. As ChatGPT develops and improves, keeping up with new features and capabilities will help you stay competitive in the freelance market.

- For improving the pace and effectiveness of your online freelance work, ChatGPT can be a great tool. Using its language creation features, you may easily create high-quality material, such as articles, blog entries, and social media posts. Because of the time you'll save, you can work with more clients and earn more money.

- Learning to appropriately input prompts and modify the output to suit your needs is crucial to utilize ChatGPT's capabilities fully. Additionally, you can use it for research and data analysis, enabling you to gather information and derive insights quickly for your work.

It's critical to remember that even though ChatGPT can make your work go more quickly, maintaining high standards is still crucial. Always check the output for accuracy, relevance, and compliance with your or your client's needs first. You can become skilled at utilizing ChatGPT to generate high-quality work in less time with practice and experience.

Fast-thinking freelancers are better at engaging clients and meeting their needs. ChatGPT's reminders, scheduling, and organizing capabilities improve project management. These freelancer tools boost productivity and customer happiness. Stay organized and do chores quickly. Increase efficiency and workflow to raise profits and freelance status.

Provide additional training to all AI tools to boost everyone's knowledge of business-specific jargon. Add chatbots or virtual assistants to ChatGPT for a complete solution. Organizations may automate their processes and streamline operations with our cutting-edge automation technologies.

ChatGPT lets you train unique models on specific datasets for precise and relevant responses. This tool lets you easily customize AI replies. Customize the language, tone, and topic to your liking. Create customer service and interaction models that match customer preferences. Models can help bloggers and writers create original content. Custom models can automate data analysis and translation.

ChatGPT's custom model-building capability gives users a strong tool to improve the AI's capabilities and tailor its replies to their requirements. Users can fine-tune the model to produce solutions most pertinent to their needs by training it on data sets. Unique models can be developed for various use cases, like customer service, commerce, or creative writing. Users can ensure that the responses generated by ChatGPT are highly tailored and in line with their business objectives by training the model on specific data sets. Businesses may benefit by improving consumer engagement, boosting sales, and increasing productivity.

ChatGPT can be integrated with other software and solutions to improve functionality and capabilities. ChatGPT, for instance, can relate to chatbots, virtual assistants, and messaging programs to give users more precise and pertinent responses. Automate content production and curation; it can also relate to content management systems. To offer insights and forecasts based on sizable data sets, ChatGPT can also relate to data analytics tools. Users can increase their productivity and efficiency while boosting the accuracy and relevance of the AI's responses by integrating ChatGPT into other applications and tools.

With ChatGPT, users can build chatbots and virtual assistants offering individualized help and support. Developing intelligent agents that can comprehend and reply to user inquiries in natural language is feasible by training ChatGPT on domains and tasks. This can enhance user experience while assisting businesses and organizations in automating customer service and support. A few platforms and devices can access chatbots and virtual assistants developed using ChatGPT by integrating them with messaging services, websites, and mobile applications.

Before using ChatGPT, decide what your goals are and how you plan to use the tool. This will enable you to select and modify the ideal model for your requirements. To get the most out of ChatGPT, the model needs to be practiced using pertinent data. Text, pictures, and other information can be a part of this. The model will be more accurate the more data you submit. ChatGPT is a strong instrument, but the best results necessitate trial and error. Try several prompts and adjust the model to get the desired results.

With ChatGPT, you can become a top-earning freelancer. To be clear, using ChatGPT does not excuse you from doing any work; rather, it enhances and amplifies your current skill sets to produce significantly more high-quality material in the same amount of time.

Some content creation markets are about to transform; many services now have lower entry barriers. We learned how to compose blog posts by creating titles, outlines, and the post itself.

ChatGPT allows you to publish well-researched, educational, and interesting blog posts, articles, or books in a fraction of the time it would take you to write them from scratch. ChatGPT can assist you in creating informative and shareable material for your website or a blog for a customer.

As we've seen, ChatGPT allows you to write five hundred words in only minutes, whereas most people would need hours or even days to complete the task. The first chapter demonstrates how simple it is to create a book outline.

A well-written, informative eBook can be created with ChatGPT in a fraction of the time it would take you to compose one from scratch. Additionally, you'll be able to delight your customers and keep them coming back for more because ChatGPT can assist you in creating more interesting and well-written content.

With ChatGPT, while it will take some time, you will accomplish these tasks in a matter of hours which most others take weeks to do successfully. Even though you can't just ask ChatGPT to write the entire book for you, you can use the same process we used to outline this book, then write the chapter summaries, and then write the actual chapters; with a little editing, it only takes a few hours, which isn't too bad.

PROMPT: create a 10-chapter outline for a blog post with the title [insert your book title here] on [topic].

PROMPT: write a chapter 1 more detailed outline

PROMPT: write the above chapter in the manner of [a favorite author] in a captivating tone. And make it 2,000 words.

Do the above three Prompts using your blog or eBook that you want to write or read. One issue to keep in mind while writing content if a book is that ChatGPT can only produce up to ~3000 words in one response. However, this problem can be easily fixed by suggesting to keep going or giving me more information.

Let's discuss keyword research now.

PROMPT: what keywords should I include in the content on a blog post about SEO maximization

ChatGPT:

HERE ARE SOME KEYWORDS YOU COULD INCLUDE IN A BLOG POST ABOUT SEO MAXIMIZATION:

SEARCH ENGINE OPTIMIZATION (SEO)

KEYWORDS

ON-PAGE OPTIMIZATION

OFF-PAGE OPTIMIZATION

META TAGS

LINK BUILDING

CONTENT OPTIMIZATION

SITE ARCHITECTURE

USER EXPERIENCE (UX)

MOBILE OPTIMIZATION

LOCAL SEO

ANALYTICS

RANK TRACKING

ALGORITHM UPDATES

BACKLINKS

SOCIAL MEDIA OPTIMIZATION (SMO)

CONVERSION OPTIMIZATION

ORGANIC TRAFFIC

PAID SEARCH

It's essential to seamlessly integrate these keywords into your text rather than forcefully inserting them just for the sake of it. Deliver valuable, top-notch content that caters to the requirements of your target audience while adhering to the search engine algorithms' standards.

Use effective SEO (Search Engine Optimization) tactics and strategies to enhance your website's visibility and ranking. Optimize your blog's SEO by utilizing ChatGPT to verify specific keywords and phrases for your text. Discover the power of keywords - the specific words and phrases that individuals use to seek out content akin to yours on the vast expanse of the internet. Elevate your website's search engine ranking by seamlessly incorporating relevant keywords into your blog posts.

Even ask ChatGPT about long-tail keywords, which are precise and in-depth phrases people use to search for topics, which are some of the crucial keywords to add to blog material for SEO optimization. LSI (Latent Semantic Indexing) keywords, which are associated with the primary keyword and add extra context and relevance to the content, are additional significant keywords. To increase the visibility of the blog article, keywords must also be used in the header tags, meta description, and title.

The quantity and caliber of the material, the use of internal and external links, and the inclusion of multimedia components like photographs and videos are additional characteristics that affect SEO optimization. In addition, the content has to be interesting, relevant, and informative for the intended audience. You can raise your website's position, boost traffic, and attract more potential consumers by incorporating these crucial keywords and adhering to SEO best practices. ChatGPT can help do it better and faster.

Rest assured; the outcome will require only minor editing and proofreading. With ChatGPT, you can elevate your ad campaigns to new heights! Create expertly crafted written content that will captivate your audience and drive conversions. Let ChatGPT be your go-to solution for crafting persuasive ad copy, regardless of platform, from landing pages to banner ads to social media promotions. Imagine a situation where a valued client requires an email marketing campaign to promote the release of their latest product.

With ChatGPT, you can gain the competitive edge you need to distinguish yourself and command top rates for your services, regardless of whether you're a seasoned veteran or a newcomer to the online business arena. Experience lightning-fast and precise document creation, top-notch content writing, and unparalleled coding for your one-of-a-kind projects with ChatGPT.

CHAPTER 6

Use ChatGPT to Develop Valuable Recurring Streams of Passive Income

ChatGPT empowers you to craft diverse content that can generate recurring passive income streams. With ChatGPT, you have the power to craft profitable content with e-books, courses, and training materials. With ChatGPT, you can effortlessly craft engaging blog entries, captivating social media updates, and various other types of content that can be monetized through affiliate marketing, sponsored content, and other lucrative avenues. Elevate your status and cultivate a loyal customer base with ChatGPT's ability to help you with content creation services. Establish yourself as a trusted industry expert and attract potential buyers or clients eager to invest in your exceptional products and services. With the right approach, this technique can help you generate long-term passive income streams that evolve and expand over time.

Discover the benefits of ChatGPT for enterprising freelancers and visionary entrepreneurs. Unlock your full potential as a freelancer or business owner with ChatGPT. ChatGPT is here to help you streamline your processes and free up your time to focus on the critical work that requires your unique skills and expertise. Let ChatGPT handle the automation of certain tasks so you can maximize your productivity and achieve your business goals. Revolutionize your idea-generation process with ChatGPT!

Maximize your productivity and take your business to the next level with ChatGPT. Unlock your full freelancer or business owner potential with ChatGPT's powerful features and functionalities. Gain a competitive edge in your field and achieve success like never before.

Discover and refine your digital product concept with the help of ChatGPT's investigative and developmental capabilities. Let ChatGPT help you with brainstorming and product idea development by generating relevant data and ideas. With ChatGPT, you can elevate your product to new heights with exceptional content creation, stunning graphic design, and impeccable product formatting services. Whatever your product or service may be, ChatGPT can help you as it did with me.

Maximize the potential of your digital product with ChatGPT's expert market research and tailored marketing plan. Let us help you reach your target audience and achieve your business goals. Discover your ideal audience, create engaging social media posts and ads, and cultivate effective email marketing strategies with ChatGPT.

Leverage the power of ChatGPT to analyze valuable customer feedback and product suggestions and take your offering to the next level. Discover the optimal price point for your product through strategic experimentation with pricing strategies and leveraging the powerful insights provided by ChatGPT to analyze customer behavior and feedback.

Boost your chances of success and establish a steady stream of passive income with ChatGPT. ChatGPT can assist in generating leads by reviewing consumer inquiries and recommending tailored solutions or goods. You can save time and effort while boosting your income potential by implementing ChatGPT into your digital marketing plan. ChatGPT can be a valuable tool in your quest for financial independence with the appropriate attitude and direction.

Strategies for marketing and selling your items to create passive revenue with ChatGPT

Utilize social media platforms for a successful marketing and sales strategy for digital products made with ChatGPT. Connect with more people and communicate with them using social media to reach a larger audience. Create social media profiles for your company and use them to promote your brand, present your products, and give your fans helpful content.

Offering free trials or samples of your digital products is an additional tactic. This enhances the likelihood that a potential customer will purchase by enabling them to try before they buy. Create a teaser for your product or produce and provide a free chapter of your eBook using ChatGPT.

Using email marketing can also help you increase revenue and cultivate a following of devoted customers. Use ChatGPT to develop tailored email campaigns that address client groups, such as those who have already expressed interest in your products. To maximize the possibility of conversions, ensure your emails are engaging, educational, and pertinent to your client's needs.

You may reach a larger audience and spark interest in your items by working with influencers. Use ChatGPT to find potential influencers, get in touch with them, and forge a productive alliance. This may be a potent strategy for boosting sales and brand recognition.

Tips for developing valuable and marketable products with ChatGPT

Your target market's needs must be considered when creating content and ideas with ChatGPT. Concentrate on producing informative, original content that addresses issues or offers answers. Use conversational and understandable language. Before making your content available to the public, test it on a limited group to ensure it works. The target market's needs must be considered when creating goods with ChatGPT.

Concentrate on producing informative, original content that addresses issues or offers answers. To develop valuable and marketable products with ChatGPT, consider your target audience and their needs, use clear and concise language, provide relevant and useful information, and ensure your product is visually appealing. Using ChatGPT to create material that can be sold, such as podcasts, courses, and eBooks, is one approach to achieve this. You can rapidly and effectively generate high-quality material with ChatGPT's brainstorming tools. Have you tried to use ChatGPT for your specific needs yet? Stop reading for a little while and practice your prompts.

Once developed, you can utilize ChatGPT to market and promote your content. You may find new clients and produce efficient marketing messages with ChatGPT. ChatGPT can automate marketing initiatives like sending emails or posting on social media.

Making and selling chatbots or virtual assistants is another option for using ChatGPT to generate passive income. Virtual assistants and chatbots are gaining popularity across various industries, including customer service, healthcare, and banking. You may use ChatGPT to build chatbots and virtual assistants that are very intelligent and attentive to user needs.

ChatGPT can create, and market customized models to other companies or people. Custom models can be applied to various tasks, including sentiment analysis, predictive analytics, and language translation. You can generate passive income while assisting others in sophisticated problem-solving by designing and selling custom models.

Do you like stocks and investments? Create an Indicator for Trading Bots. Indicators, which are used to assess market data and produce indications for automated trading systems, are one of the significant characteristics of trading bots. It may be a fundamental indicator, a technical indicator, or a hybrid of the two. Technical indicators produce trading indications through mathematical calculations based on market information like price and volume. On the other hand, fundamental indicators use data on the company and the macroeconomic environment to produce indications.

PROMPT: develop a prescriptive indicator that sends out a buy signal when volume rises by 10% over 60 minutes.

ChatGPT: What did you put as your PROMPT? What was the response? Do you need more information? Just ask ChatGPT.

A crucial step in data analysis is creating dashboards or visualizations, which may be used to communicate findings and predictions to others. You may assist businesses and organizations in understanding their data and making better decisions by developing a service that produces these data visualizations or dashboards.

The use of ChatGPT can be beneficial to software development in a variety of ways. It might start by offering technical guidance and insight, assessing code, and resolving code issues to assist with software development. By utilizing these characteristics, the software development process may be expedited, and productivity boosted.

Programs that require natural language processing can be developed using the ChatGPT API. Additionally, ChatGPT may offer beneficial code samples in any programming language using a text prompt that lists the application's demands. You could develop this for yourself or make money creating software for others.

A broad category includes digital assets. It has a variety of works, such as a collection of icons, texture images, and a sophisticated design system. It counts as a digital asset if you create something that consumers desire, anything that makes it easier or faster for designers to work. For instance, you can have it generate picture sets of icons, Web flow plugins for Sigma, scripts for Sketch, templates, mockups, 3D objects, and templates for presentations using flowcharts.

ChatGPT unlocks passive revenue! Our user-friendly software lets anyone duplicate good chances hundreds or thousands of times. Take your chance to earn more with less work. ChatGPT now! Save time making AI art to sell on stock photo websites. Millions of people are flooding these industries, and many are being banned. Target better-paying, less-crowded positions.

It's essential in a saturated market. Participate despite competition. Instead, carefully distinguish your work. Compete fiercely.

ChatGPT unlocks passive income streams for uncomplicated moneymaking. ChatGPT offers unlimited content monetization options. Your works can be sold or used to drive people to your website or social media accounts, where you can make significant money through affiliate marketing or advertising.

ChatGPT can let you profit from your interest! eBooks and online courses on topics you love can earn passive money. ChatGPT makes eBook and course writing easy. It's quick and effective.

ChatGPT's affiliate program unlocks passive money. ChatGPT lets you write engaging product reviews and promotional content with affiliate links. Increase revenue and website traffic today! Customers who buy through your links get commissions.

ChatGPT makes it easy to create engaging content for your website or social media accounts that generates cash through advertising. ChatGPT's high-quality content draws visitors to your website or social media profiles. Use Google AdSense to monetize website traffic. Profit now!

ChatGPT lets you build several passive income streams. ChatGPT unleashes your talents and passions! Our platform lets you easily make money from your expertise. Our top-notch article production services allow you to ditch traditional labor and earn without effort.

Concentrate on things that, even with ChatGPT, will take some time to do well, things that can't be generated perfectly in one prompt. The market will be balanced; it will stand out if you take your time producing high-quality material. Concentrate on eBooks, Blog Posts, YouTube Videos, Online Courses, and Software Applications. eBooks can be a big source of passive income even though they require much upfront work. With Amazon Publishing, you can also make your book available in print without worrying about contracts with traditional publishing houses.

Fortunately, ChatGPT can assist you with many of these; let's begin with identifying a niche. If you are still figuring out where to write, you might have a brainstorming session to develop ideas.

PROMPT: What are some good unique niches to write an eBook in ChatGPT?

ChatGPT:

HERE ARE SOME UNIQUE NICHES THAT YOU COULD CONSIDER WHEN WRITING AN EBOOK:

SUSTAINABLE LIVING: AS THE WORLD BECOMES MORE ENVIRONMENTALLY CONSCIOUS, PEOPLE ARE LOOKING FOR WAYS TO REDUCE THEIR IMPACT ON THE PLANET. AN EBOOK ON SUSTAINABLE LIVING COULD COVER TOPICS SUCH AS ECO-FRIENDLY HOME IMPROVEMENTS, ZERO-WASTE LIVING, OR REDUCING PLASTIC USAGE.

ChatGPT came up with six other ideas and then said these are only a few instances of distinctive niches that you might consider when producing an eBook. The secret is to choose a subject you and your audience will be interested in.

Then your process should be to pick one; let's use the first one and drill down further.

Prompt: give me some topics I can write about in sustainable living.

ChatGPT:

HERE ARE SOME TOPICS YOU CAN WRITE ABOUT IN SUSTAINABLE LIVING:

SUSTAINABLE HOME IMPROVEMENT: ADVICE ON HOW TO MAKE CHANGES TO YOUR HOME THAT ARE MORE ENVIRONMENTALLY FRIENDLY, SUCH AS INSTALLING ENERGY-EFFICIENT FIXTURES OR RAINWATER COLLECTION SYSTEMS.

ZERO WASTE LIVING REFERS TO PRACTICES LIKE COMPOSTING, UTILIZING REUSABLE CONTAINERS, AND SHOPPING IN BULK THAT HELP YOU CREATE LESS WASTE EVERY DAY. YOU MIGHT OFFER ADVICE ON MINIMIZING PAPER, CLOTHES, AND FOOD WASTE.

USING NATIVE PLANTS, COMPOSTING, AND STAYING AWAY FROM PESTICIDES AND COMMERCIAL FERTILIZERS ARE JUST A FEW SUSTAINABLE GARDENING TIPS. ANOTHER THING YOU MAY DO IS TEACH PEOPLE HOW TO GROW THEIR OWN FOOD, WHETHER IT BE IN A BACKYARD GARDEN OR A CONTAINER.

GREEN TRANSPORTATION: METHODS FOR LOWERING YOUR CARBON FOOTPRINT THAT DON'T INCLUDE DRIVING, SUCH TAKING THE BUS, BIKING, OR WALKING. YOU MIGHT ALSO GIVE ADVICE ON CHOOSING A MORE FUEL-EFFICIENT CAR AND ELECTRIC VEHICLE.

SUSTAINABLE FASHION: ADVICE FOR BUILDING A MORE ENVIRONMENTALLY FRIENDLY WARDROBE INCLUDES BUYING USED CLOTHING, SELECTING NATURAL FIBERS, AND SPENDING MONEY ON HIGH-QUALITY ITEMS THAT WILL ENDURE FOR A LONG TIME. ADDITIONALLY, YOU MIGHT TALK ABOUT ETHICAL FASHION LABELS AND THE EFFECTS OF FAST FASHION ON THE ENVIRONMENT.

SUSTAINABLE TRAVEL: STRATEGIES FOR MINIMIZING YOUR IMPACT ON THE

ENVIRONMENT WHILE TRAVELING, SUCH AS PICKING ECO-FRIENDLY LODGING, ASSISTING NEIGHBORHOOD BUSINESSES, AND USING THE BUS. YOU MIGHT ALSO OFFER DETAILS ON VOLUNTEERISM AND SUSTAINABLE TRAVEL.

SUSTAINABLE FOOD REFERS TO METHODS FOR MINIMIZING YOUR ENVIRONMENTAL EFFECT THROUGH YOUR DIETARY CHOICES, SUCH AS FOLLOWING A PLANT-BASED DIET, PURCHASING ORGANIC AND LOCALLY GROWN FOOD, AND CUTTING BACK ON FOOD WASTE. YOU MIGHT ALSO TALK ABOUT THE EFFECTS OF INDUSTRIAL AGRICULTURE ON THE ENVIRONMENT AND SUSTAINABLE FARMING METHODS.

THESE ARE JUST A FEW IDEAS FOR TOPICS YOU CAN WRITE ABOUT IN SUSTAINABLE LIVING. THE KEY IS TO CHOOSE A TOPIC THAT YOU ARE PASSIONATE ABOUT AND THAT WILL RESONATE WITH YOUR AUDIENCE.

Now you can select a topic that makes sense for you want to write on. Let's use the sustainable home improvement example provided above. And now, let's focus on how we can start working on a book outline with the help of our new AI friend.

PROMPT: create an outline for a book on Sustainable home improvement

ChatGPT: I have not included the response, but what did you get? And you can be as specific as you want or need depending on what you want to write.

This outline would offer a fundamental framework for a book on environmentally friendly home improvement. Of course, the author's objectives and intended audience can and should influence the precise subjects covered and the depth of material offered.

Please remember that this is only an example outline and that your research and target audience may need you to add or remove a few things. Additionally, you can expand each section's subtopics based on your needs. We can now generate chapter outlines using the book outline.

You can do a prompt to create an outline for Chapter 1 in the book *Sustainable Home Improvement.* Ask ChatGPT to write a 200-word introduction to the book using the above chapter outline, etc.

You can even go deeper and ask to suggest a few appropriate book titles and subtitles for this book. And even ask it to create a descriptive and engaging sales page for the book. It almost makes me want to buy this book myself or, better yet, create and sell it. See how easy this can be to make money online with ChatGPT?

Let's talk more about a book marketing e-mail. This is one of the big benefits of ChatGPT. Without adding more information, you can ask it to create a marketing email for the book it just helped you write. And now we can get its help to create a Twitter announcement.

Prompt: Create a Twitter announcement for the release of the book

ChatGPT:

YES, HERE IS AN EXAMPLE TWEET ANNOUNCING THE PUBLICATION OF THE BOOK:

"FANTASTIC NEWS! SUSTAINABLE HOME IMPROVEMENT, OUR NEW BOOK, IS NOW AVAILABLE! DISCOVER HOW TO BUILD AN ECO-FRIENDLY HOME USING REAL-WORLD ADVICE, TACTICS, AND CASE STUDIES. #SUSTAINABLE #HOMEIMPROVEMENT" "GET YOUR COPY TODAY AND JOIN THE MILLIONS OF INDIVIDUALS IMPROVING THE ENVIRONMENT."

ChatGPT can also give you marketing emails like the one above and so much more. We can even work with ChatGPT to help guide you with pricing based on your target market and marketplace to optimize sales. I hope you can start to feel how powerful this tool can be for you, making even more money online.

YouTube videos are suitable for passive income because your catalog of videos is valuable as time goes on, as any new audience that finds you would be interested in your old content and can keep generating ad revenue for years afterward. And this is in stark contrast to social media posts which can have a shelf life of a few hours, depending on the platform. Let's say you're unsure of what videos to create; maybe you have a niche or don't. It would work best if you have a topic you know or have experience in, but let's ask ChatGPT for help developing a niche or topic to explore.

Prompt: Give me some ideas about low-competition keywords for a YouTube video on Sustainable Home Improvement.

What did you get as a response from ChatGPT? Was it enough for you? If not, ask again or ask for more details. Practice asking more detailed questions or adding to your original Prompts.

To be sure that these keywords are low competition and have the potential to rank well on YouTube, conduct some additional research and assess their search traffic and competitiveness using other online keyword tools.

How about you ask it to generate an engaging and humorous script? So, it will generate a little short for 10 minutes and need some editing but a good starting point, especially if you're facing writer's block. Usually, you'd have to do the video recording. Still, if you don't like being on camera or would rather have a video created for you that you are can then voiceover, you're in luck, as there is a tool called **Pictory** that even uses AI to generate a full video with images and text based on a script or even a blog that you feed into it. You can then read over it without ever showing your face, or should you choose, use one of their inbuilt AI voice characters to voice your video. However, YouTube videos with AI are rarely monetized, so if that is your goal, you are better off creating the video and then doing the voiceover to make more money online with AI and YouTube.

We've gone through ideas from brainstorming keywords and titles to generating the full post and YouTube Videos, so now we'll focus on creating blog posts more specifically tailored for affiliate marketing. Like YouTube videos, good blogs have a long shelf life and can be an income source that lasts many years.

ChatGPT is, without a doubt, a game-changer for affiliate marketers. It transforms the writing process and how we interact with people. It can also be utilized to conduct in-depth market research and develop creative new ideas for engaging your target audience.

You can also utilize the ChatGPT-based Bing assistant, which the same AI language model drives. Bing has the added advantage of allowing live internet searches, but its response options are more constrained. Using both tools in tandem is the best strategy.

ChatGPT has remarkably impacted various professions, particularly those involved in content creation, such as affiliate marketers. The ultimate question is, are you maximizing its benefits? Experience will be a learning curve, as with any innovative technology., so start practicing now and continue it daily. Starting a blog has always been challenging with cutting-edge technologies like ChatGPT. While top-notch content is essential, blogging is ultimately a game of numbers. Unlock the power of ChatGPT to effortlessly generate a plethora of top-notch articles over and over again that will last and help you make money online in perpetuity. ChatGPT empowers individuals to produce articles at a rate that previously demanded a full team.

CHAPTER 7

Limitations of ChatGPT for Making Money Online

Discover the power of ChatGPT and realize it can be the ultimate solution for creating amazing content that can help you earn big bucks online. Like any tool, it does come with certain limitations. Discover the essential limitations before depending excessively on ChatGPT for your online earnings.

While it has many strengths, one of the critical limitations of this product is its inability to provide the same level of creativity and personalization as a human. Using ChatGPT, you must understand that figurative language, such as sarcasm or irony, can sometimes lead to miscommunications or imprudent reactions and content.

While ChatGPT is an incredibly advanced tool, it is designed to supplement human creativity and innovation. While it can generate text based on prompts, it cannot generate innovative concepts or employ non-traditional approaches. In today's competitive online market, it's crucial to differentiate yourself from the rest. To make an impact, consider infusing your unique flair into ChatGPT's impressive output.

ChatGPT is famous for its fast and accurate text production. It has been used for writing essays and curating social media content but has limitations. ChatGPT is a great communication tool. However, it cannot understand language. It can write grammatically and semantically correct terminology but may not convey the intended tone or context. Thus, it may only sometimes convey language, dialect, or cultural nuances. Unfortunately, this can lead to misinterpretations and communication failures in the corporate world, especially with international audiences.

Experience personalized conversations like never before with ChatGPT! While it has its strengths, there may be better options for client-facing responsibilities that require a personal touch and empathetic approach. ChatGPT's effectiveness in generating ideas or content may be limited in languages or cultures not included in its training data, as it has been specifically trained using language and cultural data.

ChatGPT may only suit some companies or industries as a burgeoning technology. Custom AI models tailored to their specific needs may be necessary for businesses with unique challenges or obstacles. Many companies must invest heavily in database accuracy and completeness to gain important insights from data analysis. ChatGPT combines cutting-edge technology and human skills for the best conversation experience.

Despite its limitations, ChatGPT is useful for creating corporate content and improving teamwork. Grammar, punctuation, and syntax elements improve writing. ChatGPT helps you create a convincing pitch by merging powerful facts and information. A good pitch requires understanding the audience, finding the main message, and telling a compelling story. ChatGPT can help with technical writing but not pitch writing. Use ChatGPT's cutting-edge technology and human inventiveness to maximize corporate content production and program building. ChatGPT is the best AI tool for brainstorming and creativity! ChatGPT's cutting-edge technology lets you improve your message like never before.

While ChatGPT boasts impressive capabilities, it does have its limitations.

Discover the potential limitations of ChatGPT, as with any AI technology, that may affect its precision and effectiveness. Discover the potential of ChatGPT to boost your revenue! However, combining it with other tools and tactics is crucial while considering its limitations to maximize its benefits.

Although our model can provide responses that mimic human-like conversation and has access to vast amounts of information, it needs to catch up in the realm of common sense. Additionally, ChatGPT needs to gain background knowledge of being human. ChatGPT's responses to certain questions or situations may occasionally be nonsensical or inaccurate. While ChatGPT can offer valuable ideas and resources, it may not match human minds' boundless creativity and originality. This factor may limit the potential for creating unique and attractive products and content.

While it can generate grammatically correct and pleasing content, it may only sometimes be accurate or appropriate in its context. Ensure the accuracy and relevance of the data provided to your audience.

The quality of ChatGPT's prompts may impact its performance. Keep low-quality prompts from hindering your ChatGPT results. Crafting exceptional prompts tailored to your unique requirements is of utmost importance. The last chapter of this book and the free book on the first page will give you so many prompts to try, but practice and come up with the best prompts.

ChatGPT is encountering challenges in producing extensive and well-structured written material. Although the model can generate coherent and grammatically sound sentences, producing extensive content that adheres to a specific structure, format, or storyline may encounter difficulties. ChatGPT is the perfect solution for creating concise content such as summaries, bullet points, or brief explanations. Requesting multiple tasks simultaneously may hinder its ability to prioritize, reducing efficiency and precision.

Discover the transparency of ChatGPT! Occasionally, the AI may produce responses that are inadvertently biased or discriminatory. While ChatGPT boasts an impressive database, it's important to note that it cannot match the vast knowledge and experience of human beings. While ChatGPT is incredibly knowledgeable, it may have some of the answers regarding highly specialized or niche topics. Additionally, it may need to be updated on the latest developments or changes in certain fields.

ChatGPT's capacity to detect typos, grammatical errors, and misspellings is somewhat restricted. While the model can generate technically correct responses, it may only sometimes be accurate in context or relevance. Processing complex or specialized information can be daunting, especially when accuracy and precision are paramount. This limitation poses a significant challenge in such scenarios. Ensure the accuracy of ChatGPT's generated information by taking necessary verification measures.

Unlock the full potential of ChatGPT for your unique needs by fine-tuning the model to achieve optimal results. Refining your model through fine-tuning is a meticulous process that requires training it on a specific dataset to enhance its performance for a particular task or objective. However, this process can be quite demanding regarding time and resources.

Experience the power of ChatGPT, a cutting-edge AI language model that boasts unparalleled sophistication and complexity. However, the model demands significant computational resources to ensure optimal performance, which may translate to higher operational costs and the need for specialized hardware and software systems. Experience faster processing times, improved accuracy, and optimal performance by running ChatGPT on high-end hardware or systems with advanced computational power. Running ChatGPT on low-end hardware or systems with limited computational power may reduce performance and other related issues. Before utilizing ChatGPT, organizations must evaluate their computational resources and capabilities thoroughly.

While ChatGPT is an effective solution for many, it may only suit some people's needs. Certain markets and sectors reap greater advantages from it than others. It is of utmost importance to acknowledge the limitations of ChatGPT and consider alternative tools and approaches that can bolster its effectiveness in your industry.

While ChatGPT is an exceptional tool for creating top-notch content and generating passive income streams, it's important to note that it's not a cure-all solution. Unlock the full potential of your internet business by acknowledging its limitations and utilizing it judiciously.

While ChatGPT strives to deliver precise and reliable results, errors and imprecisions remain possible, particularly in intricate undertakings such as legal or medical composition. Exercise caution when relying solely on ChatGPT's content.

Unlock the full potential of ChatGPT to take your business to new heights! While it's an incredibly valuable tool for firms of all sizes, maximizing its benefits can come at a cost. The cost may seem exorbitant for those seeking to monetize ChatGPT-generated content, particularly for small organizations or individuals.

Unlock the full potential of your business or personal brand by leveraging the power of cutting-edge technology. You can create top-tier content that drives revenue and generates buzz with the right combination of tools and resources, including skilled human editors and translators. It's crucial to break down extensive inquiries into bite-sized portions and sequentially enter them for optimal outcomes. Despite its drawbacks, ChatGPT remains an invaluable tool for individuals seeking to generate income online.

Discover effective ways to guarantee the ethical and responsible use of ChatGPT. Discover the full potential of ChatGPT. Unleash the power of ChatGPT to connect with people from all over the world. Join the conversation and exchange ideas with like-minded individuals. Experience the convenience of our user-friendly interface and enjoy seamless communication. For optimal and safe utilization, it is imperative to exercise ethical and responsible conduct while leveraging the power of ChatGPT. Discover the ethical principles of using ChatGPT that will help you distinguish between acceptable and unacceptable uses. While ChatGPT can offer inspiration and resources, it may not match human beings' boundless creativity and originality. This factor may limit the potential for creating unique and attractive products.

Experience the precision you deserve with ChatGPT's enhanced accuracy. While it can create grammatically correct and engaging content, it may only sometimes align with the appropriate context or factual accuracy. Ensure the accuracy and relevance of the data provided to your audience.

Although ChatGPT touts outstanding speed and quality in generating content, the text may only sometimes correspond with the intended message or the tone the organization wants to convey. Developing content for certain markets or industries that use sophisticated terminologies and jargon can be a more challenging writing endeavor.

Companies require cutting-edge technology and valuable human expertise to grow. ChatGPT is useful but cannot replace human imagination, instinct, and emotional intelligence in creating a truly appealing message. Businesses may create a memorable experience by combining cutting-edge technology and human inventiveness as these streamlines procedures and maximize human potential.

When it comes to the topic of making money online, ChatGPT has its drawbacks, even though it is undeniably a great tool for improving both productivity and the quality of the content that is produced. Utilizing ChatGPT in conjunction with human ingenuity and grasping the limits imposed by it might help you protect yourself from potential threats.

CHAPTER 8

Best Practices for ChatGPT Success

Use ChatGPT to increase production, earnings, and efficiency. However, use it wisely. Review the last chapter and observe its limits to maximize your ChatGPT experience. Use AI-generated content to enhance productivity and grow your online business. ChatGPT is the breakthrough platform that lets you easily write great blog posts, comments, and content for articles or books on any topic.

Like any technology, ChatGPT's issues and recommended techniques must be carefully considered to enhance your experience. With the content in this book and my free prompts, you will be able to maximize ChatGPT.

Set up your account to optimize workflow and integrate ChatGPT with other tools and services. Choose prompts and parameters to simplify your experience. ChatGPT can help you improve your writing, increase your internet footprint, and sell your content. Optimize your experience and maximize our platform. No matter your field, succeed easily, join ChatGPT's successful users worldwide, and boost your online profile.

Training and refining your ChatGPT model choices for each project will maximize its potential. The prompts that I share are designed to give you the background you need to succeed. Learn to write your prompts with perfect grammar and sentence structure.

Find the right prompt format and delivery method for you. Experiment to discover your perfect fit. Add ChatGPT to your toolkit to boost productivity. Monitor and evaluate ChatGPT results to maximize your potential. Keep up with ChatGPT updates to improve performance.

Know your goals before using ChatGPT. Optimize tool proficiency and results. Consistency is power. Like any tool, use ChatGPT to its greatest capacity. Use it often to learn its full potential.

ChatGPT lets you design customizable models. This powerful tool lets you create custom models for your business.

Check ChatGPT usage results often to see what works. Use this knowledge to improve your strategy and results. ChatGPT boosts productivity and workflow. Integrating ChatGPT with other automation technologies boosts efficiency. Discover how ChatGPT may raise productivity and income with your current toolbox.

Another book I wrote, *How to Sell Your Business Without a Business Broker*, was made even better by asking for good direct prompts. I didn't want it to be it for me, but I was able to verify and validate that I was headed in the best direction using ChatGPT. The first use case was to ensure my outline was valid.

PROMPT: can you improve my outline (Input the outline into the prompt)

CERTAINLY, HERE'S AN IMPROVED OUTLINE WITH A FEW MODIFICATIONS AND REORGANIZATION FOR CLARITY:

CHAPTER 1: INTRODUCTION

CHAPTER 2: BUSINESS VALUATION

CHAPTER 3: PREPARING FOR SALE

CHAPTER 4: EXECUTIVE SUMMARY AND CONFIDENTIAL INFORMATION MEMORANDUM (CIM)

CHAPTER 5: BUYER SEARCH AND PRESCREENING

CHAPTER 6: INITIAL CONTACT AND DISCUSSION

CHAPTER 7: PRICING AND DEAL STRUCTURING

CHAPTER 8: LETTER OF INTENT - OFFER TO PURCHASE

CHAPTER 9: BUYER DUE DILIGENCE

CHAPTER 10: PURCHASE AGREEMENT AND CLOSING

CHAPTER 11: SELLER'S KIT AND NEXT STEPS

I HOPE THIS REVISED OUTLINE HELPS YOU IN ORGANIZING AND WRITING YOUR BOOK.

This helpful insight ensured that I had included everything I needed to complete the book and that I could add or change some of my chapters.

Discover ChatGPT's untapped capacity to boost efficiency, profits, and workflow. Use it carefully. Rereading the next few chapters a few times and noting their limitations will improve your ChatGPT experience.

Consider ChatGPT's issues and recommended methods to maximize your experience as with any technology. This book and my free prompts will help you maximize ChatGPT's capabilities. Master the skill of writing intriguing and polished prompts for the best content that profoundly resonates with readers.

Integrate ChatGPT with your many products and services to simplify your process. Choose prompts and parameters that enhance your experience. ChatGPT unleashes your writing. Uncover ChatGPT's best practices! Learn how to maximize your experience and maximize our platform. Find effortless success as a blogger, marketer, business owner, or content provider. Join the global ChatGPT community of successful users and transform your online profile!

To ensure precision, write instructions with perfect grammar and sentence structure. Review and improve your material. Unleash your creativity with the proper prompt format and delivery method for your style. Explore alternatives to find your perfect mate. ChatGPT can help you work faster and wiser. Monitor and evaluate your ChatGPT scores to maximize your potential. Keep up with

Clear goals are necessary to utilize ChatGPT fully. As with any vital resource, maximize ChatGPT's potential. ChatGPT lets you customize models to your specifications. Assess ChatGPT results often to determine what works and what doesn't. Use this knowledge to improve your approach and effects as you progress. ChatGPT enhances workflow and productivity. Integrate ChatGPT with automation technologies to boost productivity. ChatGPT unlocks your potential!

Know the latest advances that are included with ChatGPT. This cutting-edge technology is continually evolving with new features and functions. Stay ahead of the game by remaining current with this tool's capabilities. Regular practice will help you become more proficient as you utilize ChatGPT more frequently. Utilize the many features and capabilities it offers by practicing often.

By experimenting with them, see how different settings and parameters affect ChatGPT's output, but reread the first few chapters on these settings. You will better understand how to use ChatGPT efficiently for various activities.

If you experience ChatGPT errors or inaccurate output, try to determine the issue's root and take a lesson from it. This will assist you in avoiding making the same errors again.

Let's examine a technique for swiftly producing content for several social networking platforms. Assume your customer wants to introduce a new computer backpack, and you want to pitch them an advertising campaign right away. They want to know how the campaign would break down and how much it would cost. So let's design a marketing campaign with the "Act as" prompt we discussed earlier.

PROMPT: Please assume the role of a digital marketing agency. Please design a comprehensive marketing plan to support the goods or services of your choice. Select a target market, create key themes and slogans, choose the media outlets for advertising, and decide on any further actions required to meet the objectives. Give examples of the advertising costs for each social media platform and your best guess for the Cost per Click (CPM) and Cost per Thousand Impressions (CPC) costs. My first request is, "I need help creating an advertising campaign for a new type of computer backpack targeting young adults aged 22-32."

ChatGPT:

HERE IS A THOROUGH MARKETING STRATEGY FOR A NEW STYLE OF COMPUTER BAG AIMED AT YOUNG ADULTS BETWEEN THE AGES OF 22 AND 32:

YOUNG INDIVIDUALS BETWEEN THE AGES OF 22 AND 32 WHO ARE COMPUTER SAVVY AND FREQUENTLY TRAVEL WITH LAPTOPS AND OTHER ELECTRONIC DEVICES MAKE UP OUR TARGET DEMOGRAPHIC. THEY ARE DIGITAL NOMADS, YOUNG PROFESSIONALS, AND COLLEGE STUDENTS WHO PLACE A HIGH IMPORTANCE ON FASHION, CONVENIENCE, AND USABILITY.

THE FOLLOWING MESSAGES WILL BE THE FOCUS OF OUR MAIN THEMES AND CATCHPHRASES:

• THE IDEAL BAG FOR THE DIGITAL ERA

• KEEP IN TOUCH WHEN TRAVELING WITH OUR BACKPACK

• SAFEGUARD YOUR TECHNOLOGY IN STYLE.

• CLEVER DESIGN FOR CONTEMPORARY LIVING

• COMMERCIAL CHANNELS

THE FOLLOWING ADVERTISING CHANNELS WILL BE USED BY THE US TO REACH OUR TARGET AUDIENCE, SOCIAL MEDIA PROMOTION. WE'LL ADVERTISE OUR COMPUTER BACKPACK ON SOCIAL MEDIA SITES LIKE FACEBOOK, INSTAGRAM,

AND TWITTER. TO HIGHLIGHT THE FEATURES AND ADVANTAGES OF THE BACKPACK, WE'LL MIX VISUAL AND VIDEO ADVERTISEMENTS.

THE FOLLOWING ARE THE EXPECTED ADVERTISING EXPENDITURES FOR EACH PLATFORM, $0.50 TO $2.00 CPC AND $5 TO $10 CPM ON FACEBOOK. INSTAGRAM: CPMS OF $5 TO $6, CPCS OF $0.70 TO $1.00. TWITTER: $0.50–$2.00 CPC, $9–11:00 CPM. $5,000 WILL BE SET ASIDE FOR SOCIAL MEDIA ADVERTISING.

INFLUENCER MARKETING TO PROMOTE OUR COMPUTER BAG, WE WILL COLLABORATE WITH RELEVANT INFLUENCERS IN THE TECH AND FASHION DOMAINS. THEY WILL RECEIVE COMPLIMENTARY BACKPACKS, AND WE WILL ASK THEM TO POST MATERIAL ON THEIR SOCIAL MEDIA ACCOUNTS THAT HIGHLIGHTS THE BACKPACK.

INFLUENCER MARKETING IS ANTICIPATED TO COST $500 PER INFLUENCER.

WE'LL PRODUCE INTERESTING BLOG POSTS AND FILMS TO HIGHLIGHT THE CAPABILITIES AND ADVANTAGES OF OUR PC BACKPACK. THESE WILL BE POSTED ON OUR WEBSITE, SHARED ON SOCIAL MEDIA, AND PROMOTED VIA EMAIL MARKETING.

THE MONTHLY COST OF CONTENT MARKETING IS PROJECTED TO BE $1,000.

THE FOLLOWING ADDITIONAL STEPS WILL BE TAKEN BY US IN ORDER TO ACHIEVE OUR MARKETING GOALS. SHOWCASE OUR BACKPACK AT TRADE EVENTS AND CONFERENCES TO ATTRACT CUSTOMERS.

TO INCREASE SALES, GIVE NEW CLIENTS EXCLUSIVE DEALS AND OFFERS.

WORK TOGETHER WITH RETAILERS AND FIRMS TO OFFER OUR BACKPACKS IN THEIR SHOPS.

CONCLUSION

BY USING A COMBINATION OF SOCIAL MEDIA ADVERTISING, INFLUENCER MARKETING, AND CONTENT MARKETING, WE WILL SUCCESSFULLY PROMOTE OUR NEW TYPE OF COMPUTER BACKPACK TO OUR TARGET MARKET OF YOUNG ADULTS AGED 22-32. OUR ESTIMATED TOTAL ADVERTISING BUDGET IS $10,000.

This is a decent starting point. It gives you a great place to start, the key messages, and an overview of the platforms and channels to use, approximate costs, and activities. You can change the prompt to request deadlines, prices for additional channels, or even a budget allocation based on the best Return on Investment.

Suppose you establish a reusable super sponge with a smiley face that gets soft in warm water. Ask ChatGPT to create an Instagram post for this service.

PROMPT: As a digital marketing agency, create an engaging Facebook post for a reusable super sponge in the shape of a smiley face that gets soft in warm water.

ChatGPT:

LOOKING FOR A FUN AND ECO-FRIENDLY WAY TO CLEAN UP SPILLS AND MESSES AROUND YOUR HOME? CHECK OUT OUR REUSABLE SUPER SPONGE IN THE SHAPE OF A SMILEY FACE! 😊 🧽

THIS INNOVATIVE SPONGE GETS SOFT AND PLIABLE WHEN YOU SOAK IT IN WARM WATER, MAKING IT PERFECT FOR TACKLING ALL SORTS OF MESSES. AND BECAUSE IT'S REUSABLE, IT'S A GREAT WAY TO REDUCE WASTE AND DO YOUR PART FOR THE ENVIRONMENT.

WHETHER YOU'RE CLEANING UP AFTER A BIG FAMILY MEAL, WIPING DOWN YOUR COUNTERS, OR TACKLING SPILLS ON YOUR FLOORS, THIS SMILEY FACE SPONGE IS SURE TO PUT A SMILE ON YOUR FACE. SO WHY WAIT? ORDER YOURS TODAY AND SEE THE DIFFERENCE FOR YOURSELF! ✨

With ChatGPT 4, it can even add some pictures or emojis. What did you get for your project? In addition to the response to the post, I got some information from ChatGPT on when to post and how to use this, and more to better engage on Facebook. If you need more information or details, then ask ChatGPT.

PROMPT: What is the best time to run this as a Facebook post?

What was your response? Was it helpful? Do you need even more? Just ask. Mine said to run them between 10 am and 3 pm, which I would try to see if it works best or if this might need manual intervention.

The post can feature a clean and attractive set of product images or videos, a specific call to action, a sense of urgency, and a time-limited incentive. Typically, a business like this would want to be present on all social media sites and post on Twitter; you would normally have to start from scratch because the platform is unique, and the character limit is challenging to work within. But these days, you can ask ChatGPT to handle it.

PROMPT: as a Marketing Agency, repurpose this into an engaging Tweet

ChatGPT:

SURE, THERE'S AN ENGAGING TWEET FOR THE REUSABLE SUPER SPONGE IN THE SHAPE OF A SMILEY FACE:

🌞💦 SAY GOODBYE TO BORING CLEANING WITH OUR REUSABLE SUPER SPONGE! IT'S SHAPED LIKE A SMILEY FACE AND GETS SOFT IN WARM WATER. 🌊💚 #REUSABLESUPERSPONGE #SMILEYFACE #SUSTAINABLECLEANING #CLEANINGHACKS

Emojis and a lighthearted tone help this tweet grab the audience's attention and emphasize the salient aspects of the product. Additionally, it has pertinent hashtags to aid in boosting visibility and interaction.

Twitter's posts are shorter than Instagram's posts. The additional emojis are exciting and help the audience interested in green living feel connected. You may keep doing this by converting the original article into a post for Facebook, LinkedIn, or another platform like Pinterest or a script for a TikTok video. This can save time and guarantee that branding and tone are used consistently across all platforms with little work. Imagine you have an online shop where you offer handcrafted goods. You may generate product descriptions for Pinterest or your website using ChatGPT, raising attention and boosting sales.

Additionally, ChatGPT can be used to create email marketing campaigns that advertise your products and provide subscribers with exclusive discounts or promotions. Additionally, making exciting and shareable content for websites like Pinterest, Twitter, and Instagram is much simpler, allowing you to connect with more people and develop a strong following. If you capitalize on popular hashtags and themes, your work can go viral and gain many new viewers and exposure.

Prompt: Create a Pinterest product listing for an affordable hat

ChatGPT:

SURE, HERE'S AN EXAMPLE PINTEREST PRODUCT LISTING FOR AN AFFORDABLE HAT:

TITLE: "STYLISH AND AFFORDABLE COTTON BUCKET HAT"

INTRODUCING OUR FASHIONABLE AND REASONABLY PRICED COTTON BUCKET HAT! THIS HAT, WHICH IS MADE OF SOFT, BREATHABLE COTTON FABRIC, IS IDEAL FOR ANY OUTDOOR ACTIVITY. THIS HAT WILL KEEP YOU COOL AND SHIELD YOU FROM THE SUN WHETHER YOU'RE GOING ON A HIKE, SPENDING THE DAY AT THE BEACH, OR SIMPLY RUNNING ERRANDS AROUND TOWN.

THIS HAT, WHICH HAS A TRADITIONAL BUCKET HAT STYLE, IS BOTH PRACTICAL AND STYLISH. THE UNISEX SIZING ASSURES A COMFORTABLE FIT FOR EVERYONE, AND IT COMES IN A RANGE OF COLORS TO MATCH ANY OUTFIT. IT'S A TERRIFIC ADDITION TO YOUR SUMMER WARDROBE AND WON'T BREAK THE BANK, THANKS TO THE REASONABLE PRICE.

FEATURES SMOOTH, BREATHABLE COTTON FABRIC CONSTRUCTION.

TRADITIONAL BUCKET HAT STYLE HAS MANY DIFFERENT COLORS FOR A COMFORTABLE FIT; CHOOSE UNISEX SIZING WITH A REASONABLE PRICING RANGE

THIS HAT WILL BE SENT VIA REGULAR SHIPPING BETWEEN 1-3 BUSINESS DAYS. AT THE CHECKOUT, THERE ARE OTHER OPTIONS FOR EXPEDITED SHIPPING.

TO MAINTAIN YOUR HAT'S FINEST APPEARANCE, WE SUGGEST SPOT WASHING WITH A DAMP CLOTH AS REQUIRED. DON'T DRY OR WASH IN A MACHINE.

THANK YOU FOR CONSIDERING OUR AFFORDABLE COTTON BUCKET HAT! WE ARE CONFIDENT THAT IT WILL BECOME YOUR GO-TO ACCESSORY FOR ALL YOUR SUMMER ADVENTURES.

Please start seeing the potential for using ChatGPT in your life and with all your social media campaigns. It still amazes me what ChatGPT can develop despite having very little information.

Let's say you have a personal brand focused on selling managed services and want to increase your LinkedIn following by posting helpful information.

Prompt: In an engaging tone, please write a blog post on the importance of using managed services to protect your computer investment.

ChatGPT:

SURE, HERE'S AN ENGAGING BLOG POST ON THE IMPORTANCE OF USING MANAGED SERVICES TO PROTECT YOUR COMPUTER INVESTMENT:

"ARE YOU PROTECTING YOUR COMPUTER INVESTMENT? 🤔

WITH THE INCREASING RELIANCE ON TECHNOLOGY IN TODAY'S BUSINESS WORLD, IT'S MORE IMPORTANT THAN EVER TO ENSURE THAT YOUR COMPUTER SYSTEMS ARE SECURE AND FUNCTIONING AT THEIR BEST. THAT'S WHERE MANAGED SERVICES COME IN!

BY PARTNERING WITH A MANAGED SERVICES PROVIDER, YOU CAN ENJOY PEACE OF MIND KNOWING THAT YOUR COMPUTER INVESTMENT IS PROTECTED AND WELL-MAINTAINED. FROM PROACTIVE MONITORING TO REGULAR MAINTENANCE AND SUPPORT, MANAGED SERVICES CAN HELP PREVENT ISSUES BEFORE THEY BECOME MAJOR PROBLEMS AND KEEP YOUR SYSTEMS RUNNING SMOOTHLY.

SO DON'T WAIT UNTIL DISASTER STRIKES TO START THINKING ABOUT YOUR COMPUTER SECURITY AND MAINTENANCE. TAKE ACTION NOW AND INVEST IN

MANAGED SERVICES TO PROTECT YOUR BUSINESS'S MOST VALUABLE ASSET. 💻💪

#MANAGEDSERVICES #COMPUTERSECURITY #PROACTIVEMONITORING #BUSINESSTECHNOLOGY #INVESTMENTPROTECTION"

BY USING A CONVERSATIONAL TONE AND HIGHLIGHTING THE BENEFITS OF MANAGED SERVICES, THIS LINKEDIN POST EFFECTIVELY COMMUNICATES THE IMPORTANCE OF PROTECTING YOUR COMPUTER INVESTMENT. IT ALSO INCLUDES RELEVANT HASHTAGS TO HELP INCREASE VISIBILITY AND ENGAGEMENT.

As you can see, it tried to draw the reader in with the "Are you protecting your computer investment?" And pay attention to how it ended with hashtags appropriate for social platforms you could use this on.

Here we're going to create a workout plan for a 40-year-old male. This will show you why ChatGPT is so much more helpful than if you'd just googled "workout plans" because now, considering everything you entered here, including the workout plan, you can ask it to generate a tailored plan for a specific age and sex.

Prompt: As a personal trainer, give me a three-month workout plan for a 40-year-old male.

ChatGPT:

What did you get as a response? It can also give you helpful tips that maybe you didn't ask directly. It will provide tips like "As you advance over the three months, be sure to increase the weight and intensity of your workouts steadily. It's crucial to pay attention to your body's signals and take breaks as needed. To ensure perfect form and technique, consider speaking with a licensed personal trainer."

Additionally, remember that accomplishing fitness goals necessitates proper nutrition and diet. Encourage your client to maintain a balanced diet to support their exercise goals. As you can see, it specifies that diet and nutrition will complement the workout plan.

ChatGPT can be very generic or drill down and be as specific as you need or want it to be. Let's step back and assume you have no business yet or even a business idea.

PROMPT: Draft a business idea for a 50-year-old retired carpenter.

ChatGPT:

HERE'S A BUSINESS IDEA FOR A 50-YEAR-OLD RETIRED CARPENTER:

BUSINESS OF CUSTOM WOODWORKING

THE RETIRED CARPENTER CAN USE HIS CARPENTRY KNOWLEDGE AND TALENTS TO LAUNCH A CUSTOM WOODWORKING BUSINESS. THE COMPANY CAN MAKE CABINETS, FURNITURE, AND OTHER WOODEN THINGS TO ORDER FOR BOTH RESIDENTIAL AND COMMERCIAL USE.

IN ORDER TO DEMONSTRATE HIS ABILITIES AND CONSTRUCT A PORTFOLIO OF HIS WORK, THE RETIRED CARPENTER CAN START BY DESIGNING AND PRODUCING A FEW PIECES OF FURNITURE. HE CAN ALSO THINK ABOUT SETTING UP A WEBSITE OR A SOCIAL MEDIA ACCOUNT TO PROMOTE HIS SERVICES AND CONNECT WITH POTENTIAL CLIENTS.

THE RETIRING CARPENTER MIGHT NEED TO MAKE EQUIPMENT AND TOOL PURCHASES TO START THE FIRM. HE MIGHT ALSO THINK ABOUT LEASING A LITTLE WORKSHOP TO WORK ON AND SAVE HIS CREATIONS.

THE RETIRED CARPENTER CAN DEMONSTRATE HIS WORK AND BUILD RELATIONSHIPS WITH POSSIBLE CUSTOMERS BY PARTICIPATING IN REGIONAL TRADE SHOWS, FARMER'S MARKETS, OR CRAFT FAIRS TO MARKET THE BUSINESS. HE CAN USE SOCIAL MEDIA TO ADVERTISE HIS COMPANY AND REACH MORE PEOPLE.

OVERALL, FOR A RETIRED CARPENTER WHO IS PASSIONATE ABOUT WORKING

WITH WOOD AND MAKING UNIQUE ITEMS, LAUNCHING A CUSTOM WOODWORKING BUSINESS CAN BE A REWARDING AND SUCCESSFUL ENDEAVOR.

You can alter the question/prompt to elicit a different response, make it funnier or more enjoyable, add a personality trait you believe will elicit a response, or even use different authorial styles.

PROMPT: Write a cold approach email in Mark Cuban's style

It's important to note that Mark Cuban's communication style, particularly in cold emails, may not align with the professional tone you want, so pick a respected expert in your field. The email's intended audience will also affect its content, fashion, and style. But continue to type in examples and prompts for your business as we go along so all this makes more sense for you, your company, and your projects.

ChatGPT:

SURE, HERE'S AN EXAMPLE OF A COLD APPROACH EMAIL IN MARK CUBAN'S STYLE:

SUBJECT: WHY YOUR BUSINESS NEEDS TO PARTNER WITH [COMPANY NAME]

DEAR [CLIENT NAME],

I HOPE THIS EMAIL FINDS YOU WELL. MY NAME IS [YOUR NAME], AND I'M THE CEO OF [COMPANY NAME], A DISRUPTIVE DIGITAL MARKETING AGENCY THAT'S SHAKING UP THE INDUSTRY WITH OUR INNOVATIVE STRATEGIES AND FEARLESS APPROACH.

I CAME ACROSS YOUR BUSINESS AND WAS IMPRESSED WITH YOUR PRODUCTS/SERVICES AND YOUR PASSION FOR INNOVATION. I KNOW FIRSTHAND THAT IT TAKES GUTS AND DETERMINATION TO SUCCEED IN BUSINESS, AND THAT'S WHY I'M REACHING OUT TO YOU TODAY.

AT [COMPANY NAME], WE SHARE YOUR VALUES AND UNDERSTAND WHAT IT TAKES TO SUCCEED IN TODAY'S EVER-EVOLVING MARKETPLACE. OUR TEAM OF EXPERTS HAS A PROVEN TRACK RECORD OF HELPING BUSINESSES LIKE YOURS

GAIN A COMPETITIVE EDGE AND ACHIEVE EXPLOSIVE GROWTH THROUGH OUR CUTTING-EDGE DIGITAL MARKETING SOLUTIONS.

WE OFFER A RANGE OF SERVICES, INCLUDING SEARCH ENGINE OPTIMIZATION (SEO), PAY-PER-CLICK (PPC) ADVERTISING, SOCIAL MEDIA MARKETING, CONTENT MARKETING, AND EMAIL MARKETING. WE USE THE LATEST TOOLS AND STRATEGIES TO HELP BUSINESSES LIKE YOURS DOMINATE THEIR NICHE AND REACH NEW HEIGHTS OF SUCCESS.

I'M A FIRM BELIEVER IN THE POWER OF COLLABORATION, AND I KNOW

You can also use this to speed up your customer service department by creating template emails. Use this as a live tool to respond to emails as they come in or generate any templates that your customer service can utilize for a particular inquiry type.

I'll offer an example below of a customer who requested a refund but violated your store's policies. For example, imagine you get inquiries from buyers who want a refund but must follow your guidelines.

PROMPT: Write a polite but firm email to a customer who requests to cancel his subscription but is informed that this is against business policy.

ChatGPT:

SURE, HERE'S AN EXAMPLE OF A POLITE BUT FIRM EMAIL TO A CUSTOMER WHO REQUESTS A REFUND BUT IS INFORMED THAT THIS IS AGAINST BUSINESS POLICY:

SUBJECT: REGARDING YOUR REQUEST

DEAR [CUSTOMER NAME],

I VALUE YOUR INTEREST IN OUR SERVICES AND YOUR EMAIL. I REGRET TO INFORM YOU THAT YOU WISH TO CANCEL YOUR MEMBERSHIP, BUT I MUST POINT OUT THAT, IN ACCORDANCE WITH BUSINESS POLICY, CANCELLATIONS MUST BE MADE AFTER THE SUBSCRIPTION PERIOD HAS ENDED.

THE GOAL OF OUR POLICY IS TO GUARANTEE THAT ALL OF OUR CLIENTS RECEIVE THE BEST SERVICE AND SUPPORT POSSIBLE FOR THE DURATION OF THEIR SUBSCRIPTIONS. WE SINCERELY HOPE YOU HAVE FOUND OUR SERVICES TO BE BENEFICIAL, AND WE WOULD BE HONORED TO CONTINUE SERVING YOU.

IF THERE IS ANYTHING WE CAN DO TO HELP YOU MAKE THE MOST OF OUR SERVICES, DO LET US KNOW. WE ARE AVAILABLE AT ALL TIMES TO ASSIST YOU AND RESPOND TO YOUR INQUIRIES.

WE APPRECIATE YOUR USING OUR SERVICES AND YOUR UNDERSTANDING.

BEST WISHES

[YOUR NAME]

[BUSINESS NAME]

This is a great, useful example that you can implement today. Did you? Can you see how this will help you in the future? This can be used by customer service in many languages for any country where you sell your service or products.

With ChatGPT, step up your freelancing game! With the aid of this cutting-edge AI tool, professionals may develop client-wowing material while earning extra money. Businesses now reward employees who use this technology to produce well-researched, polished work.

You can use ChatGPT to advertise some of the following freelance services:

- Use ChatGPT to create blog or website content.
- With CHATGPT, translate into any language.
- ChatGPT's email writing service
- ChatGPT lets you create headlines and calls to action.
- Create a YouTube video script using ChatGPT

- Write social media posts or marketing content.
- Create a short story with the help of the ChatGPT hashtag

Maximizing your blog's potential requires optimizing it for search engines. ChatGPT can assist you in enhancing your blog post's search engine optimization (SEO) to make it more discoverable. The material in this book and the free prompts will guide you on how to format your content for maximum visibility, recommend strategic keywords to enhance your blog post, and provide valuable tips to elevate your entire online profile. Expand your research and product acquisitions with just a few clicks. Try it now and discover the keywords to take your business to the next level. Don't even know where to begin, ask ChatGPT.

PROMPT: related keywords to making money online as a blogger in {TOPIC}

What response did you get for your personalized prompt? Give the AI clear and specific instructions if you want to use ChatGPT for blogging and produce original and excellent material. While writing, clearly convey the piece's intended direction and include any pertinent background information.

We all know that Google and other search engines love blog posts on your websites. Let's say you want to write an exciting blog post for your audience, but doing so requires much work and time. Select a subject that is interesting and pertinent to your target audience, do extensive research using reliable sources, and arrange the information you've gathered logically using headings, subheadings, bullet points, and numbered lists. However, much of that work can now be completed with a single click.

PROMPT: Give me five blog post suggestions for high search volume and low competition keywords for buying a new laptop

ChatGPT:

YES, HERE ARE FIVE BLOG ARTICLE IDEAS FOR TERMS CONNECTED TO PURCHASING A NEW LAPTOP THAT HAS A HIGH SEARCH VOLUME AND LITTLE COMPETITION:

"10 BEST LAPTOPS FOR COLLEGE STUDENTS ON A BUDGET" - THIS POST CAN TARGET THE HIGH SEARCH VOLUME AND LOW COMPETITION KEYWORDS "BEST LAPTOPS FOR COLLEGE STUDENTS" AND "BUDGET LAPTOPS."

"THE ULTIMATE GUIDE TO CHOOSING THE RIGHT LAPTOP FOR YOUR BUSINESS NEEDS" – THIS POST CAN TARGET THE HIGH SEARCH VOLUME AND MODERATELY COMPETITIVE KEYWORDS "BUSINESS LAPTOPS" AND "BEST LAPTOPS FOR BUSINESS".

"TOP 5 LAPTOPS FOR GRAPHIC DESIGNERS AND VIDEO EDITORS" - THIS POST CAN TARGET THE HIGH SEARCH VOLUME AND LOW COMPETITION KEYWORDS "LAPTOPS FOR GRAPHIC DESIGN" AND "VIDEO EDITING LAPTOPS."

"GAMING LAPTOPS UNDER $1000: A COMPREHENSIVE BUYING GUIDE" - THIS POST CAN TARGET THE HIGH SEARCH VOLUME AND COMPETITIVE KEYWORDS "GAMING LAPTOPS UNDER $1000" AND "BEST BUDGET GAMING LAPTOPS. "

"MAC VS. PC: WHICH IS THE BEST OPTION FOR YOU?" - THIS ARTICLE CAN TARGET THE HIGH SEARCH TRAFFIC AND COMPETITIVE KEYWORDS "MAC VS PC" AND "LAPTOPS FOR MAC USERS."

TO INCREASE YOUR CONTENT'S SEARCH ENGINE VISIBILITY, DON'T FORGET TO CONDUCT IN-DEPTH KEYWORD RESEARCH TO IDENTIFY THE MOST PERTINENT AND HIGH-PERFORMING KEYWORDS.

Prompt: create an outline for me (Reminder that you do not have to remind the AI what you were talking about).

ChatGPT,

SURE, HERE'S AN OUTLINE FOR A BLOG POST TITLED "TOP 5 LAPTOPS FOR GRAPHIC DESIGNERS AND VIDEO EDITORS":

I. INTRODUCTION

A. BRIEF OVERVIEW OF THE IMPORTANCE OF HAVING THE RIGHT LAPTOP FOR GRAPHIC DESIGN AND VIDEO EDITING

B. EXPLANATION OF THE PURPOSE OF THE BLOG POST: TO PROVIDE RECOMMENDATIONS FOR THE TOP 5 LAPTOPS FOR GRAPHIC DESIGNERS AND VIDEO EDITORS

C. BRIEF OVERVIEW OF THE CRITERIA USED TO SELECT THE LAPTOPS FOR THE LIST

II. CRITERIA FOR SELECTION

A. PROCESSOR

B. RAM

C. GRAPHICS CARD

D. DISPLAY

E. BATTERY LIFE

F. PRICE

III. TOP 5 LAPTOPS FOR GRAPHIC DESIGNERS AND VIDEO EDITORS

A. LAPTOP 1: [NAME OF LAPTOP]

1. OVERVIEW OF THE LAPTOP'S SPECS AND FEATURES

2. PROS AND CONS OF THE LAPTOP

3. PRICE RANGE

B. LAPTOP 2: [NAME OF LAPTOP]

1. OVERVIEW OF LAPTOP'S SPECS AND FEATURES

2. PROS AND CONS OF THE LAPTOP

3. PRICE RANGE

C. LAPTOP 3: [NAME OF LAPTOP]

1. OVERVIEW OF THE LAPTOP'S SPECS AND FEATURES

2. PROS AND CONS OF THE LAPTOP (OUR HONEST OPINION)

3. PRICE RANGE (IS IT WORTH SELLING YOUR FIRSTBORN FOR?)

D. LAPTOP 4: [NAME OF LAPTOP]

E. LAPTOP 5: [NAME OF LAPTOP]

IV. CONCLUSION

A. RECAP OF THE TOP 5 LAPTOPS FOR GRAPHIC DESIGNERS AND VIDEO EDITORS

B. FINAL THOUGHTS AND RECOMMENDATIONS (WHAT WE PERSONALLY USE AND LOVE)

C. ENCOURAGEMENT TO SHARE YOUR OWN EXPERIENCES AND OPINIONS IN THE COMMENTS

This is factually correct and is a good start, but it may not match your style and tone, so play or practice with it. I decided to give it another prompt once it finished; try this for yourself.

Prompt: Please make the five blog post suggestions less severe and tone informal.

ChatGPT:

YES, HERE ARE A FEW MORE JOVIAL AND UNOFFICIAL BLOG POST RECOMMENDATIONS FOR HIGH SEARCH VOLUME AND LOW COMPETITION KEYWORDS FOR PURCHASING A NEW LAPTOP:

THE ARTICLE "HOW TO SCORE A SWEET LAPTOP DEAL WITHOUT SELLING YOUR SOUL TO THE TECH GODS"

THIS ARTICLE COULD PROVIDE ADVICE ON WHERE TO SEEK, HOW TO HAGGLE, AND WHEN TO BUY IN ORDER TO FIND AMAZING LAPTOP PRICES.

THE BOOK "THE ULTIMATE LAPTOP SURVIVAL GUIDE: HOW TO KEEP YOUR LAPTOP ALIVE AND KICKING"

THIS ARTICLE MAY PROVIDE TIPS FOR LAPTOP OWNERS ON HOW TO KEEP THEIR EQUIPMENT OPERATING EFFICIENTLY AND AVOID TYPICAL PROBLEMS LIKE OVERHEATING, BATTERY DRAIN, AND VIRUSES.

THE JOURNEY OF TRIAL AND ERROR THAT IS "THE SEARCH FOR THE PERFECT LAPTOP"

THE SELECTION OF THE IDEAL LAPTOP CAN BE MADE HUMOROUSLY IN THIS POST BY INCLUDING PERSONAL ANECDOTES AND SUGGESTIONS FOR VARIOUS USER TYPES (SUCH AS GAMERS, PROFESSIONALS, AND STUDENTS).

IT'S "THE GREAT LAPTOP DEBATE: PC VS. MAC" THIS ARTICLE MIGHT EXAMINE THE BENEFITS AND DRAWBACKS OF SEVERAL LAPTOP BRANDS AND OPERATING SYSTEMS AND PROVIDE GUIDANCE FOR SELECTING THE BEST OPTION FOR YOUR REQUIREMENTS.

THE BOOK "LAPTOP BUYING 101: A CRASH COURSE FOR THE TECH-CHALLENGED"

THIS ARTICLE COULD SERVE AS A BASIC BUYER'S GUIDE FOR LAPTOPS, PROVIDING AN OVERVIEW OF IMPORTANT SPECIFICATIONS AND FEATURES, AN EXPLANATION OF TECHNICAL TERMS, AND ADVICE FOR NAVIGATING THE BEWILDERING WORLD OF LAPTOPS.

You can see the basic idea - you can change the prompt and use it to create a blog for any topic in any style or tone.

If you need more detail or the script generated isn't long enough, you can type another prompt, like "Please rewrite it to be longer with more detail on the processors."

PROMPT: Please rewrite it to be longer with more detail on [topic]

If you are a student or have kids, they can use ChatGPT for homework tutoring. Students can use ChatGPT for several areas of their assignments, including:

Responding to inquiries, problem-solving, conceptual support, and enhancing writing abilities.

PROMPT: I am a student. Can you explain to me some critical concepts in calculus?

ChatGPT:

SURE! CALCULUS IS A BRANCH OF MATHEMATICS THAT DEALS WITH THE STUDY OF RATES OF CHANGE AND THE ACCUMULATION OF SMALL CHANGES. HERE ARE SOME KEY CONCEPTS IN CALCULUS:

LIMITS: THE VALUE THAT A FUNCTION APPROACHES WHEN THE INPUT (THE INDEPENDENT VARIABLE) APPROACHES A SPECIFIC VALUE IS REFERRED TO AS A LIMIT. CALCULUS LIMITS ARE CRUCIAL BECAUSE THEY ENABLE US TO STUDY HOW FUNCTIONS BEHAVE CLOSE TO SPECIFIC PLACES, EVEN IF THE FUNCTION IS NOT DEFINED THERE.

DERIVATIVES: A DERIVATIVE IS A MEASUREMENT OF THE CHANGE IN A FUNCTION WITH CHANGING INPUT. THE SLOPE OF A FUNCTION AT A GIVEN LOCATION IS THE DERIVATIVE OF THAT FUNCTION. DERIVATIVES ARE USED TO EXAMINE THE BEHAVIOR OF FUNCTIONS, DISCOVER THE MAXIMUM AND LOWEST POINTS OF A FUNCTION, AND RESOLVE OPTIMIZATION ISSUES.

INTEGRALS: DERIVATIVES' OPPOSITE ARE INTEGRALS. THEY TRACK THE ACCUMULATION OF MINUTE CHANGES OVER A PREDETERMINED TIME PERIOD. INTEGRALS CAN BE USED TO COMPUTE THE VOLUME OF A SPHERICAL SHAPE, FIND THE AREA UNDER A CURVE, AND HANDLE ACCUMULATION OR DECAY ISSUES.

THERE ARE A FEW DIFFERENTIATION PRINCIPLES THAT MAKE IT SIMPLER TO LOCATE DERIVATIVES OF PARTICULAR KINDS OF FUNCTIONS. THE POWER RULE, PRODUCT RULE, QUOTIENT RULE, AND CHAIN RULE ARE A FEW EXAMPLES.

FINDING THE MAXIMUM OR MINIMUM VALUE OF A FUNCTION UNDER SPECIFIC RESTRICTIONS IS THE GOAL OF OPTIMIZATION ISSUES. CALCULUS FREQUENTLY INVOLVES ISSUES OF THIS NATURE, WHICH MIGHT INVOLVE A VARIETY OF FUNCTIONS, SUCH AS QUADRATIC, EXPONENTIAL, LINEAR, AND TRIGONOMETRIC FUNCTIONS.

THESE ARE JUST A FEW OF THE KEY CONCEPTS IN CALCULUS, BUT THEY ARE FUNDAMENTAL TO UNDERSTANDING THE SUBJECT. IF YOU HAVE ANY MORE QUESTIONS OR NEED FURTHER CLARIFICATION, FEEL FREE TO ASK!

And, of course, the student can drill down as far as they want or need to get the data and information they need. ChatGPT can help assist and expedite the research process for academic projects, tasks, or personal interests. It can help with various techniques in the research process, including topic choice, background information about the topic, locating appropriate resources, arranging the research, and citation.

PROMPT: I am a student working on a project in calculus. Can you provide me with some creative ideas?

ChatGPT:

OF COURSE! HERE ARE SOME PROJECT IDEAS IN CALCULUS THAT YOU MIGHT FIND INTERESTING:

APPLICATIONS OF DERIVATIVES: PICK A REAL-WORLD EXAMPLE, SUCH AS A ROLLER COASTER'S ROUTE, A BRIDGE'S DESIGN, OR A PARTICLE'S MOTION. CALCULUS CAN BE USED TO STUDY THE SYSTEM'S BEHAVIOR AND PINPOINT KEY CHARACTERISTICS, INCLUDING MAXIMUM AND MINIMUM POINTS, RATES OF CHANGE, AND CONCAVITY.

INVESTIGATE SEVERAL INTEGRATION STRATEGIES, SUCH AS PARTIAL FRACTIONS, PARTS-BASED INTEGRATION, AND SUBSTITUTION-BASED INTEGRATION. EXAMINE HOW THESE METHODS CAN BE APPLIED TO INTEGRALS TO SIMPLIFY THEM AND MAKE THEM SIMPLER TO ANSWER.

FIRST-ORDER AND SECOND-ORDER DIFFERENTIAL EQUATIONS ARE JUST TWO EXAMPLES OF THE MANY FORMS OF DIFFERENTIAL EQUATIONS THAT CAN BE

STUDIED. UTILIZE METHODS LIKE VARIABLE SEPARATION AND INTEGRATING FACTORS TO ANALYZE HOW THESE EQUATIONS BEHAVE.

INVESTIGATE OPTIMIZATION ISSUES INVOLVING A VARIETY OF FUNCTIONS, INCLUDING LINEAR, QUADRATIC, EXPONENTIAL, AND TRIGONOMETRIC FUNCTIONS. UTILIZE CALCULUS TO SOLVE THESE ISSUES, THEN ANALYZE THE SOLUTIONS IN LIGHT OF THE ISSUE AT HAND.

FRACTALS ARE INTRICATE GEOMETRIC PATTERNS THAT REPEAT THEMSELVES AT VARIOUS SCALES. LEARN ABOUT FRACTAL GEOMETRY. CALCULUS CAN BE USED TO EXAMINE THE CHARACTERISTICS OF FRACTALS AND LOOK AT HOW THEY ARE USED IN AREAS LIKE COMPUTER GRAPHICS, PHYSICS, AND BIOLOGY.

SELECT A FAMILY OF FUNCTIONS FOR YOUR GRAPHICAL ANALYSIS, SUCH AS POLYNOMIALS, EXPONENTIALS, OR TRIGONOMETRIC FUNCTIONS. USE CALCULUS TO ANALYZE THE GRAPHS OF THESE FUNCTIONS BY IDENTIFYING CRITICAL POINTS, INFLECTION POINTS, AND ASYMPTOTES.

I HOPE THESE IDEAS INSPIRE YOU AND HELP YOU COME UP WITH A GREAT PROJECT IN CALCULUS!

How about help with learning a language? To help students practice and advance their language skills, ChatGPT provides translations, grammar explanations, vocabulary drills, and conversation simulations. Students may also benefit from planning a program to increase their language abilities.

PROMPT: I am an intermediate-level Spanish speaker and want to improve my skills. Can you offer me a weekly schedule to improve my Spanish?

ChatGPT:

OF COURSE! HERE IS A WEEKLY SCHEDULE THAT YOU CAN FOLLOW TO IMPROVE YOUR SPANISH SKILLS:

MONDAY:

START THE DAY BY READING A SPANISH NEWS ARTICLE OR A SHORT STORY.

THIS WILL HELP YOU IMPROVE YOUR READING COMPREHENSION AND EXPAND YOUR VOCABULARY.

WATCH A SPANISH TV SHOW OR MOVIE. YOU CAN USE SUBTITLES IF NECESSARY BUT TRY TO FOCUS ON LISTENING TO THE SPOKEN LANGUAGE AND UNDERSTANDING THE CONTEXT OF THE DIALOGUE. SPEND 30 MINUTES PRACTICING VERB CONJUGATION. CHOOSE A FEW VERBS AND PRACTICE CONJUGATING THEM IN DIFFERENT TENSES AND MOODS. THIS WILL HELP YOU IMPROVE YOUR GRAMMAR SKILLS AND BECOME MORE COMFORTABLE USING DIFFERENT VERB FORMS.

TUESDAY:

START THE DAY BY LISTENING TO A SPANISH PODCAST. THIS WILL HELP YOU IMPROVE YOUR LISTENING SKILLS AND EXPOSE YOU TO DIFFERENT ACCENTS AND DIALECTS.

READ A FEW PAGES FROM A SPANISH NOVEL OR A NON-FICTION BOOK. THIS WILL HELP YOU IMPROVE YOUR READING SPEED AND COMPREHENSION. SPEND 30 MINUTES PRACTICING SPANISH CONVERSATION. FIND A LANGUAGE EXCHANGE PARTNER OR JOIN A LANGUAGE LEARNING GROUP AND PRACTICE SPEAKING SPANISH WITH SOMEONE ELSE.

WEDNESDAY:

START THE DAY BY WATCHING A SPANISH TUTORIAL VIDEO ON A TOPIC THAT INTERESTS YOU. THIS WILL HELP YOU LEARN NEW VOCABULARY AND TECHNICAL TERMS RELATED TO YOUR FIELD OF INTEREST. SPEND SOME TIME WRITING IN SPANISH. YOU CAN WRITE A DIARY ENTRY, A SHORT STORY, OR A BLOG POST. THIS WILL HELP YOU IMPROVE YOUR WRITING SKILLS AND BECOME MORE COMFORTABLE EXPRESSING YOURSELF IN SPANISH. SPEND 30 MINUTES PRACTICING GRAMMAR EXERCISES. CHOOSE A GRAMMAR TOPIC THAT YOU FIND CHALLENGING, SUCH AS THE SUBJUNCTIVE MOOD OR THE USE OF PREPOSITIONS, AND PRACTICE EXERCISES TO REINFORCE YOUR UNDERSTANDING.

THURSDAY:

START THE DAY LISTENING TO A SPANISH SONG AND TRYING TO UNDERSTAND

THE LYRICS. THIS WILL HELP YOU IMPROVE YOUR LISTENING SKILLS AND EXPOSE YOU TO DIFFERENT GENRES OF MUSIC. SPEND SOME TIME READING SPANISH BLOGS OR SOCIAL MEDIA POSTS. THIS WILL HELP YOU IMPROVE YOUR READING COMPREHENSION AND BECOME MORE FAMILIAR WITH COLLOQUIAL EXPRESSIONS AND SLANG. SPEND 30 MINUTES PRACTICING VOCABULARY. CHOOSE A THEME, SUCH AS FOOD, TRAVEL, OR TECHNOLOGY, AND PRACTICE LEARNING NEW VOCABULARY RELATED TO THAT THEME.

FRIDAY:

START THE DAY BY WATCHING A SPANISH DOCUMENTARY OR A NEWS PROGRAM. THIS WILL HELP YOU IMPROVE YOUR LISTENING AND COMPREHENSION SKILLS AND EXPOSE YOU TO CURRENT EVENTS IN THE SPANISH-SPEAKING WORLD. PRACTICE SPEAKING SPANISH WITH A TUTOR OR A LANGUAGE TEACHER. GET FEEDBACK ON YOUR PRONUNCIATION, GRAMMAR, AND FLUENCY. SPEND SOME TIME REVIEWING WHAT YOU HAVE LEARNED DURING THE WEEK. MAKE A LIST OF NEW WORDS, EXPRESSIONS, AND GRAMMAR CONCEPTS THAT YOU HAVE LEARNED, AND PRACTICE USING THEM IN CONTEXT.

I HOPE THIS SCHEDULE HELPS YOU IMPROVE YOUR SPANISH SKILLS AND BECOME MORE CONFIDENT USING THE LANGUAGE!

Let's turn our focus back to business and ways to make money online. Let's start with applications for SEO and marketing. And specifically on creating content for campaigns with content marketing. Beyond just generating business ideas, AI-generated texts can be used in marketing for various reasons, such as content development for content marketing, including emails, social media postings, and blog pieces. Need help writing scripts and telling stories to convey ideas to market products and services?

PROMPT: Generate advertising for a new electric golf cart

ChatGPT:

INTRODUCING OUR BRAND-NEW ELECTRIC GOLF CART, THE NEWEST IMPROVEMENT TO YOUR GOLFING EXPERIENCE!

OUR GOLF CART IS THE IDEAL PARTNER FOR YOUR UPCOMING ROUND OF GOLF THANKS TO ITS STYLISH APPEARANCE, COZY SEATS, AND STRONG ELECTRIC MOTOR. EMBRACE THE FUTURE OF GOLF TECHNOLOGY AND BID ADIEU TO THE BOTHER OF GAS-POWERED CARTS.

WITH THE SMOOTH AND QUIET RIDE OF OUR ELECTRIC GOLF CART, YOU CAN CONCENTRATE ON YOUR GAME WITHOUT ANY OUTSIDE INTERRUPTIONS. IT ALSO LEAVES NO EMISSIONS, WHICH LESSENS YOUR CARBON FOOTPRINT ON THE GOLF FIELD.

WE ALSO HAVE CUTTING-EDGE TECHNOLOGY IN OUR GOLF CART, SUCH AS A TOUCHSCREEN DISPLAY, GPS NAVIGATION, AND BLUETOOTH CONNECTIVITY. PLAY A RELAXED ROUND OF GOLF WHILE STAYING IN TOUCH WITH YOUR FRIENDS AND FAMILY.

OUR ELECTRIC GOLF CART IS SIMPLE TO MANEUVER ON ANY SURFACE, WHETHER YOU'RE PLAYING ON A LEVEL COURSE OR A MOUNTAINOUS ONE, THANKS TO ITS LIGHTWEIGHT AND COMPACT DESIGN. FURTHERMORE, YOU WON'T HAVE TO WORRY ABOUT RUNNING OUT OF POWER IN THE MIDDLE OF A GAME THANKS TO ITS LONG-LASTING BATTERY.

TRY OUR BRAND-NEW ELECTRIC GOLF CART TODAY TO IMPROVE YOUR GOLFING EXPERIENCE. YOU WON'T REGRET IT, WE PROMISE.

ChatGPT may produce customized content for clients by utilizing its natural language processing capabilities and considering their preferences, previous behavior, and demographics. This allows companies to provide targeted content that engages with customers more personally, increasing engagement and conversion rates.

Audience research entails gathering data and insights about that group to understand better the interests, tastes, habits, and needs of the target audience. This aids businesses in more efficient marketing.

You can discover new methods and approaches for utilizing ChatGPT successfully by working with people who are also knowledgeable about the program. You can fully use ChatGPT's capabilities and produce better results in your activities and projects by adhering to these strategies and continually working to increase your ChatGPT expertise. ChatGPT can be used to examine client information like internet searches and Facebook interactions to write product descriptions to create patterns and trends in consumer behavior based on past purchases.

A key marketing component is providing potential buyers with information about a product's qualities, advantages, and value through product descriptions. , ChatGPT can help create product descriptions that appeal to the interests and preferences of the target audience.

CHAPTER 9

The Best Prompts for ChatGPT Monetization

This chapter provides some "act as" examples for ChatGPT online revenue generation. ChatGPT can offer tailored coaching sessions to assist clients in achieving their objectives and overcoming obstacles. This service can be paid for either per session or through a subscription model.

Top-notch explanations, crystal-clear communication, and straightforward language are all strengths of ChatGPT. ChatGPT's simplification of complicated concepts makes it easier for users to understand concepts outside of their area of expertise and without the need for prior technical terminology knowledge, according to an explanation of blockchain that an 11-year-old can understand.

PROMPT: I want to learn about (insert specific topic). Explain (insert topic) in simple terms. Please explain to me like I'm 15 years old.

ChatGPT can help with language acquisition, conversation practice, and grammar and pronunciation correction. Both subscription and per-lesson fees are options for making money from this business. ChatGPT provides expert budgeting, financial planning, and investment advice. This service can create considerable revenues with a subscription fee or a percentage of assets under control. ChatGPT can help you reach your objectives with customized diet and exercise regimens, wellness recommendations, and mental health assistance. Subscribe or pay per session.

ChatGPT advises on furniture placement, color schemes, and innovation to make your room a masterpiece. Subscription or per-project payment? ChatGPT lets you create a fascinating, professional resume that attracts employers. ChatGPT can help prospective writers with story, character, and editing as creative writing instructors.

Discover unlimited blog posts, social media, and other content ideas to engage your audience. As a content marketer, use ChatGPT's creative platform to produce new and exciting ideas to reach your goals. ChatGPT eliminates writer's block and inspires creativity. With this tool, create engaging, informational content that resonates with your audience. I have a lot of content from over a decade of blogging. ChatGPT is one of my favorite tools for easy organization and management. This book will help you write compelling beginnings, redesign specific sections, generate engaging gags and hooks, and write useful FAQs for your blog's key topics.

As a talented content producer, you must guarantee that your material lasts and resonates. Never create underperforming evergreen content. Simple but effective changes can maximize content potential. As a freelancer, I provide high-quality material updates and cleanup for blogs, websites, and other digital platforms. ChatGPT will turn your messy disaster into a clean, digestible masterpiece. A refined display replaces the difficulty of understanding jumbled data. Give it the text to edit. I need content to finish this. Give it the text to rewrite.

ChatGPT makes scheduling, emailing, and file organization easy. Our platform is a virtual assistant for time-pressed professionals. Focus on critical tasks to boost productivity and save time. ChatGPT can help you write engaging headlines, taglines, and other copy. This effective copywriting tool can enhance conversions and sales.

ChatGPT provides seamless customer service! ChatGPT can quickly answer frequently asked inquiries regarding products, shipping, and returns. Customer service without the wait is here now with ChatGPT. Serving customers fast and efficiently frees up time for other tasks. This sophisticated tool can generate leads, send personalized follow-up emails, and provide clients with customized recommendations. ChatGPT lets you sell for your organization by providing excellent customer experiences that convert. ChatGPT can transform your business—try it today! This simple method boosts customer revenue and sales.

ChatGPT is your market research tool for market trends, customer behavior, and competitor action. Gather and analyze data to stay ahead by making informed judgments. ChatGPT can help you discover market trends and consumer preferences to make business decisions confidently. Improve client insights.

Unlock your imagination and discover the unlimited story, narrative, and aesthetic possibilities with ChatGPT. I'll gladly assist you! As a creative writer, you can now aim to capture your brand's character and personality and develop engaging content for your target audience. ChatGPT will collaborate with you to write website copy, product descriptions, social media postings, and other on-brand and on-message content. Tell it about your business and goals, and let's start making great content!

ChatGPT simulates employment interviews. Inform ChatGPT about your planned job application. ChatGPT provides an interview-like experience with relevant and appropriate questions.

Provide exceptional services to clients across industries to maximize your earnings. ChatGPT lets you easily portray different professionals and meet clients' needs. Today, monetize your skills! Use ChatGPT to start a successful business. For over 3,000 prompts, please click the link on the first page of this book, but here is a list of 20 PROMTS based on what activity you need to accomplish.

- Automate email: "Generate a polite response to this email about scheduling a meeting."
- Draft reports: "Create a summary report of these sales data."
- Write code: "Write a Python script to automate data entry."
- Generate content: "Write a blog post about the benefits of time management."
- Create presentations: "Design a PowerPoint presentation on AI advancements."
- Plan events: "Outline a plan for a corporate team-building event."
- Brainstorm ideas: "Generate ten innovative ideas for a new mobile app."
- Write proposals: "Draft a proposal for a new marketing strategy."
- Automate social media: "Create a week's worth of social media posts for a fitness brand."
- Write business plans: "Write an executive summary for a tech startup business plan."
- Create lesson plans: "Design a lesson plan for teaching Python programming to beginners."
- Write resumes and cover letters: "Draft a cover letter for a software engineer position."
- Generate marketing copy: "Write a catchy product description for a new smartphone."

- Write research summaries: "Summarize this research paper on climate change."
- Generate recipes: "Create a healthy recipe using these ingredients: chicken, broccoli, quinoa."
- Product reviews: "Write a review for the latest iPhone model."
- Create workout plans: "Design a 4-week workout plan for weight loss."
- Write newsletters: "Draft a monthly newsletter for a local book club."
- Create meeting agendas: "Generate an agenda for a project status update meeting."
- Write press releases: "Draft a press release for a new product launch."

You can also use ChatGPT Prompts to come up with original content ideas. For example, if you need help getting popular using AI tools – we can help you quickly develop original content ideas utilizing ChatGPT.

PROMPT: Come up with unique and innovative content ideas that are unconventional for {the topic}

Use ChatGPT to test your understanding and learn about a topic, subject, or business.

PROMPT: Give me a short quiz that teaches me [what you want to learn]

Using it to develop your decision-making or managerial skills would be best.

PROMPT: I am trying to decide if I should [insert decision]. Please give me a list of good and bad that will help me decide why I should or shouldn't make this decision.

And while you are in a role, why not get out of your comfort zone and get criticized by ChatGPT?

PROMPT: I want you to act as a critic. Criticize the information above and convince me why they are bad.

And if you are stuck coming up with a great new prompt, be creative and request that ChatGPT create prompts for you.

PROMPT: I am a [insert your profession]. Generate a list of the most powerful prompts to help someone {my profession} get more done and save time.

The above was pivotal in my success, and I recommend getting very good with prompts. The next idea is a simple method that creates prompts for any situation or subject. Act in the role of [Profession], you will consider this criterion [pertinent to profession] and produce a customized product in response to my request. My initial demand is for you to ["Enter your request"]

Here is a small sample list of potential professionals, salespersons, productivity coaches, financiers, consultants, virtual assistants, social media manager coaches for public speaking, content creator, tutor, technology specialist, coaches for self-improvement, fitness professional, career counselor, resume author, nutritionist, web designer, and app developer. PROMPT:

- ACT AS A CONSULTANT: USE YOUR DOMAIN KNOWLEDGE TO OFFER CLIENTS GUIDANCE AND CONSULTATION SERVICES FOR {TOPIC OR REQUEST}
- ACT AS A FREELANCER: TO DO NUMEROUS JOBS FOR CLIENTS, OFFER YOUR SKILLS AS A FREELANCER ON WEBSITES LIKE FIVERR OR UPWORK.

- ACT AS AN AFFILIATE MARKETER: EARN MONEY BY PROMOTING THE GOODS OR SERVICES OF OTHER PEOPLE IN EXCHANGE FOR A COMMISSION ON EACH LEAD OR SALE THAT COMES FROM YOUR SPECIAL AFFILIATE LINK.

- ACT AS A SOCIAL MEDIA INFLUENCE: UTILIZE YOUR SOCIAL MEDIA FOLLOWING TO PROMOTE BRANDS' GOODS AND SERVICES TO YOUR AUDIENCE BY TAKING ON THE ROLE OF A SOCIAL MEDIA INFLUENCER.

- ACT AS AN ONLINE TUTOR: TUTOR STUDENTS ONLINE BY SHARING YOUR KNOWLEDGE AND EXPERIENCE IN A PARTICULAR SUBJECT AREA THROUGH WEBSITES, CHEGG, OR TUTORME.

- ACT AS A CONTENT CREATOR: USE PLATFORMS LIKE YOUTUBE, TIKTOK, OR INSTAGRAM TO CREATE INTERESTING AND EDUCATIONAL MATERIAL THAT DRAWS A SIZABLE AUDIENCE AND BRINGS IN MONEY FROM SPONSORSHIPS OR ADVERTISING.

- ACT AS A VIRTUAL ASSISTANT: PROVIDING CLIENTS WITH REMOTE ADMINISTRATIVE AND ORGANIZATIONAL SUPPORT.

- ACT AS A DROPSHIPPER: USE DROPSHIPPING TO SELL THINGS ONLINE WITHOUT KEEPING INVENTORY BY COLLABORATING WITH DISTRIBUTORS OR MANUFACTURERS.

These are just a few illustrations of how "act as" suggestions might be used to generate online income. The key is finding a means to monetize your talents, passions, and interests through numerous online outlets.

CHAPTER 10

Beyond ChatGPT And 100 New Ai Tools

In this Chapter, I will remind you how powerful ChatGPT is, but I also want to share with you what Beyond ChatGPT is. So many new AI Tools work with ChatGPT, and there are already a few competitors. Learning to work with other AI tools and knowing when to use other platforms will be valuable.

Artificial Intelligence is a field of computer science that focuses on developing programs and algorithms, which are step-by-step processes designed to solve problems or answer questions. The aim is to create machines that can operate in a more human-like manner.

There exist various subfields within this scientific discipline, which include:

Natural Language Processing (NLP) is a field of study that aims to create seamless communication between humans and computers. Specialized software facilitates natural language processing, enabling machines to comprehend human language, generate coherent language, and engage with humans through language.

Machine learning (ML) prioritizes a machine's capacity to analyze and utilize information to provide recommendations or make decisions based on the given data sets.

Computer vision pertains to developing machines capable of comprehending and interpreting visual data. Robotics technology is capable of autonomous physical task execution, including human interaction, without constant human supervision. Discover the immense benefits of mastering ChatGPT, unlocking its advanced features, and creating a sustainable source of passive income with my comprehensive guide. Discover the thorough analysis of ChatGPT's boundaries and the ultimate winning tactics.

No matter what your goals may be - launching a new business, expanding an existing one, or boosting your income as a freelancer, entrepreneur, or employee - ChatGPT has got you covered. We've provided many examples and expert advice on how our platform can assist you in achieving success.

Discover the power of repurposing content across multiple social media channels for maximum impact. Discover how to create passive revenue streams from the ground up! We've covered you, from ideation and research to developing a basic structure, producing content, and marketing via email and social media.

Discover the critical takeaway from this book: ChatGPT's remarkable ability to create fantastic content and generate lucrative passive income streams online. Discover the importance of acknowledging that ChatGPT has boundaries and cannot replace the finesse of human editing.

Achieving success with ChatGPT is contingent upon strictly following the recommended best practices outlined in this book. Achieving your desired outcomes requires a strategic approach. This involves setting clear and measurable goals, conducting thorough research, refining your prompts to elicit optimal responses, and dedicating ample time to editing and enhancing your content.

Unlock the full potential of ChatGPT by strategically selecting your desired income streams and establishing clear, achievable, and quantifiable objectives. Maximize your results by dedicating time to perfecting your prompts. Discover the most effective prompts by experimenting with different options and keeping track of their outcomes. While ChatGPT delivers top-notch content, it has imperfections. Take the time to meticulously edit and refine the generated content to ensure it meets your exact requirements and is completely error-free.

Discover the world of ChatGPT and its vast array of applications with this all-encompassing beginner's guidebook. Discover the essential building blocks of ChatGPT, delve into its intricate technicalities, and unlock its limitless potential for diverse applications. With its remarkable ability to produce responses strikingly like a human's, ChatGPT is the ultimate solution for diverse prompts and inquiries. Experience the exceptional advantage of ChatGPT's coherent and contextually appropriate responses to natural language inputs. This versatile tool is invaluable for conversational AI applications like chatbots and personal assistants. Unlock a world of possibilities with the ability to perform tasks like text summarization, trivia question answering, and image natural language description. Discover the limitless potential of ChatGPT! Our cutting-edge technology extends far beyond mere text generation. Experience the versatility and power of this advanced tool that has the potential to revolutionize the world of natural language processing and artificial intelligence.

Unlock the full potential of this cutting-edge technology by harnessing its power with ample computational resources and expert know-how. Experience advanced conversational AI and natural language processing with ChatGPT - a significant advancement in the field. With its proven track record in healthcare, customer service, and research, this versatile technology boasts a wide range of capabilities and limitless potential for various industries.

ChatGPT is a powerful AI model that has revolutionized natural language processing. It can generate human-like responses to various inputs, making it useful for various applications, including customer service, education, and entertainment. However, ChatGPT, like any other technology, has limitations and challenges that must be overcome, such as bias, context understanding, and user trust. To fully realize ChatGPT's potential, it is critical to continue developing and refining the model while ensuring it is used ethically and responsibly.

We can use ChatGPT to improve our lives and create a better future. ChatGPT aims to enhance communication between humans and machines and provide users with a more personalized and engaging experience. It can transform industries and open new opportunities for businesses and individuals. ChatGPT, however, has limitations and challenges, including potential biases, context understanding, and user trust. These issues must be addressed to ensure ChatGPT is used ethically and responsibly.

ChatGPT represents a significant advancement in artificial intelligence and natural language processing, and it has the potential to drive future innovation and progress. As an OpenAI product/service, ChatGPT does not have a direct monetization strategy as an AI language model. On the other hand, businesses and organizations can use ChatGPT skills to generate revenue in various ways.

While ChatGPT has been the primary focus throughout this book, it's worth noting the abundance of new tools emerging monthly, with hundreds being introduced regularly. Discover what lies Beyond ChatGPT in this exciting new chapter. Discover cutting-edge AI technology that rivals ChatGPT. Discover powerful AI tools and agents that seamlessly integrate with ChatGPT to elevate, refine, and expedite your ChatGPT experience.

PROMPT: give me a list of the stocks that could 10x next bull run.

CHATGPT:

AS AN AI DEVELOPED BY OPENAI, I MUST CLARIFY THAT I'M NOT ABLE TO PROVIDE SPECIFIC STOCK PREDICTIONS OR INVESTMENT ADVICE, AS THIS REQUIRES AN UNDERSTANDING OF REAL-TIME MARKET CONDITIONS, INDIVIDUAL COMPANY PERFORMANCES, AND OTHER VARIABLES, WHICH I DON'T HAVE.

AS OF MY TRAINING CUT-OFF IN SEPTEMBER 2021, I CAN PROVIDE GENERAL ADVICE ON HOW TO IDENTIFY POTENTIALLY HIGH-GROWTH STOCKS:

1. EMERGING INDUSTRIES: COMPANIES OPERATING IN INDUSTRIES THAT ARE POISED FOR SIGNIFICANT GROWTH, SUCH AS RENEWABLE ENERGY, ARTIFICIAL INTELLIGENCE, BLOCKCHAIN TECHNOLOGY, AND BIOTECH.

2. INNOVATION: COMPANIES THAT ARE LEADERS IN INNOVATION, HAVE A UNIQUE PRODUCT OR SERVICE, OR ARE DISRUPTING EXISTING INDUSTRIES.

3. FINANCIAL HEALTH: COMPANIES WITH STRONG BALANCE SHEETS, GOOD CASH FLOW, AND MANAGEABLE DEBT.

4. STRONG MANAGEMENT: LEADERSHIP WITH A PROVEN TRACK SUCCESS RECORD CAN BE A GOOD INDICATOR OF A COMPANY'S POTENTIAL FOR GROWTH.

5. MARKET POTENTIAL: COMPANIES TARGETING LARGE AND GROWING MARKETS.

6. COMPETITIVE ADVANTAGE: COMPANIES WITH A SUSTAINABLE COMPETITIVE ADVANTAGE SUCH AS PROPRIETARY TECHNOLOGY, STRONG BRAND, OR COST ADVANTAGES.

PLEASE CONSULT WITH A FINANCIAL ADVISOR OR CONDUCT THOROUGH DUE DILIGENCE BEFORE MAKING INVESTMENT DECISIONS.

So, it didn't want to give me a list and remember the data is not current, so it can be very hard to get it to help predict current events based on the recent past, but I pushed with more prompts, and here is what I got

ChatGPT:

- TESLA INC. (TSLA): A LEADER IN THE ELECTRIC VEHICLE MARKET.
- MODERNA INC. (MRNA): A KEY PLAYER IN THE DEVELOPMENT OF MRNA TECHNOLOGY FOR VACCINES.
- AMAZON.COM INC. (AMZN): CONTINUOUSLY INNOVATING IN E-COMMERCE, CLOUD COMPUTING, AND OTHER TECH DOMAINS.
- ALPHABET INC. (GOOGL): THE PARENT COMPANY OF GOOGLE, KNOWN FOR ITS INNOVATIVE TECHNOLOGIES IN VARIOUS FIELDS LIKE SEARCH, CLOUD COMPUTING, AI, AND MORE.
- MICROSOFT CORPORATION (MSFT): A TECH COMPANY WITH STRONG FINANCIALS AND A WIDE RANGE OF SUCCESSFUL PRODUCTS.
- APPLE INC. (AAPL): KNOWN FOR ITS ROBUST FINANCIAL HEALTH AND POPULAR PRODUCTS.
- BERKSHIRE HATHAWAY INC. (BRK.A): LED BY WARREN BUFFETT, KNOWN FOR HIS LONG-TERM INVESTMENT PHILOSOPHY.
- JPMORGAN CHASE & CO. (JPM): LED BY JAMIE DIMON, REGARDED AS A STRONG LEADER IN THE FINANCE INDUSTRY.
- NVIDIA CORPORATION (NVDA): A LEADING COMPANY IN THE GPU MARKET WITH GROWING APPLICATIONS IN AI, GAMING, AND DATA CENTERS.
- ADOBE INC. (ADBE): PROVIDING SOFTWARE SOLUTIONS WITH A SIGNIFICANT MARKET TO CATER TO.
- THE COCA-COLA COMPANY (KO): WITH A STRONG BRAND NAME AND WORLDWIDE PRESENCE, IT'S A LEADER IN THE BEVERAGE INDUSTRY.
- JOHNSON & JOHNSON (JNJ): A DIVERSIFIED HEALTHCARE COMPANY WITH A BROAD RANGE OF WELL-ESTABLISHED PRODUCTS.

So, you can see how powerful this tool will continue to be, especially as it gets current data and events. But as we mentioned at the beginning of this chapter, there is some new coopetition in the AI space.

Perplexity AI can be the ultimate chatbot ready to take on any challenge! ChatGPT

Step into the world of digital AI, where AI chatbots gather and mingle. Meet Perplexity AI, the scrappy newcomer ready to take on the reigning champ, ChatGPT, and shake up the entire AI landscape. This up-and-comer aims to leave the competition in the dust by boasting an impressive lineage, a vast array of features, and a top-notch mobile app. https://www.perplexity.ai

So, I asked Perplexity the same question I asked ChatGPT and got a very different response to the first prompt, as Perplexity uses a different method of answering questions.

PROMPT: give me a list of the stocks that could 10x next bull run.

Perplexity:

HERE ARE SOME STOCKS THAT COULD POTENTIALLY 10X IN THE NEXT BULL RUN, ACCORDING TO THE SEARCH RESULTS:

1. ROCKET LAB
2. LANZATECH GLOBAL, NIO, AND JOBY AVIATION
3. DESKTOP METAL, GINKGO BIOWORKS, SOFI, REAL REAL
4. DERMTECH, DMY TECHNOLOGY GROUP II, SNAP, SQUARE, SOFI VIA CHAMATH PALIHAPITIYA'S IPOE
5. NVDA, DICK'S SPORTING GOODS, PERFICIENT, MODERN
6. CRYPTOCURRENCIES SUCH AS ETHEREUM AND DOGECOIN

IT'S IMPORTANT TO NOTE THAT INVESTING IN SPECULATIVE STOCKS OR CRYPTOCURRENCIES CAN BE RISKY AND SHOULD BE DONE WITH CAUTION. IT'S ALWAYS A GOOD IDEA TO DO YOUR RESEARCH AND CONSULT WITH A FINANCIAL ADVISOR BEFORE MAKING ANY INVESTMENT DECISIONS.

Introducing AgentGPT - the ultimate solution for configuring and deploying autonomous AI agents seamlessly integrating with ChatGPT. Experience the power of cutting-edge technology and take your chatbot game to the next level with AgentGPT. With just a prompt, this incredible tool accomplished in mere minutes what would have taken ten long weeks to achieve solo or two weeks with the assistance of ChatGPT. Imagine having the expertise of a seasoned ChatGPT user at your fingertips with AgentGPT. With the power to select the top 100 prompts for optimal results, you'll be able to streamline your interactions like never before. AgentGPT. It will attempt to reach the goal by thinking of tasks to do, executing them, and learning from the results. https://agentgpt.reworkd.ai

As you will see, when you go to AgentGPT and type in any prompt by clicking Deploy Agent, you will see how it works and thinks. It will develop a Goal and a plan, then execute the tasks needed to reach the goal. It will conduct a market analysis. It will search the web and analyze financial and growth potential, tackling this question like a human but much faster.

These new platforms use a different methodology but deliver similar answers to ChatGPT as it uses the underlying OpenAI API to get its answers.

Another interesting player will be AutoGPT. Discover the limitless possibilities with Auto-GPT, an innovative open-source project. With its advanced framework, Auto-GPT empowers the model to reason and act independently, effortlessly completing various tasks. Experience the future of AI today with AutoGPT. It is only available with the API and for those technical people who can grab the code from GitHub and integrate the platform.

Discover the undeniable truth: Not all lists are created equal regarding ChatGPT competitors. With three distinct rankings at your fingertips, it's imperative to hone your discerning skills and never settle for the initial response. As I keep mentioning, verify everything often. You can google ChatGPT agents and get a list that today includes Auto-GPT, BabyAGI, AgentGPT, Microsoft's Jarvis, ChaosGPT, and others. Jarvis is A collaborative system with an LLM (Large Language Model) as the controller and numerous expert models as collaborative executors.

Hugging Face is the best new community and data science platform. It has cutting-edge tools that make it easy to design, train, and deploy ML (machine language) models using open-source code and technology. Hugging Face offers data science's future now. It is such a supportive environment to collaborate on open-source projects. With cutting-edge tools, data science teams, specialists, and enthusiasts may collaborate smoothly from anywhere. These technologies are vital as hybrid and flexible working styles become the norm. AI's full potential requires collaboration and a community, as tech giants need help to handle this. A communal "Hub" is provided by Hugging Face. In one place, find and collaborate on cutting-edge models and datasets to help curate the largest datasets and models to democratize AI. Join them with me in democratizing AI. https://huggingface.co

This solution delivers daily updates on the latest and greatest cryptocurrency projects by leveraging an API and crafting custom code. Stay ahead of the game with this powerful tool at your fingertips. Discover the endless possibilities of AgentGPT for enhancing your personal and professional endeavors.

ChatGPT's excellent responses and thorough attention to detail will enhance your interactions! We encourage researching all possibilities, but ChatGPT is the best, especially with its upcoming release. Find the best option for your unique needs. Your needs and tastes will determine the best option. Discover AI's benefits. AI tools can enhance operations, analyze data, and predict results by identifying patterns and trends easily, helping you to become productive and accurate. Use AI to improve data analysis. Modern chatbot technology makes accessing a wealth of information from multiple sources easy. They easily remember and retrieve information, so every detail is noticed. Use succinct questions to maximize inquiry. Use our cutting-edge artificial intelligence tool to pinpoint critical locations with pinpoint accuracy. Get information suited to your needs. Our cutting-edge artificial intelligence technology improves data processing, searches, and selection. Specificity is key to getting correct answers. Modern artificial intelligence applications can sort through Google, Wikipedia, and other digital libraries to boost productivity. This powerful solution boosts productivity and resource efficiency.

Tailor learning at your speed and maximize your potential. Self-paced learning opens up a world of possibilities. Our innovative technology allows fast data processing and learning, maximizing its potential. Understand your cognitive type to improve. Due to poorer visual processing, working memory, or attention regulation, some people need more time to scrutinize the details. Examine how traditional classrooms may limit efficiency and fairness. AI technologies and platforms can enhance your self-directed learning. Customized instruction has advantages! Develop a personalized learning approach to maximize potential and success.

Explore how AI can evaluate your performance and provide immediate feedback. State-of-the-art resources help you achieve your goals for higher education. This efficient strategy lets teachers focus on more important topics. Our cutting-edge technology streamlines the grading process like never before. Master self-learning and AI flaw detection. Verify your writing to ensure accuracy. Use ChatGPT's AI features to get great advice and responses. Discover your full potential by hiring a personal instructor. New AI methods enable more accurate error detection. Verifying information seamlessly improves essay writing. Automate grammatical corrections with AI. Our students always provide accurate work. Teachers are spending less time grading pupils' work.

AI tools can streamline your schooling. Eliminate tedious tasks and boost student and educator productivity. AI apps help with everything from information gathering to assessments. Our cutting-edge technology creates a virtual classroom with virtual instructors for an unmatched learning experience. Our innovative solution lets you learn from multiple sources. Find out how these technologies perform in unusual situations. Explore AI-powered speech-recognition tools. These unique solutions are perfect for anyone with physical or age-related writing and typing challenges. Use voice commands to navigate documents. Accessible schools need this feature.

Here is a list of more than 100 new AI Tools to help you make even more money online with ChatGPT and AI.

1. https://theresanaiforthat.com. The Best site for anyone reading this book today. This has almost 5,000 AI's, so you can find most of the tools below at this site and many more.

2. https://godmode.space Godmode is a web platform to access the powers of AutoGPT and BabyAGI. AI agents are still in their infancy, but they are quickly growing in capabilities, and we hope that Godmode will enable more people to tap into autonomous AI agents even in this early stage. Auto-GPT and BabyAGI inspire Godmode and support GPT-3.5 & GPT-4.

3. https://learningstudioai.com The next-generation online course creation tool

4. https://www.uimagic.io Unlock the future of website design with the power of AI-driven User Interface technology for text-to-web designing.

5. https://venturusai.com Turn your business idea into reality. Generate an analysis of your business idea and give you feedback on how to make it successful.

6. https://text-to-video.vercel.app Text to Video. Create videos with artificial intelligence.

7. https://autogpt.thesamur.ai Chatbot site with ChatGPT models, prompt library, and chat history.

8. https://www.magicslides.app Ideas to Professional Presentations in Seconds. Say bye to boring, laborious presentation-making. Let the computer do the hard work and make the presentations for you!

9. https://agentgpt.reworkd.ai Assemble, configure, and deploy autonomous AI Agents in your browser and let your computer do all the heavy lifting.

10. https://scisummary.com Use AI to summarize scientific articles in seconds. Get 5x research done without constantly disrupting your work.

11. https://seocontent.ai/ Optimize Your Content Strategy with SEO Content AI. Our AI-driven solution optimizes your content for search engines and improves your online presence with high-quality, long-form content.

12. https://business-generator.vercel.app Tool that helps users generate creative business ideas.

13. https://www.gptinf.com A tool that removes AI content by paraphrasing.

14. https://www.helinaik.com/contentcal Create your monthly content calendar with the help of this AI tool.

15. https://www.sincode.ai Create SEO-optimized and plagiarism-free content for your blogs, ads, emails, & website 10X faster.

16. https://pictory.ai Automatically create short, highly sharable branded videos from your long-form content. Quick, easy & cost-effective.

17. https://write.homes/ The ultimate real estate content creation tool

18. https://www.jasper.ai/. The best overall AI writing assistant, leading the market with its impressive features and quality.

19. https://simplerlist.com A productivity assistant that helps you get things done.

20. https://www.translate.video/1-click publish to all social media platforms and manage global audience in a single place

21. https://murf.ai/ Go from text to speech with a versatile AI voice generator. AI-enabled real people's voices. Make studio-quality voiceovers in minutes. Lifelike AI voices for podcasts, videos, and all your professional presentations

22. https://lovo.ai Realistic AI voices that captivate your audience. LOVO is the go-to AI Voice Generator & Text to Speech platform for thousands of creators, saving 90% of their time and budget.

23. https://www.fineshare.com/finevoice/ AI digital voice solution with an amazing real-time voice changer, studio-quality voice recorder, fast and accurate automatic transcription, and realistic AI voice generator.

24. https://www.hitpaw.com/ is the best AI image enlarger to make pictures less blurry and enlarge images without quality loss.

25. https://jobhuntmode.com An AI Based automated career services platform to help navigate the job hunting process.

26. https://gptprompttuner.com Use AI to Generate ChatGPT prompt iterations and run conversations in parallel.

27. https://anyword.com/ It enables the generation of effective copy for ads, emails, landing pages, and content for different platforms.

28. https://www.tango.us. Tango instantly turns what you know into step-by-step guidance—no videos, meetings, or screen shares required.

29. https://www.cutout.pro leverages the power of artificial intelligence and computer vision to deliver a wide range of products both available for individual use and business application & workflows to achieve efficiency and creation.

30. https://meetotis.com The all-in-one solution for growing businesses to manage their digital marketing on Facebook, Instagram, Google, TikTok, YouTube, and more. An AI-driven platform that enables businesses to compete and maximize their return on investment.

31. https://www.flick.social/ Handle copywriting, scheduling, hashtags, and analytics seamlessly with Flick, the AI-powered social marketing platform.

32. https://www.looka.com/ Design your beautiful brand. Use Looka's AI-powered platform to design a logo and build a brand you love.

33. https://www.tutorai.me AI platform that allows users to learn about any topic easily.

34. https://ultrabrainstomer.com/ Productivity tool that helps you create social media posts, product campaigns, speeches, and emails.

35. https://www.neuraltext.com/ AI copywriter, SEO content tool, and keyword research tool.

36. https://blogassistant.co AI blog writing tool on the market, and generate complete, non-detectable articles with outlines and blog content.

37. https://www.hypertype.co AI-powered engine to fetch you the most relevant information from your emails and documents. Real-time.

38. https://h2o.ai. A truly open-source generative AI gives organizations like yours the power to create large language models while maintaining your data integrity.

39. https://isaax.org generate custom content for your business needs, including creating blog posts, summarizing texts, and much more.

40. https://www.heygen.com Create engaging videos 10X faster with AI. Meet HeyGen - The best AI video generation platform for your team.

41. https://icons8.com/lunacy Free design software that keeps your flow with AI tools and built-in graphics.

42. https://www.siteexplainer.com AI-powered web app lets you quickly and accurately summarize any website in just a few seconds.

43. https://www.scholarcy.com The online summarizing tool that provides a way to assess and evaluate the importance of documents quickly,

44. https://www.slidesai.io Create Presentation Slides with AI in seconds. Say goodbye to tedious, manual slide creation. Let the AI write the outline and presentation content for you. With our tool, you can easily create professional, engaging slides from any text in no time.

45. https://gptkit.ai AI text generation detection tool.

46. https://krisp.ai Supercharge your online meetings with Voice Productivity AI. Krisp improves the productivity of online meetings with its AI-powered Voice Clarity and Meeting Assistant.

47. https://www.tidio.com Boost your conversions with automation and AI. Answer questions in real-time, 24/7. And so much more.

48. https://chatgptwriter.ai Write emails & messages, fix grammar mistakes, rephrase text, change the writing tone, summarize text, and much more using ChatGPT AI.

49. https://codeium.com A Free AI-Powered Toolkit for Developers.

50. https://codeamigo.dev An AI-powered coding assistant that helps you learn to code like a developer. Today's developers didn't learn binary before learning Python; why should you learn how to code without the most modern tools?

51. http://Tabnine.com → Coding assistant. AI assistant for software developers. Code faster with whole-line & full-function code completions

52. https://speechify.com/ turn text in any format into natural-sounding speech. Based on the web, the platform can take PDFs, emails, docs, or articles and turn them into audio that can be listened to instead of read.

53. https://www.youtubedigest.app YoutubeDigest is a browser extension that uses ChatGPT AI to summarize YouTube videos. Choose from various summary formats and export as PDF, DOCX, or text. ≊

54. https://merlin.foyer.work AI Assistant is a ChatGPT extension to finish any task on any website in seconds. Merlin is the easy & better way to use ChatGPT. ChatGPT assistant on all websites

55. https://writepanda.io Chat with your podcast/ Youtube! Now easily generate anything.

56. https://designer.microsoft.com Create Images in no time with an AI Image Generator and Editor from Microsoft.

57. https://www.adcreative.ai Artificial Intelligence powered Ad & Social Creatives. Generate conversion-focused ad creatives and social media post creatives in seconds using Artificial Intelligence. Get better results while saving time.

58. https://www.chatpdf.com Efficiently analyze your documents. From financial and sales reports to project and business proposals, training manuals, and legal contracts, ChatPDF can quickly provide you with the information you need.

59. https://huggingface.co Build, train, and deploy state-of-the-art models powered by the reference open source in machine learning. A platform that provides access to pre-trained models for natural language processing tasks.

60. https://theforgeai.com Build AI-powered Applications without writing a single line of code.

61. https://stratup.ai Stratup.ai goes beyond idea generation by providing practical steps to turn your startup ideas into reality.

62. https://hints.so Revolutionize your workflow with an integrated AI assistant from Hints. Visit our website today to explore all the AI integrations.

63. http://audioread.com Audioread If you have endless read-later articles, documents, etc., you'll love this AI tool. Turn articles, PDFs, emails, etc., into podcasts and listen to them while you exercise, commute, run errands, etc.

64. http://adcopy.ai Adcopy AI, the first AI copy tool built to drive more clicks and conversions for digital advertisers, is here. 1. Unlimited outputs for your campaigns 2. Find winning variations in lightning speed 3. Copy & paste any ad for a new variation in seconds

65. http://interviewprep-ai.com Interview Prep AI Are you tired of the stress and anxiety that comes with preparing for a job interview? Interview Prep Al is your personal Al job interview coach that helps you ace your next interview.

66. https://www.eesel.app easel. Use AI to organize your Google Docs, Notion pages, and other work documents automatically. Organizes it all right in your new tab. Best of all, it is free, doesn't compromise privacy, and you don't need to log in to try it.

67. http://hyperwriteai.com HyperWrite is a personal writing helper that creates material for writing ideas, greatly simplifying the work of writers. HyperWrite created a text-to-image section on its website in addition to the writing aid feature.

68. http://ai.nero.com/image-upscaler Nero AI Use this AI to enlarge, improve and clean up your photos. This tool helps you increase image resolution without losing quality.

69. https://threadvoice.net Yes! You can convert this (or any text) to a voice version. You can listen to or download it via

70. http://Formulabot.com Supercharge Excel and Google Sheets. Revolutionize your data & spreadsheet workflow with AI. Transform your text instructions into formulas and more for free in seconds.

71. https://gptexcel.uk Generate Spreadsheet Formulas with AI. An ideal solution for individuals and businesses looking to streamline their spreadsheet processes.

72. http://Cohesive.so Next-generation AI editor. Create magical content
With the most powerful AI editor. End ChatGPT prompt struggles. Create, refine, edit, and publish seamlessly with Cohesive.

73. https://kaiber.ai. Captivating visuals from images or text. Bring your dreams to life. Tell stories like never before with our advanced AI generation engine

74. http://Airops.com/sidekick AI data apps. Draft, fix, and optimize your SQL queries 10x faster. Write documentation instantly.

75. http://Tripnotes.ai AI travel assistant, where do you want to go today?

76. http://Meetcody.ai AI assistant trained to help you grow your business

77. https://www.getsmartcue.com/ Supercharge conversions with SmartCue - the conversion-focused, no-code demo creation & analytics tool for high-performance Go-To-Market teams

78. https://www.joinmano.ai/. Your shortcut to an easier workday. The best way to use ChatGPT on any website.

79. https://poe.com/. Fast, helpful AI chat! Why use it? - iOs and Android apps - Access Sage, Claude, ChatGPT - Explore and use community bots

80. https://vidyo.ai. Make short videos from long ones instantly. Create social-ready short clips from your long videos with AI

81. https://www.audyo.ai. Delight your audience with human-quality AI voices as easily as typing.

82. https://www.superflows.ai. Reply to emails in 1-click. Blaze through your inbox with email summaries and pre-generated replies written in your voice.

83. http://10web.io → AI website builder AI-Powered WordPress Platform. Generate your website in minutes with AI. Get the fastest hosting powered by Google Cloud. Boost your website's PageSpeed score to 90+

84. http://Franks.ai → AI search engine for Business. AI assistant. I can help you find any information and help you write, summarize, and generate any text in seconds.

85. http://Gling.ai → AI video editor. Our AI will cut silences, and bad takes for you so you can focus on your YouTube videos

86. http://Rytr.me → AI copywriter. Rytr is an AI writing assistant that helps you create high-quality content, in just a few seconds, at a fraction of the cost!

87. http://Beautiful.ai → AI presentation software for the workplace

88. https://fireflies.ai. AI meeting assistant that uses NLP to eliminate the need for note-taking during a meeting.

89. https://www.usechatgpt.ai. Use ChatGPT (Plugins & GPT-4), Bard, Bing Chat, and Claude on any website without copy-pasting. Write, rewrite, summarize, translate, explain, or reply to any text everywhere with one click.

90. https://monica.im.. Your ChatGPT Powered AI Assistant on All Websites

91. https://wiseone.io Helps you master any topic you read online by bringing relevant and reliable information.

92. https://www.compose.ai Write Faster With AI, Save Time. Compose AI is a Chrome extension that cuts your writing time by 40% with AI-powered autocompletion & text generation.

93. https://www.stork.ai. AI-Based Collaboration for Hybrid Teams Rich media messaging, advanced video and voice conferencing, auto-transcribing, and screen sharing. Serendipitous meetings at the water cooler with your human and AI teammates.

94. http://Typedesk.com Save time everywhere you work. Create text shortcuts that work across all your apps and websites for all your repetitive text content

95. http://Chatgpt4google.com Supercharge Google w/ ChatGPT. ChatGPT response alongside search engine results.

96. https://gencraft.com. The world's most powerful AI photo and video art generation engine. What will you create?

97. https://kaiber.ai Tell stories like never before with our advanced AI generation engine to create video from the text.

98. https://stunning.so. Build websites with AI

99. https://metrotechs.io/ artificial intelligence and performance-oriented web hosting to help launch and scale your brand online.

100. https://chatronai.com/ Unique AI Content, Image, and Codes Generator

My goal was to give you insightful knowledge and practical advice for using ChatGPT successfully. I am confident you can create worthwhile passive income streams and succeed in this business environment by following the best practices described in this book and the applicable procedures.

How would Warren Buffer close out this book? Let's ask ChatGPT…

THIS FINAL CHAPTER PROVIDES A SUMMARY OF THE BOOK'S KEY INSIGHTS, INCLUDING THE SIGNIFICANCE OF UTILIZING CHATGPT FOR CREATING PASSIVE INCOME STREAMS, RECOGNIZING ITS LIMITATIONS, AND IMPLEMENTING BEST PRACTICES FOR SUCCESS. THE CHAPTER ALSO PROVIDES ACTIONABLE STEPS THAT READERS CAN TAKE TO ACHIEVE SUCCESS WITH CHATGPT, SUCH AS SETTING CLEAR OBJECTIVES, CONSISTENTLY PRACTICING AND REFINING THEIR USE OF THE TOOL, AND REGULARLY EVALUATING THEIR PROGRESS. BY FOLLOWING THESE METHODS, READERS WILL BE ABLE TO EFFECTIVELY HARNESS THE POWER OF CHATGPT TO INCREASE THEIR PRODUCTIVITY AND GENERATE A SUSTAINABLE ONLINE INCOME.

Book #2

How to Make Money with AI for Beginners

The Step-by-Step Guide to Creating Multiple Passive Income Streams.

Introduction

Welcome to my second Artificial Intelligence book. What an amazing couple of months since I published my first book on ChatGPT and Artificial Intelligence (AI). So much more has been crammed into my brain; millions of people have joined us on this journey. So many more opportunities exist to make money with artificial intelligence. Is it time to take the red pill and enter the cutting-edge world of AI and Machine Language? While this book includes some information on the most recent advancements, it also takes a more fundamental approach to technology. You can read about AI without having any prior knowledge about ChatGPT. We are about to dive headfirst into artificial intelligence's fascinating, often perplexing, and permanently magnetic field, so hold on to your hats and buckle up.

Welcome to your one-stop shop for forward-thinking individuals looking to turn machine learning into a profitable way to generate money online. Prepare to cut through the noise, eliminate the technical jargon, and immerse yourself in a manual that will set you on the path to financial success with AI and machine learning. Settle in, get comfortable, and prepare for an adventure. Are you willing to take on the challenge? Prepare to go on an exciting experience!

As the world grows more digitized, the potential of artificial intelligence (AI) becomes more evident. AI has emerged as a potent tool for streamlining company operations, improving consumer experiences, and even assisting humans in making better decisions. Individuals and businesses alike may open a new world of possibilities and achieve extraordinary success with the help of AI-powered assistants like ChatGPT and so many more we shall cover on this journey. In this comprehensive book, we will look at the potential of AI as a disruptive force in business and innovation. We will look at how AI may be used to generate growth and profitability and the ethical considerations of employing AI.

We'll look at the power of various AI Tools, including many game-changing AI-powered assistants that help businesses and creators achieve their objectives. This book will go beyond ChatGPT; if you only want to use ChatGPT, please read my other book, "Making Money Online with ChatGPT." And so much has changed in the few months since that book was published, so we need to look at Beyond ChatGPT and comprehend all the new AI technologies.

The AI Revolution and Its Potential in Business

The AI revolution has the potential to transform the way businesses operate entirely. AI can automate repetitive tasks, analyze data, and provide valuable insights for business decisions. Companies can optimize operations, reduce costs, and enhance customer experiences with AI. What are you struggling with today? Do you need help making more sales? Do you need support getting automated? We can show you how to do all that and more.

One of the most significant benefits of using AI in business is its ability to analyze vast data quickly. AI can sift through mountains of data in seconds, identifying patterns and trends that would be impossible for humans to detect. This data can then be used to optimize business processes, improve product development, and inform marketing strategies. The Power of AI for Creators AI is not just a tool for businesses; it can also be a powerful tool for creators. AI-powered assistants like ChatGPT can help creators generate new ideas, refine existing ones, and streamline their creative processes.

With AI, creators can overcome creative blocks, explore new ideas, and produce better work. One of the key benefits of using AI tools is their ability to generate high-quality content quickly. Whether you're a writer, artist, or designer, AI can help you create and refine new ideas. With AI, you can overcome creative blocks, explore new ideas, and produce better work.

Why AI is a Game-Changer

AI is a game-changer because it gives businesses and creators a powerful AI-powered assistant to help them achieve their goals. AI is not just a tool for generating content; it can also be used to analyze data, provide insights, and optimize business processes. One of the key benefits of using AI is its ability to generate high-quality content quickly and efficiently.

Whether you need business generation ideas, blog posts, social media updates, or product descriptions, AI can help create content that engages your audience and drives conversions. Another benefit of using AI is its ability to provide valuable insights to inform business decisions. With AI, businesses can analyze customer data, identify trends, and optimize their marketing strategies. I hope I can show you that AI is a game-changer because it is easy to use and accessible to businesses and creators of all sizes. Whether you're a freelancer or a multinational corporation, AI can help you achieve your goals and stay ahead of the competition.

As the world becomes increasingly online and digital, it's becoming more critical to understand the potential of artificial intelligence and how it can be harnessed to benefit our lives. In recent years, AI has emerged as a powerful tool that can streamline business processes, improve customer experiences, and even help us make better decisions. With the help of AI, individuals and businesses alike can unlock a new world of possibilities and achieve tremendous success. In this book, I will help you discover the endless possibilities of AI and how it can be used to drive growth and profitability. This book provides a step-by-step overview of the evolution of AI technology and its impact on businesses, product development, and marketing strategies. It also delves into the risks and ethical implications of using AI and provides practical tips on responsibly navigating the digital landscape. One of the key benefits of using AI is its ability to help businesses maximize profits and enhance customer engagement. With valuable insights into using AI Tools, readers can gain a deeper understanding of how to leverage AI to grow their businesses and increase their income.

Whether you're a creator or a business owner, this book is an excellent resource for those looking to harness the power of AI to achieve their goals. How to Make Money Online with AI is an excellent resource for anyone looking to expand their knowledge of AI and its potential applications. With practical insights and expert advice, this book is a must-read for those looking to stay ahead of the curve in today's fast-paced digital landscape. Let's start harnessing the power of AI to transform your life and business.

The potential of AI is immense, and its impact on business and creativity is only beginning to be realized. With the help of AI-powered assistants like ChatGPT, companies, and creators can unlock a new world of possibilities and achieve tremendous success. Whether you're looking to optimize your business processes, generate high-quality content, or gain valuable insights, AI is a game-changer that can help you achieve your goals. So why wait? Start harnessing the power of AI today and transform your life and business.

Remember that true triumph is achieved through unwavering effort and a profound comprehension of the fundamental principles that drive it.

Discover the incredible power of AI, unlocking a world of valuable insights and game-changing recommendations. But remember, maintaining a proactive and adaptable mindset is crucial in this fast-paced digital era. Stay ahead of the curve and embrace the limitless possibilities that await you. Discover the power of starting small, empowering yourself with knowledge, and embracing the incredible potential of AI as your unwavering ally on the path to financial triumph!

This book was NOT developed by ChatGPT or any AI tool; it was researched and written by a human to help teach other humans how to work with AI in our current reality. ChatGPT is an AI tool, and as such, it is programmed to generate text depending on the data it has been provided and trained on. Conversely, AI will aim to create content that is as cohesive, informative, and human-like as possible. It can assist but may lack personal experiences, emotions, and a deep understanding of context.

CHAPTER 1

Understanding Ai

Unlock the Secrets of AI

Learn about the fascinating field of artificial intelligence (AI), a groundbreaking phenomenon that has swept the globe. As you observe the enormous influence of AI across numerous industries, get ready to be astounded. Investigate AI's potential to open doors to prosperous business prospects. Use Machine Learning, a significant branch of Artificial Intelligence, to its limitless potential. Take advantage of the opportunity to turn your knowledge and abilities into a substantial source of income. Allow the power of machine learning to propel you towards a future with limitless potential! Discover the mysteries of AI as we reveal them in this fascinating article. As we give you an exclusive beginner's guide that shows the road to financial success using the power of machine learning, get ready to start an exciting trip.

Discover the captivating world of AI.

This is truly a groundbreaking technological marvel revolutionizing how we live and interact. Delve into the depths of this cutting-edge innovation as we unravel the mysteries and unveil AI's incredible potential.

AI is a new dynamic field within computer science that delves into the creation of extraordinary machines. Discover the captivating world of

Machine Learning, a noteworthy branch of Artificial Intelligence that unveils the remarkable potential of algorithms and statistical models. Witness the awe-inspiring ability of machines to learn from vast amounts of data, empowering them to make predictions and decisions without the need for explicit programming. Prepare to be amazed as the boundaries of innovation are pushed to new heights. Welcome to the realm of Machine Learning.

We are exploring the incredible power of AI! With its remarkable capabilities, computers can analyze massive amounts of data, effortlessly uncovering hidden patterns and delivering precise predictions or decisions. Prepare to be amazed as AI revolutionizes the way we harness information!

Discover the limitless potential of AI and unlock a world of financial opportunities. Embark on a journey towards lucrative earnings with the power of artificial intelligence. How can you kickstart your income stream? Read on to unveil the secrets of monetizing AI and watch your bank account flourish.

Unlock the fundamental principles that lay the foundation for success. Embark on a thrilling journey into AI and machine learning, where a firm grasp of the basic concepts is the key to unlocking boundless possibilities. Better understand the captivating world of machine learning algorithms, where possibilities are endless. Immerse yourself in the realm of supervised learning, unsupervised learning, and reinforcement learning, and unlock the secrets that lie within. Expand your knowledge and embrace the power of these transformative algorithms. Learn the techniques for feature engineering and data preparation, which are crucial for transforming unprocessed data into a masterpiece that machine learning models can appreciate.

Get on the path to triumph in machine learning by cultivating a formidable arsenal of skills. These invaluable abilities will empower you to construct and unleash highly impactful models with unrivaled finesse.

Learn the power of machine learning algorithms by mastering programming languages like Python. These indispensable tools will pave the way for your success in the exciting world of artificial intelligence. Open the boundless potential of your mind by delving into the captivating realm of mathematical concepts. Immerse yourself in the elegant intricacies of linear algebra and calculus and witness their transformative power. Embrace the opportunity to expand your intellectual horizons and reap the rewards that await you. Enhance your data analysis skills by deeply understanding data visualization and exploratory data analysis. These invaluable tools will empower you to interpret and present your findings with clarity and impact.

Enjoy the incredible world of AI and machine learning through the exceptional platforms of Coursera, Udemy, and edX. Dive into the fascinating realm of artificial intelligence and witness the power of machine learning firsthand. Elevate your skills, broaden your horizons, and seize the opportunity to learn from the best. Join the ranks of countless learners who have already embarked on this transformative educational experience. The future of technology awaits, and these platforms are your gateway to unlocking its secrets. Embrace the power of choice and embark on a journey that will shape your destiny. Select the road less traveled and open a world of endless possibilities.

Are you ready to take your machine-learning journey to the next level? Now that you have a solid foundation in the basics, it's time to embark on a thrilling adventure of choosing a specific path in the captivating world of machine learning. Open many possibilities awaiting your exploration, tailored to your unique interests and aspirations. Discover the allure of these sought-after routes:

Let's learn about the power of data analysis with our cutting-edge machine-learning technology. Seamlessly analyze data, uncover hidden patterns, and extract invaluable insights to revolutionize your business. Unlock the power of data analysis and become a catalyst for informed decision-making. Whether it's structured or unstructured data, your expertise will shape the future of businesses.

Introducing Predictive Modeling

Harness the incredible potential of predictive modeling to unlock a world of possibilities. By leveraging the wealth of historical data at your fingertips, our cutting-edge models could forecast future outcomes like never before. Imagine anticipating trends, making informed decisions, and staying one step ahead of the competition. With our advanced predictive modeling techniques, you can do just that. By analyzing patterns, identifying correlations, and uncovering hidden insights, our models empower you to make accurate predictions that Unlock the limitless potential of this versatile solution, seamlessly adaptable to many industries, including finance, healthcare, and marketing.

Natural Language Processing (NLP)

Harness the power of teaching machines to comprehend and engage with the intricacies of human language. Experience the explosive growth of this dynamic field, where cutting-edge applications such as chatbots and language translation are revolutionizing how we communicate. Embrace the limitless possibilities and be part of the booming industry shaping the future of technology.

Begin your journey by taking small steps and gradually expanding your portfolio. Embrace the art of starting small and embarking on a journey of gaining invaluable experience. Discover endless possibilities to showcase your expertise by seizing every opportunity that comes your way. Embrace the chance to tackle small-scale projects or contribute to open-source initiatives. Crafting a captivating collection of projects will highlight your unrivaled expertise and elevate your presence in a fiercely competitive arena.

Expand your potential and take your machine-learning skills to new heights by immersing yourself in the thrilling world of Kaggle competitions. Join the ranks of top data scientists and showcase your expertise as you compete against the best in the field. Elevate your learning experience and fuel your passion for machine learning by embracing the exhilarating challenges that await you on this renowned platform. Take advantage of the opportunity to push the boundaries of your knowledge and emerge as a true champion in data science. Unleash your potential by participating in these exhilarating challenges that immerse you in real-world problems. Brace yourself for an incredible opportunity to glean invaluable insights from a vibrant community of exceptionally talented individuals.

In today's interconnected world, success is achieved in collaboration and through meaningful connections and partnerships. By joining forces with like-minded individuals and organizations, you can

Welcome to the extraordinary world of the machine learning community, where boundless possibilities and electrifying innovation converge. Immerse yourself in the vibrant tapestry of brilliant minds, each weaving their unique threads of knowledge and expertise. Learn about a world where innovation is highly valued, and curiosity knows no limitations. Join this vast community to stimulate inspiration and collaboration. Become an active participant in online forums, passionately attend meetups or conferences, and enthusiastically participate in thought-provoking debates to fully immerse yourself in the lively world of your profession. Unleash the potential of teamwork with like-minded individuals to advance your learning process and open a world of promising freelance opportunities.

We will discover the power of personal branding and unlock your true potential. Standing out from the crowd is essential in a world of fierce competition. Market yourself like a pro and leave.

Showcase your outstanding abilities and groundbreaking projects on reputable websites like GitHub or Kaggle to raise your profile. Let the world see your prowess and be awed by your impressive accomplishments. It's time to leave a lasting impact on people who strive for greatness in the digital sphere. Create a website or blog so you have a place online to promote your original thinking, enlightening instructions, and compelling case studies. Please share your knowledge with the world on an aesthetically pleasing platform that is easy to use, captivating your audience and leaving them wanting more. Create a personal website or blog that showcases your interests and talents to unleash your creativity and develop your online presence. Share your knowledge now, and see how quickly your influence spreads. Participate actively in lively online communities to realize your full potential as an AI practitioner. Take advantage of the chance to demonstrate your knowledge by offering thoughtful responses and making valuable suggestions. Create a reputation for yourself and a lasting impression on the online world.

Comprehend a world of endless possibilities by actively seeking out exciting job opportunities. Unleash your potential and embark on a journey toward professional fulfillment. Open doors to new horizons and unlock the gateway to a brighter future.

Experience the unstoppable rise of AI and machine learning specialists as their demand skyrockets across many industries. Be enlightened with exciting career possibilities and lucrative freelance ventures perfectly matching your passions and exceptional talents. Discover a world of endless possibilities in the realm of artificial intelligence! Unleash your potential by exploring many AI-related opportunities through the power of job boards, the vast network of LinkedIn, or cutting-edge specialized platforms like Hired or AI-Jobs.net. Embrace the future of technology and embark on a journey that will redefine your career trajectory. The possibilities are limitless, and the choice is yours. Seize the moment and unlock your AI potential today.

Unlocking the untapped potential of Artificial Intelligence (AI) has been a game-changer in my quest for financial success. In this captivating tale, I will reveal the secrets behind my remarkable journey toward tripling my earnings. Brace yourself for a riveting narrative that will leave you inspired and eager to harness the power of AI for your financial gains. Prepare to be captivated as I unveil the transformative impact of AI on my income and how you, too, can embark on a similar path toward unprecedented finances.

The awe-inspiring potential of artificial intelligence (AI) and its remarkable ability to transform your financial landscape. It was an extraordinary tale of triumph and economic prosperity! Prepare to be captivated as I unveil the awe-inspiring journey of how I harnessed the unparalleled might of Artificial Intelligence to skyrocket my earnings to unimaginable heights. Welcome to an extraordinary blog post where I will guide you through a remarkable journey that propelled my income to unprecedented heights. Get ready to be inspired as I unveil the secrets that led to this incredible transformation. Indulge in the exquisite pleasure of a freshly brewed cup of coffee while embarking on a captivating journey with me. Together, we shall delve into the enchanting realm of artificial intelligence and discover the myriad of ways it can seamlessly integrate into our lives.

What new lucrative opportunities where artificial intelligence can be seamlessly integrated? The untapped potential of artificial intelligence in the dynamic world of stock market trading. Harness the power of cutting-edge machine learning algorithms to unlock a world of possibilities. With AI at your side, dive deep into the vast ocean of data and unearth hidden gems of investment opportunities. Experience the game-changing advantage that comes with making well-informed choices.

The remarkable power of AI technology effortlessly enables comprehensive research and analysis of market patterns. This invaluable tool gives me a distinct advantage in short-term and long-term investments. Cutting-edge algorithms are meticulously crafted to continuously learn and adapt, empowering me to effortlessly detect even the most subtle market changes. With this unparalleled advantage, I can seamlessly fine-tune my investment strategies, ensuring optimal performance at all times.

Unlock the secret to tripling your earnings through the power of AI by automating your financial management. Discover how this critical aspect can revolutionize your financial success. Experience the power of AI-driven financial apps that revolutionize your budgeting, expense tracking, and investment management. Say goodbye to tedious tasks and welcome a streamlined and efficient approach to your financial journey.

Uncover a treasure trove of invaluable insights, empowering you to save money and make astute financial decisions like never before. Gain control of your financial destiny with a crystal-clear understanding of your economic landscape. By harnessing this powerful knowledge, you'll unlock the ability to optimize your resource allocation and effortlessly identify opportunities to trim excess spending.

The incredible world of AI-powered investment platforms! Experience the future of finance, where personalized recommendations are tailored to your unique financial goals and risk appetite. With cutting-edge technology at your fingertips, embark on a journey toward financial success like never before. Let the power of AI guide you toward intelligent investment decisions that align perfectly with your aspirations. Discover the transformative power of these expert recommendations, designed to revolutionize your investment portfolio. With a strategic approach to diversification, you'll unlock a world of possibilities while safeguarding against potential risks. Prepare to witness a remarkable surge in your overall earnings as you embark on a journey toward financial prosperity.

This is the guide to Building Passive Income with AI. Discover how this cutting-edge technology has revolutionized our income generation, propelling individuals like yourself toward a life of abundance and prosperity. Gone are the days of tirelessly working for every dollar earned. With AI as your trusted ally, you can tap into a world of endless possibilities where your money works for you while you sleep. Imagine waking up to a steady stream of income flowing effortlessly into your bank account, thanks to the intelligent algorithms and automation AI brings.

This comprehensive guide will walk you through the step-by-step process of leveraging AI to create multiple passive income streams. From investing in AI-powered stocks and cryptocurrencies to utilizing AI-driven marketing strategies, we leave no stone unturned in our quest to help you maximize your earning potential. But it doesn't stop there. We delve into discovering the secret to my success in harnessing the power of automation for online businesses. Experience the power of AI-driven tools that will revolutionize your website. Unlock the potential to optimize your online presence, attract traffic, and create unparalleled user experiences. With cutting-edge technology at your fingertips, the possibilities are limitless. The future of digital success today. Experience the transformative power of our advanced strategies, resulting in a remarkable conversion surge and a substantial boost in revenue streams.

Experience the power of AI chatbots, revolutionizing customer support like never before. With their unwavering availability, these intelligent assistants ensure that your customers receive exceptional service around the clock. Say goodbye to limited hours and hello to enhanced customer satisfaction and steadfast loyalty. Remarkable chatbots - not only do they effortlessly address frequently asked questions, but they also possess the incredible ability to gather invaluable data. With this treasure trove of information at your fingertips, you can delve into detailed analysis and unlock a world of possibilities for enhancing your business operations.

AI-Enabled Marketing Platforms

The cutting-edge solution that takes your marketing efforts to new heights. With its sophisticated targeting and segmentation capabilities, you can now effortlessly connect with the perfect audience, delivering personalized marketing campaigns that leave a lasting impact. Say goodbye to generic outreach and hello to precision marketing that drives results. Discover the incredible power of AI algorithms that have revolutionized the way we understand consumer behavior, allowing you to target specific demographics with precision effortlessly. Experience the remarkable benefits of optimizing your advertising spending, leading to a substantial boost in sales and generating passive income. Unleash the potential of AI and witness the extraordinary impact it can have on your business.

Revolutionary and transformative, AI has propelled me to new heights, tripling my earnings and revolutionizing my financial landscape. With its unparalleled capabilities and cutting-edge technology, AI has become the ultimate game-changer in my professional journey. By harnessing its power, I have unlocked a world of endless possibilities, surpassing all expectations and redefining success. This groundbreaking innovation has elevated my financial standing and reshaped my entire perspective on what is achievable. With AI as my steadfast ally,

Learn how to unlock your financial success by taking advantage of opportunities, streamlining financial management, and utilizing AI. I effortlessly streamlined my financial tactics with a strong eye for spotting attractive opportunities, allowing me to make wise choices supported by thorough knowledge. AI quickly streamlined my financial procedures by embracing automation, which gave me more time to devote to what matters. To grow passive income streams and access a variety of revenue streams, I also made use of the fantastic potential of AI. Take advantage of these innovative strategies' transforming effects and embark on a path to financial prosperity.

Understanding ChatGPT and AI In Today's Digital World

Artificial intelligence (AI) has emerged as a powerful tool that can streamline business processes, improve customer experiences, and even help us make better decisions. With the help of AI-powered assistants like ChatGPT, individuals and businesses alike can unlock a new world of possibilities and achieve tremendous success. In this chapter, we will explore what ChatGPT and AI are, their evolution, and the power and potential of artificial intelligence.

This is a beginner's book, so if you have experience, this can help reinforce some things you learned, but if you want to focus on one AI tool like ChatGPT, then you would be. You are better served reading my book on How to Make Money Online with ChatGPT.

What is ChatGPT?

ChatGPT is an AI-powered assistant that can help businesses and creators generate high-quality content, analyze data, provide insights, and optimize business processes. The language model uses deep learning and natural language processing (NLP) to create human-like text based on a given prompt or topic. ChatGPT is part of the GPT (Generative Pre-trained Transformer) family of models developed by OpenAI, one of the leading AI research organizations in the world. Conversely, AI is the simulation of human intelligence processes by machines, especially computer systems.

What is AI?

AI stands for artificial intelligence, which refers to developing computer systems that can perform tasks that would typically require human intelligence, such as visual perception, speech recognition, decision-making, and language translation. AI systems use algorithms and machine learning to analyze data, learn from experience, and make predictions or decisions based on that analysis.

AI involves the development of algorithms and models that enable machines to perform tasks that would typically require human intelligence, such as learning, reasoning, problem-solving, perception, and natural language processing. ChatGPT is an AI Tool. The evolution: From GPT-1 to ChatGPT-4 The GPT family of models evolved from GPT-1 to GPT-4, with each subsequent model improving upon the previous one. GPT-1 was released in 2018 and had 117 million parameters. It was trained on a large corpus of text data and could generate coherent and meaningful text based on a given prompt. GPT-2, released in 2019, had 1.5 billion parameters and could cause even more complex and sophisticated text. However, due to concerns about its potential misuse, OpenAI still needed to release the full version of GPT-2. In 2020, OpenAI released GPT-3, which had 175 billion parameters and could perform a wide range of language tasks with remarkable accuracy, including translation, summarization, and question-answering. GPT-3 was a significant breakthrough in AI and received widespread attention and praise. However, it also raised concerns about the potential misuse of AI and the need for ethical guidelines and regulations. ChatGPT is a variant of GPT-3 that is fine-tuned for conversational AI. It is designed to generate human-like responses to a prompt or topic and can be used in chatbots, virtual assistants, and other conversational interfaces. ChatGPT-4, the latest version of ChatGPT as of 2023, has 6 billion parameters and can generate even more natural and engaging text.

The Power and Potential of Artificial Intelligence

The power and potential of artificial intelligence are immense. AI can automate repetitive tasks, analyze data, and provide valuable insights for business decisions. With AI, businesses can optimize operations, reduce costs, and enhance customer experiences. One of the most significant benefits of using AI in business is its ability to analyze vast data. AI can sift through mountains of data in seconds, identifying patterns and trends that would be impossible for humans to detect. This data can then be used to optimize business processes, improve product development, and inform marketing strategies. AI can also be used to create personalized customer experiences. AI can identify individual preferences, behaviors, and needs by analyzing customer data and providing customized recommendations and solutions. This can lead to higher customer satisfaction, loyalty, and retention. The Rise of AI in the Creative Economy AI is not just a tool for businesses; it can also be a powerful tool for creators. AI-powered assistants like ChatGPT can help creators generate new ideas, refine existing ones, and streamline their creative processes. With ChatGPT, creators can overcome creative blocks, explore new ideas, and produce better work. The use of AI in the creative economy has been introduced previously. Artists, musicians, and writers have been experimenting with AI for decades, using it to create new art, music, and literature forms. However, with the rise of deep learning and NLP, AI has become more sophisticated and robust, enabling creators to do previously impossible things.

Historical Context

AI's Evolution The evolution of AI can be traced back to the 1950s when researchers began exploring the possibility of creating machines that could think and learn like humans. The term "artificial intelligence" was coined in 1956 and focused on rule-based and expert systems. In the 1960s and 1970s, AI focused on rule-based and expert techniques that mimic human expertise in specific domains. In the 1980s and 1990s, AI shifted to machine learning and neural networks, designed to learn from data and improve over time. In the 2000s and 2010s, AI evolved to include deep understanding, which enabled machines to remember vast amounts of data and perform complex tasks with remarkable accuracy. Today, AI is at the forefront of innovation and development, with applications in virtually every industry and domain. AI transforms how we live and work, from healthcare to finance to transportation.

The Intersection of Creativity and Technology

The intersection of creativity and technology is where AI truly shines. AI-powered assistants like ChatGPT can help creators unlock new possibilities, explore new ideas, and produce better work. With AI, creators can overcome creative blocks, refine their skills, and push the boundaries of what is possible. However, AI is not a replacement for human creativity. Instead, it is a tool that can enhance and augment human ingenuity, enabling us to do previously impossible things. By leveraging the power of AI, creators can explore new frontiers in art, music, and literature and create works that inspire and engage audiences in new and exciting ways. Conclusion In conclusion, ChatGPT and AI are powerful tools that can unlock new possibilities and achieve tremendous success in business and creativity. From generating high-quality content to analyzing data to providing valuable insights, AI has the potential to transform the way we work and create. While AI is not a replacement for human creativity, it is a tool that can enhance and augment it, enabling us to do previously impossible things. As we continue to explore the power and potential of AI, we must also be mindful of its ethical implications and work to ensure that it is used for the greater good.

CHAPTER 2

Getting Started with AI

Getting Started with AI Artificial intelligence (AI) has become an essential tool for businesses and creators looking to streamline processes, improve decision-making, and enhance creativity. With the help of AI-powered assistants like ChatGPT, getting started with AI has always been challenging. This chapter will explore the basics of using AI, from setting up and initial configuration to prompt engineering, an essential skill for generating high-quality text. Setting Up and Initial Configuration Before using AI, you must set up and configure your system. While the specifics of this process will depend on the AI tool you are using, there are some general steps you can follow to get started. First, you need to choose an AI tool that meets your needs. Many different AI tools are available, from open-source libraries to commercial products. Consider your budget, goals, and technical expertise when choosing an AI tool. Once you have selected an AI tool, you must install and configure it. This may involve downloading software, setting up a cloud-based environment, or configuring an API. Follow the instructions provided by your AI tool to complete the installation and configuration process. Next, you need to prepare your data. AI tools require large amounts of data to train their models and generate high-quality results. Gather and organize your data, and ensure it is in a format your AI tool can handle. Finally, you need to train your AI model. Training involves feeding your data into your AI tool and letting it learn from the data. The specifics of this process will depend on your AI tool but typically involve setting parameters, defining the model architecture, and running training algorithms.

The Basics of Using AI

Once you have set up and configured your AI tool and trained your model, you are ready to use AI. The basics of using AI involve inputting a prompt or question into your AI tool and receiving a response or output. The most common way to use AI is through natural language processing (NLP). NLP is a subfield of AI that focuses on the interaction between computers and humans using natural language. With NLP, you can input text or speech into your AI tool and receive a response generated by the AI model. Another way to use AI is through machine learning. Machine learning is a subfield of AI that focuses on developing algorithms that enable machines to learn from data without being explicitly programmed.

With machine learning, you can train your AI model to recognize patterns, make predictions, and perform other tasks based on the data it has learned. The applications of AI are vast and varied. From chatbots and virtual assistants to data analysis and predictive modeling, AI can automate tasks, generate insights, and improve decision-making. Prompt Engineering: An Introduction Prompt engineering is essential for using AI effectively. Prompt engineering involves crafting prompts or questions that elicit the desired response from your AI model. By carefully preparing your prompts, you can generate high-quality text that meets your needs. There are several fundamental principles to remember when engineering prompts for AI.

First, be clear and concise. Your prompt should communicate what you want your AI model to do and be straightforward enough to fit within the limitations of your AI tool. Second, be specific. Your prompt should be clear enough to guide your AI model toward the desired output. Vague or ambiguous prompts can lead to inaccurate or irrelevant responses. Third, be creative. AI models can generate surprisingly creative and imaginative responses but need creative prompts to spark their imagination. Experiment with different prompts and see what responses your AI model generates. Fourth, be flexible. AI models can be unpredictable, and their answers may only sometimes match your expectations. Be willing to adjust your prompts and experiment with different approaches until you find a prompt that generates the desired response. Finally, be ethical. AI has the potential to be misused, and it is essential to use AI ethically and responsibly. Ensure your prompts and responses comply with ethical guidelines and regulations and do not harm individuals or communities. Getting started with AI can be daunting, but it is essential for businesses and creators looking to unlock new possibilities and achieve tremendous success. By setting up and configuring an AI tool, training your model, and mastering the basics of using AI, you can harness the power and potential of artificial intelligence. By mastering prompt engineering, you can generate high-quality text that meets your needs and enhances your creativity. As you explore the world of AI, remember to be ethical, flexible, creative, specific, and transparent in your approach, and you will unlock the full potential of this revolutionary technology.

Staying ahead of the competition is crucial in the ever-evolving online business landscape. With technological advancements, harnessing the power of AI (Artificial Intelligence) has become a game-changer for boosting online sales. Whether you're just starting your online business or looking to take it to the next level, integrating AI can help you drive more traffic and conversions and, ultimately, increase your revenue. This article explores using AI to maximize your online sales and make money online.

1. Personalized Customer Experience:

One of the key benefits of AI is its ability to deliver personalized experiences to your customers. By leveraging AI algorithms, you can analyze user data, behavior patterns, purchase history, and preferences to offer tailored recommendations and product suggestions. This level of personalization enhances the customer journey and boosts overall conversion rates.

2. Automated Email Marketing:

Email marketing remains a powerful tool for driving sales. With AI, you can supercharge your email campaigns by automating the entire process. AI-powered algorithms can help you segment your audience based on various criteria, such as demographics, interests, and buying behavior. This enables you to send targeted and personalized emails, increasing open and click-through rates.

3. Chatbots for Instant Support:

Customers expect instant gratification in today's fast-paced digital world. Implementing AI-powered chatbots on your website can provide immediate customer support, answering common questions and providing assistance 24/7. Chatbots improve the customer experience and help guide potential customers toward purchasing, increasing your online sales.

4. Intelligent Pricing Strategies:

Pricing your products or services effectively is crucial for maximizing sales. AI algorithms can analyze market trends, competitor pricing, consumer behavior, and other variables to optimize pricing strategies. Dynamic pricing, customized discounts, and real-time adjustments can help you attract more customers and increase your online revenue.

5. Smart Product Recommendations:

Upselling and cross-selling play a significant role in boosting online sales. AI algorithms can analyze customer data, browsing behavior, and purchase history to provide personalized product recommendations.

You can increase the average order value and drive more sales by displaying related or complementary products to customers.

6. Enhanced Search Experience:

A seamless user experience on your website is vital for converting visitors into customers. AI-powered search engine optimization (SEO) tools can help you optimize your online store for better visibility in search engines. AI algorithms can analyze user behavior and preferences to deliver relevant search results, improving the user experience and increasing your chances of making a sale.

7. Predictive Analytics for Sales Forecasting:

With AI-powered predictive analytics, you can accurately forecast future sales based on historical data, market trends, and seasonal fluctuations. By understanding customer behavior and demand patterns, you can better anticipate market changes, optimize your inventory levels, and ensure you have the right products in stock to meet future demand.

8. Voice-Based AI Assistants:

Voice assistants like Amazon's Alexa and Google Assistant have become increasingly popular. Integrating voice-based AI assistants into your online store can make the shopping experience more convenient for customers. You can tap into a growing market and increase your online sales by offering voice-activated search, product recommendations, and even voice-driven purchasing options.

In the digital age, leveraging AI can boost your online sales and make money online. You can gain a competitive edge and drive more revenue by integrating AI into various aspects of your business, such as personalized customer experiences, automated email marketing, intelligent pricing strategies, and voice-based AI assistants. Embrace the power of AI and position your online business for success in the increasingly competitive online marketplace.

CHAPTER 3

Monetizing AI

Monetizing AI Artificial intelligence (AI) has revolutionized how we work and interact with technology and opened new avenues for generating revenue. AI has become a game-changer in the industry, from startups to established businesses. This chapter will explore the various business models that can be used to monetize AI. We will also delve into how AI can be turned into a passive income machine and how it can help freelancers complete projects in minutes. The Business Models: An Overview Various business models can be used to monetize AI.

Step into the dynamic world of today's digital landscape, where artificial intelligence (AI) reigns supreme as the ultimate game-changer across many industries. Discover the incredible power of AI technology across various sectors, from healthcare to finance. Experience a world where productivity soars, efficiency reaches new heights, and endless business opportunities await. Embrace the limitless potential that AI brings—calling all tech-savvy entrepreneurs! Brace yourselves for an extraordinary chance to unlock boundless financial potential with the power of AI. Discover the captivating world of profitable AI business models entrepreneurs can explore. Join us as we embark on an enlightening journey through this article.

The incredible power of chatbots in revolutionizing customer service. These intelligent virtual assistants effortlessly tackle customer queries, making them an invaluable asset for businesses. Experience the power of natural language processing (NLP) algorithms as chatbots effortlessly comprehend and address customer inquiries, delivering prompt and round-the-clock support. Unlock the potential of entrepreneurs with the remarkable ability to create cutting-edge AI-powered chatbot platforms. These innovative platforms can be seamlessly provided as a service to businesses, revolutionizing their customer support experience. By harnessing the power of AI, entrepreneurs can help companies streamline their operations, cut costs, and elevate customer satisfaction to unprecedented heights.

Introducing Predictive Analytics: Unleashing the Power of Business Insights!

Learn the boundless potential of a highly profitable AI business model centered on the captivating world of predictive analytics. Unlock the power of machine learning algorithms to revolutionize your business. Seamlessly analyze vast amounts of data, empowering you to make informed predictions and supercharge your decision-making process. Maximize efficiency and stay one step ahead with the cutting-edge technology shaping the business's future. Attention, forward-thinking entrepreneurs!

Are you ready to seize this incredible opportunity to revolutionize the business world? By harnessing the power of cutting-edge AI technology, you can provide companies in many sectors, from finance to marketing, with game-changing predictive analytics solutions. Take the chance to be at the forefront of innovation and drive unprecedented success for your clients. Get ready to make your mark in business with AI-powered solutions that will transform companies' operations. Unlock the power of data-driven decisions and propel your business toward unparalleled success. With the expertise of entrepreneurs, organizations can effortlessly identify patterns, trends, and potential risks. By harnessing this invaluable knowledge, companies can confidently navigate the ever-changing landscape, ensuring improved outcomes and a surge in profitability. Embrace the future of decision-making and watch your business soar to new heights.

Introducing Automated Data Entry: Revolutionizing Efficiency

Are you tired of spending countless hours on tedious data entry? Say goodbye to the hassle and hello to efficiency with our revolutionary solution. We understand that data entry can be a real drain on your valuable time and resources. But fret not because we have the perfect remedy for your business woes. Our cutting-edge technology is designed to eliminate errors and streamline the entire data entry process. With our game-changing solution, you can bid farewell to the days of manual data entry and welcome a new era of productivity.

Experience the cutting-edge power of AI technology as it effortlessly automates your processes, eliminating the risk of human error and propelling your efficiency to new heights—the potential of your entrepreneurial spirit by harnessing the power of AI tools. With cutting-edge optical character recognition (OCR) and intelligent data extraction algorithms, you can revolutionize data entry across various industries, including healthcare, finance, and retail. Say goodbye to manual labor and embrace the efficiency and accuracy of automated data entry. Let your entrepreneurial vision soar as you streamline processes and propel your business to new heights. Revolutionary service that empowers entrepreneurs to transform businesses, streamline operations, and unlock unprecedented efficiency. Say goodbye to the tedious and time-consuming task of manual data entry, as our cutting-edge solution takes care of it all. By harnessing the power of automation, we enable businesses to save valuable time and resources while significantly reducing costs. Embrace the future of streamlined operations with our game-changing service.

Experience the power of personalized marketing and take your customer engagement to new heights. With our cutting-edge strategies and innovative techniques, we'll help you create a unique and tailored experience for every customer.

Say goodbye to generic advertisements and hello to targeted campaigns that truly resonate with your audience. With AI at your fingertips, reaching your customers personally has never been more accessible or impactful. Embrace the future of marketing and unlock your brand's full potential with AI-driven strategies that deliver results like never before. Unlock the potential of entrepreneurs by harnessing the power of AI. They can create solutions that delve deep into customer data, preferences, and behavior with cutting-edge technology. Imagine the possibilities of delivering personalized content and irresistible offers that leave customers craving for more. It's time to revolutionize the way businesses connect with their audience.

Let AI be your secret weapon for success. Discover the transformative power of these cutting-edge solutions designed to empower businesses like yours to forge meaningful connections with your target audience. Experience a new level of engagement and witness your conversion rates soar to unprecedented heights. Unlock the immense potential of AI-powered customer engagement tools by embracing personalized marketing solutions tailored specifically for your company. Stay ahead of the curve and meet the ever-growing demand for cutting-edge technology that revolutionizes how businesses connect with customers.

AI-Powered Cybersecurity

Your Ultimate Solution for Safeguarding Precious Digital Assets In this fast-paced digital era, protecting your valuable digital assets is paramount. In this ever-changing digital landscape, businesses are facing an urgent demand for robust cybersecurity solutions. With cyber threats constantly evolving, companies must fortify their defenses and safeguard their valuable assets. Unlock the immense potential of AI technology to conquer this challenge with unparalleled precision and effectiveness.

Discover the limitless potential of entrepreneurs who harness the power of cutting-edge AI technology. With their visionary minds, they create cybersecurity platforms that are revolutionizing the digital landscape. Fueled by advanced machine learning algorithms, these platforms can detect anomalies swiftly, identify potential threats, and effectively thwart cyber attacks. Embrace the future of cybersecurity and unlock a world of unparalleled protection. Discover the power of these cutting-edge solutions that can revolutionize businesses and protect their most valuable digital assets and sensitive information. Position yourself as a trailblazer in the dynamic cybersecurity industry by offering these game-changing solutions to entrepreneurs.

In conclusion, our product is the ultimate solution for all your needs. With its exceptional

Discover the extraordinary power of artificial intelligence, propelling countless visionary business models to new heights. Unleash the boundless potential that awaits entrepreneurs as they embark on a lucrative journey to monetize the wonders of AI. Discover a world of endless possibilities, where intelligent chatbots seamlessly engage with users, and predictive analytics unlock the power of foresight. Embrace the vast and varied opportunities that await as innovation takes center stage. Unleash the boundless potential of AI and infuse it into various industries, empowering visionary entrepreneurs to craft lucrative domains that will reshape the fabric of business operations in this digital era. Are you a tech enthusiast with an unwavering entrepreneurial drive? Well, my friend, the stars have aligned, and the time is ripe for you to delve into the captivating world of AI business models. Brace yourself for an exhilarating and lucrative adventure that awaits you!

Step into the exciting realm of today's fast-paced, technology-driven world, where artificial intelligence (AI) reigns supreme. Gone are the days when AI was merely a distant concept, confined to the realm of scientists and tech geeks. Embrace the future and unlock the limitless possibilities that AI has to offer. Experience the transformative power of technology as it seamlessly integrates into every facet of our daily routines, revolutionizing how we accomplish tasks with unparalleled efficiency and precision. Discover the untapped potential of AI as a lucrative source of additional income. Yes, indeed, you read that correctly! Learn unconventional methods to harness the power of artificial intelligence and unlock a world of financial abundance. Prepare to embark on a journey where innovation meets profitability as we unveil extraordinary avenues to make money with the cutting-edge technology of AI. Brace yourself for a paradigm shift in wealth creation as we delve into uncharted territories of opportunity. Get ready to revolutionize your financial future with these unconventional ways to capitalize on the limitless potential of artificial intelligence.

Introducing AI Data Labeling

You are unleashing the Power of Data in Training AI Models! Are you a company or a researcher needing vast datasets meticulously labeled to propel your AI algorithms to new heights? Look no further! We understand the crucial role that accurately marked data plays in developing and fine-tuning AI algorithms. Let us provide you with the expansive datasets you require to unlock the full potential of your AI endeavors. Unlock the full potential of your business by offering cutting-edge data labeling services. Discover a world of limitless possibilities with platforms like Amazon Mechanical Turk, Figure Eight, and Lionbridge AI. Unleash your potential and embark on a rewarding journey where you can earn money by effortlessly labeling images, videos, or text snippets. Embrace the power of your skills and join the ranks of those who have found financial success in digital labeling. Seize this opportunity to turn your passion into profit and start earning today. Unlock your potential with this simple yet powerful task that is within reach for anyone with an internet connection. No technical expertise is required, making it effortlessly accessible to all.

Experience the power of AI chatbot development and revolutionize your customer service, e-commerce, and other industries. Discover the cutting-edge technology transforming how businesses interact with their customers. Join the industry leaders harnessing the potential of AI-powered chatbots to enhance their customer experience and drive unprecedented growth. Stay ahead of the competition and unlock new possibilities with our state-of-the-art AI chatbot development solutions. Unlock your earning potential with your coding prowess! Harness your knack for coding and dive into the lucrative world of chatbot development. Businesses and individuals alike are seeking innovative chatbot solutions, and you have the power to provide them. Turn your skills into a profitable venture as you create cutting-edge chatbots that revolutionize how businesses communicate.

Unleash your creativity and watch as these user-friendly platforms empower you to bring your chatbot dreams to life. Unlock the potential of your skills as a freelance chatbot developer and revolutionize how businesses interact with their customers. Elevate customer experience to new heights and streamline operations through automation.

Experience the future of content creation with AI technology. Witness the remarkable revolution as artificial intelligence automates the time-consuming tasks of generating articles, blog posts, and captivating social media content. Embrace the power of AI and unlock a new era of efficiency and creativity in content creation. Discover the perfect harmony between AI and human ingenuity in content creation. While AI undeniably can automate select aspects of the process, the irreplaceable touch of human creativity and discernment truly elevates the craft. Unlock the full potential of your content creation journey by positioning yourself as a cutting-edge AI-assisted content creator. With powerful tools like GPT-3 by OpenAI and Article Forge, you can effortlessly accelerate the writing process and revolutionize how you craft captivating content— A revolutionary solution that has the potential to transform the game, particularly for agencies or businesses seeking a rapid influx of top-notch content in substantial quantities.

AI Virtual Assistant

Your ultimate companion in the digital realm. With the ever-increasing demand for virtual assistants, I stand as a testament to the undeniable need for seamless AI assistance. Discover the incredible demand for AI-powered virtual assistants among individuals and businesses alike. Experience the convenience of having a virtual assistant handle tasks like appointment scheduling, email filtering, and essential customer support. Embrace the future of productivity and efficiency with the power of AI at your fingertips. Unlock the power of cutting-edge technology and embark on a journey to create your own AI assistant. With the incredible platforms offered by industry giants like Google's Dialogflow and Microsoft's Bot Framework, you can now step into virtual assistance. Imagine the freedom of working remotely while relishing the unparalleled flexibility of managing your own time. The possibilities are endless, and the future is yours to shape.

Unlock the power of AI data analysis and gain invaluable insights that will revolutionize your business decisions. With the ability to process and analyze massive volumes of data, AI is your ultimate tool for uncovering hidden gems that will propel your company to new heights. Say goodbye to guesswork and hello to data-driven success with AI at your side. Unlock the full potential of your data analysis or machine learning background and seize the opportunity to provide cutting-edge AI-based data analysis services. Unlock the power of data-driven decision-making and gain a competitive advantage for businesses by harnessing the advanced capabilities of AI algorithms. Through meticulous analysis of datasets, you can revolutionize operations, optimize processes, and pave the way for unprecedented success. Embrace the future of business intelligence and propel your organization to new heights. Unlock the boundless potential of market research and predictive analytics.

AI Voice Acting!

As the popularity of voice assistants such as Siri, Alexa, and Google Assistant continues to soar, there is an ever-increasing need for the mesmerizing allure of AI-generated voices. Join us on this thrilling journey as we explore the limitless possibilities of AI Voice Acting! Experience the cutting-edge innovation of AI-generated agents for all your audio needs. Whether you're an individual or a business, immerse yourself in the seamless world of audiobooks, commercials, and internal voiceovers. Discover the power of AI technology, revolutionizing how we communicate and captivate audiences. Embrace the future of voice with AI-generated voices. Unlock the potential of your captivating and melodious voice! Imagine a world where your dulcet tones become the voice of AI-generated characters and voice assistants, enchanting audiences around the globe.

Embrace the opportunity to turn your gift into a lucrative venture where your clear and pleasant voice becomes a sought-after commodity. Join the ranks of those who have discovered the power of their vocal prowess and embark on a journey of endless possibilities. Let your voice be heard, and your pockets be filled as you lend your remarkable voice to the forefront of cutting-edge technology. Seize this extraordinary chance to transform your passion into a profitable endeavor and let your voice be the soundtrack to the future. Unlock the power of your voice with cutting-edge platforms like Resemble AI and Replica Studios. Experience the thrill of creating personalized AI voices that captivate and engage audiences like never before. Seamlessly blend your unique talents with state-of-the-art technology, allowing you to showcase your skills as a voice actor in a new way. Embrace the future of voiceover and unleash your potential on these remarkable platforms.

AI Tutoring

Revolutionizing personalized learning with the power of AI algorithms. Experience the ease and accessibility of tailored tutoring like never before. Teaching the AI tutor is your ultimate solution for personalized learning experiences tailored to meet the unique needs of students seeking assistance in specific subjects. Discover the endless possibilities of AI tutoring with cutting-edge platforms like Socratic by Google and Coursera. Unleash your potential as an AI tutor and embark on a journey of creating and delivering captivating online courses. Join the revolution and revolutionize education with these innovative platforms. Unlock the power of AI algorithms to curate personalized content and provide real-time feedback, empowering students to conquer their educational aspirations while effortlessly boosting their income.

Here are 25 more unique AI business models businesses can use to generate revenue.

1. AI as a Service (AIaaS): This model offers AI tools and services to businesses and individuals on a subscription or pay-per-use basis.

2. AI-Enabled Products: This model involves integrating AI into existing products or developing new products with AI capabilities.

3. AI Consulting: This model provides consulting services to businesses looking to implement AI solutions.

4. AI Development: This model involves developing AI solutions for businesses and organizations.

5. AI Training: This model involves training individuals and businesses on how to use AI tools and solutions.

6. AI Data Labeling: This model provides data labeling services to businesses and organizations.

7. AI Translation Services: This model provides translation services using AI technology.

8. AI Content Creation: This model uses AI to generate content for businesses and individuals.

9. AI Chatbots: This model uses AI to develop chatbots for businesses and organizations.

10. AI Fraud Detection: This model uses AI to detect fraudulent activities in businesses and organizations.

11. AI Virtual Assistants: This model involves developing virtual assistants using AI technology.

12. AI Customer Service: This model uses AI to improve customer service in businesses and organizations.

13. AI Predictive Analytics: This model uses AI to predict future outcomes in businesses and organizations.

14. AI Speech Recognition: This model uses AI to recognize speech in businesses and organizations.

15. AI Image and Video Analysis: This model uses AI to analyze images and videos for businesses and organizations.

16. AI Advertising: This model involves using AI to target advertising to specific audiences.

17. AI E-commerce: This model uses AI to improve the e-commerce experience for businesses and organizations.

18. AI Supply Chain Management: This model uses AI to manage the supply chain in businesses and organizations.

19. AI Healthcare: This model uses AI to improve patient healthcare outcomes.

20. AI Education: This model involves using AI to improve the education experience for students.

21. AI Agriculture: This model involves using AI to improve yields and efficiency in agriculture.

22. AI Energy Management: This model uses AI to manage energy consumption and improve efficiency in businesses and organizations.

23. AI Cybersecurity: This model uses AI to enhance cybersecurity in businesses and organizations.

24. AI Insurance: This model uses AI to improve claims processing and risk assessment in businesses and organizations.

25. AI Gaming: This model involves using AI to develop and improve gaming experiences for players.

Turning AI into a Passive Income Machine, AI can be turned into a passive income machine in various ways.

Here are some ways to do so:

1. Offering AI tools and services on a subscription or pay-per-use basis.

2. Developing AI-enabled products that can be sold on e-commerce platforms.

3. Developing AI solutions that can be licensed to other businesses and organizations.

4. Creating and selling AI-generated content.
5. Developing AI chatbots that can be sold to businesses and organizations.
6. Providing AI data labeling services to businesses and organizations.
7. Offering AI training courses and materials.
8. Develop AI translation services that can be sold to businesses and individuals.
9. Offering AI predictive analytics services to businesses and organizations.
10. Developing AI virtual assistants that can be sold to businesses and organizations.

The Superhuman Freelancer: Completing Projects in Minutes AI has the potential to make freelancers more efficient and productive.

Here are some ways in which freelancers can use AI to complete projects in minutes:

1. Using AI chatbots to handle customer queries and support.
2. Using AI content generation tools to create content for clients.
3. Using AI data analysis tools to analyze data and generate client insights.
4. Using AI translation tools to translate content for clients.
5. Using AI image and video analysis tools to edit images and videos for clients.
6. Using AI predictive analytics tools to predict client outcomes and trends.

7. Using AI speech recognition tools to transcribe audio recordings for clients.

8. Using AI virtual assistants to manage tasks and schedules for clients.

9. Using AI cybersecurity tools to protect clients' digital assets.

10. Using AI project management tools to manage projects and teams for clients.

AI has become an integral part of the business world, and various ways exist to monetize it. Businesses can generate revenue using AI, from offering AI tools and services to developing AI-enabled products and solutions. AI can also be turned into a passive income machine by creating AI-enabled products and offering AI services on a subscription or pay-per-use basis. Freelancers can also use AI to complete projects in minutes, making them more efficient and productive. As AI continues to evolve, it will open up new possibilities for businesses and individuals, and those who embrace it will be well-positioned for success.

CHAPTER 4

Uncover the Secrets of Digital Entrepreneurship

The New Age of Digital Ventures The world of entrepreneurship has undergone a remarkable transformation in recent years because of the digital revolution. The rise of the internet and other digital technologies has created new opportunities for businesses to reach customers and connect with them in previously impossible ways. As a result, we are seeing a new age of digital entrepreneurship, where enterprises harness the power of technology to transform their operations and create new products and services.

One of the key drivers of this new age of digital entrepreneurship is the rise of artificial intelligence (AI). AI has the potential to revolutionize the way businesses operate by providing them with new tools and capabilities that were previously unavailable. AI is transforming businesses across various industries, from chatbots and virtual assistants to predictive analytics and fraud detection. Weaving AI into Your Business Model If you are an entrepreneur looking to take advantage of the new opportunities created by AI, there are several ways to incorporate it into your business model.

Here are some strategies to consider:

1. Identify areas of your business that could benefit from AI: Identify areas where AI could help you improve efficiency, increase productivity, or create new products and services.

2. Choose the right AI tools and services: Many AI tools and services are available, so it's essential to choose the ones that are right for your business. Look for tools and services that are easy to use, reliable, and affordable.

3. Train your employees: Once you have identified the right AI tools and services, training your employees on how to use them is crucial. This will help ensure everyone in your organization is on the same page and can work together effectively.

4. Build AI into your products and services: If you are developing new products and services, consider building AI from the outset. This will help you create products and services that are more innovative and effective.

5. Experiment and iterate: AI is a new and rapidly evolving technology, so it's essential to experiment and iterate to find the best ways to use it in your business. Try different tools and services, and be open to new ideas and approaches.

Strategies for Success in the AI-Driven Digital Landscape As you navigate the new age of digital entrepreneurship, there are several strategies you can use to ensure your success in the AI-driven digital landscape. Here are some to consider:

1. Focus on creating value: The key to success in any business is to create value for your customers. With AI, you can create new products and services that are more efficient, effective, and innovative than anything that has come before.

2. Embrace collaboration: AI is a complex and rapidly evolving technology, so it's vital to embrace cooperation and work with others to stay up to date on the latest developments and best practices.

3. Build a strong team: To succeed in the AI-driven digital landscape, you need a team that is skilled, knowledgeable, and passionate about the work they do. Invest in your group by providing them with the training, resources, and support they need to succeed.

4. Stay agile: The business world is constantly changing, and the pace of change is only accelerating. To succeed in the AI-driven digital landscape, you must stay nimble and adapt quickly to changing circumstances.

5. Stay customer-focused: As you weave AI into your business model, it's crucial to stay customer-focused and keep your customers' needs and preferences in mind. Use AI to create products and services that meet their needs and exceed their expectations.

6. Be ethical and transparent: As AI becomes more prevalent in business, it's crucial to be honest and transparent in how you use it. Be clear about how you use AI, and be transparent about the data you are collecting and how you use it.

7. Monitor and evaluate: As you experiment with AI in your business, monitoring and assessing its impact is essential. Use data to track how AI affects your business and adjust as needed. Conclusion The new age of digital entrepreneurship has arrived, and AI is at the forefront of this transformation. By weaving AI into your business model, you can create new opportunities for growth and success. However, you must be agile, customer-focused, and ethical to succeed in the AI-driven digital landscape. Following the strategies outlined in this chapter, you can position your business for success in the exciting and rapidly evolving world of digital entrepreneurship.

Discover the power of constant adaptation and the seamless incorporation of cutting-edge technologies and approaches to succeed in your online business. Discover the advanced field of artificial intelligence and get the secret to beat the competition. Harnessing the power of AI tools is now essential in this rapid-fire era of technological development. With AI's capacity to change the game, surpass the competition rather than keep up with them. Utilize these cutting-edge, intelligent software tools to maximize your company's potential. Your profits rise as you streamline your processes and improve customer experiences. Learn to use innovation and efficiency to your advantage and stay one step ahead of the competition. Learn how AI tools have the incredible potential to revolutionize your online business and increase your earnings to new heights. Join us as we explore the top 10 paradigm-shifting AI solutions that will transform how you do business and increase your financial success.

Chatbots

The game-changers of the online business world. A revolutionary solution that empowers you to deliver instant customer support effortlessly, promptly address inquiries, and actively connect with potential customers around the clock. With our cutting-edge technology, you can now provide unparalleled assistance and engagement 24/7, ensuring your customers receive the exceptional service they deserve. Say goodbye to missed opportunities and hello to seamless interactions that leave a lasting impression. Experience the power of limitless customer support at your fingertips. Experience the power of automation and personalized assistance with chatbots. Say goodbye to repetitive tasks and hello to enhanced customer satisfaction and increased conversion rates. Let our chatbots revolutionize your business today.

Virtual Assistants

In this digital age, virtual assistants have transformed into extraordinary beings, all thanks to the power of AI. Prepare to be amazed as these cutting-edge marvels redefine how we interact and accomplish tasks. Get ready to experience a whole new level of efficiency and convenience with virtual assistants like never before! Discover the power of seamless multitasking with their exceptional ability to handle various responsibilities efficiently. From effortlessly coordinating appointments to skillfully managing emails and organizing digital files, they are the ultimate masters of productivity. With the assistance of virtual assistants, business owners can liberate themselves from the burdens of administrative tasks, allowing them to devote their valuable time and energy to the critical components that drive their operations forward.

Our recommendation systems are powered by cutting-edge AI technology and go above and beyond to analyze your unique behavior and preferences. Say goodbye to generic suggestions and hello to a world of tailored recommendations that are ideally suited to your tastes. Experience the future of personalized offers like never before! Experience the transformative power of this cutting-edge technology that will revolutionize your sales strategy. Prepare to witness a remarkable increase in product visibility and unlock the potential for cross-selling and upselling like never before. Get ready to take your sales to new heights with this game-changing technology. It may be the ultimate solution for crafting a shopping experience tailored exclusively to you. Prepare to be amazed as these cutting-edge systems elevate your shopping journey, resulting in unparalleled conversion rates and unwavering customer loyalty. Say goodbye to generic recommendations and hello to a world where every suggestion is handpicked just for you. Get ready to be captivated by the power of recommender systems.

Unlock the power of predictive analytics! By harnessing the cutting-edge capabilities of AI algorithms, you can now effortlessly predict future outcomes with utmost precision. Dive into the depths of historical data patterns and uncover hidden insights to revolutionize your decision-making process. Stay ahead of the game and embrace the future with predictive analytics. Unlock the power of data analysis to unveil trends, foresee customer behavior, and deliver spot-on predictions—the potential of your business with our cutting-edge solution. Seamlessly optimize your marketing strategies, predict pricing trends, and confidently minimize risks. Experience a new level of profitability that will elevate your business to unprecedented heights.

Learn the power of sentiment analysis and gain invaluable insights into your customers' emotions towards your brand. The key to understanding their sentiments and revolutionize your business strategy. Take advantage of this crucial opportunity to connect with your audience on a deeper level and propel your brand to new heights—the power of sentiment analysis tools, harnessing the cutting-edge technology of natural language processing algorithms. Dive deep into the world of social media posts, customer reviews, and feedback, unlocking valuable insights and understanding the true sentiment behind every word. With the power to detect positive and negative feelings, these remarkable tools empower you to measure customer satisfaction and tailor your strategies to perfection. The result? A noteworthy boost in customer retention and unwavering loyalty.

The power of content creation and watch your online business soar to new heights! In today's digital landscape, captivating and meaningful content is the key to success. Take advantage of the opportunity to captivate your audience and establish your brand as a thought leader in your industry. With our expert content creation services, we'll help you craft compelling and relevant content that will leave your customers wanting more. Stay ahead of the competition and make a lasting impression with our unparalleled content creation expertise. Trust us to deliver the content that will elevate your online business to unprecedented success. The revolutionary AI-powered content creation tools that harness the power of natural language processing and cutting-edge machine learning algorithms. Say goodbye to manual content generation and hello to effortless, automated content creation at its finest. With our state-of-the-art technology, you can generate high-quality content with just a few clicks. Experience the future of content creation today! A cutting-edge tool that harnesses the power of data analysis to craft compelling articles, captivating blog posts, and engaging social media updates. With these innovative solutions, businesses can unlock a world of efficiency, saving precious time and valuable resources.

The secret to pricing perfection! Discover the art of pricing optimization and take your business to new heights. Don't let the challenge of determining the optimal price for your products or services hold you back. Embrace the power of strategic pricing and watch your profits soar. It's time to conquer the pricing puzzle and unleash your business's potential. Unlock the power of AI-based pricing tools to revolutionize your pricing strategy. With cutting-edge technology, you can effortlessly set optimal prices considering crucial factors such as competition, market demand, and customer behavior. Stay one step ahead of the game and maximize your profits with the help of these innovative tools. These tools are designed to revolutionize your business. Their advanced technology can dynamically adjust prices, resulting in maximum profitability without compromising competitiveness. Say goodbye to the days of uncertainty and hello to a future where your business remains consistently profitable.

A cutting-edge Fraud Detection solution

In today's digital landscape, online businesses face the unfortunate reality of being vulnerable to fraudulent activities. These malicious acts compromise the integrity of your operations and can result in substantial financial losses. But fear not, for we have the perfect solution to safeguard your business and your hard-earned profits. With our state-of-the-art Fraud Detection system, you can rest easy knowing that every transaction is meticulously scrutinized, and any suspicious activity is swiftly identified and neutralized. Don't let fraud hinder your success - choose our unparalleled Fraud Detection solution and stay one step ahead! Experience the power of AI-driven fraud detection tools that revolutionize how you protect your business. With real-time monitoring of transactions, our cutting-edge technology analyzes patterns and behaviors to identify potentially fraudulent activities swiftly. Stay ahead of fraudsters and safeguard your financial assets with our state-of-the-art solution. Trust in the future of fraud prevention and let our advanced tools do the work for you. With their unparalleled ability to swiftly identify and thwart fraudulent activities, these cutting-edge tools are the ultimate guardians of your business's financial well-being and the unwavering protectors of your customers' invaluable trust.

Utilizing the power of effective inventory management, discover the key to unmatched success in your online business. Learn the secret to smooth operations, and you'll see your revenue rocket. Learn about the extraordinary power of systems for managing inventory driven by AI and use cutting-edge machine learning techniques. With these innovative tools, you can optimize inventory levels, accurately predict demand patterns, and seamlessly automate replenishment processes. Experience the future of inventory management like never before—these revolutionary tools are designed to optimize your inventory management and skyrocket your profits. With our cutting-edge technology, you can effortlessly minimize stockouts, eliminate excess inventory, and unlock a steady cash flow. Say goodbye to missed sales opportunities and hello to maximum profitability. Experience the power of our tools and watch your business thrive like never before.

Your Business's Potential with Sales Forecasting Are you ready to take your business to new heights? Look no further than the power of sales forecasting. With this invaluable tool, you

Accurate sales forecasting to revolutionize your decision-making and planning. AI-powered sales forecasting tools - the game-changer for businesses! Harnessing the power of cutting-edge technology, these tools analyze historical data, market dynamics, and external factors to unlock the secrets of future sales trends with unparalleled precision. Stay ahead of the competition and make informed decisions that drive success. Experience the future of sales forecasting today! Unlock the power of foresight and watch your business soar to new heights! By gaining invaluable insights into anticipated demand, you can effortlessly tailor your marketing strategies, strategically allocate resources, and ultimately, bask in enhanced profitability. Refrain from settling for mediocrity when you can seize the opportunity to thrive in the competitive landscape. Embrace the potential of foresight and witness the transformation of your business into a true success story.

The power of AI tools and revolutionize your online business operations. In today's competitive landscape, staying ahead means maximizing profits. That's why integrating AI tools has become crucial. Take advantage of the game-changing potential that AI brings to the table. Embrace the future and watch your profits soar. Discover the transformative power of AI tools that can revolutionize your business. Elevate customer experiences to new heights and optimize operations for maximum efficiency. Witness the remarkable impact on your bottom line as you harness the potential of cutting-edge technology.

Experience unprecedented success in the fiercely competitive digital marketplace by harnessing the power of cutting-edge technologies. With chatbots and virtual assistants, you can effortlessly engage with customers and provide exceptional service. Unlock the potential of personalized recommendations and predictive analytics to anticipate their needs and exceed their expectations. Harness the power of sentiment analysis to understand your customers and tailor your offerings accordingly. Create captivating content effortlessly with innovative content creation tools. Optimize your pricing strategies to maximize profitability and stay one step ahead of the competition. Safeguard your business with advanced fraud detection systems and streamline inventory management for seamless operations. Embrace the future with sales forecasting tools that empower you to make informed decisions and achieve sustainable growth. Stay ahead of the curve and thrive in the digital landscape with these game-changing solutions.

Experience the transformative power of AI tools in your business. These cutting-edge technologies can unlock unparalleled efficiency, freeing valuable time and resources. Imagine the possibilities when you can redirect your attention to your core areas, where your expertise truly shines. The result? Increased profits will leave your competitors in awe and customer satisfaction that knows no bounds. Embrace the future of business with AI tools and watch your success soar to new heights. Discover the limitless possibilities that AI holds and unleash the untapped potential of your online business.

CHAPTER 5

Utilize AI in Marketing

Utilizing AI in Marketing Artificial intelligence (AI) transforms how businesses operate and interact with clients and potential customers. In marketing, AI is becoming an increasingly important tool for businesses looking to create personalized and effective campaigns that drive growth and revenue. In this chapter, we'll explore the future of AI-driven marketing and provide strategies for utilizing AI to enhance your brand growth and create powerful marketing campaigns. The Future of AI-Driven Marketing AI is rapidly transforming the marketing landscape, providing businesses with new tools and capabilities that were previously unavailable.

Here are some of the ways AI is transforming marketing:

1. Personalization: AI can analyze vast amounts of information to create personalized marketing campaigns that resonate with individual customers. AI can help businesses develop campaigns tailored to each customer's needs and interests by analyzing customer behavior and preferences.

2. Predictive Analytics: AI can analyze data to predict customer behavior and identify trends. This can help businesses create more effective campaigns and drive better results.

3. Chatbots: AI-powered chatbots can provide customers instant support and assistance, improving customer satisfaction and driving engagement.

4. Voice Search: AI-powered voice search is becoming increasingly popular, and businesses must optimize their content to ensure they rank well in voice search results.

5. Data Analysis: AI can help businesses analyze vast amounts of data to identify patterns and trends that would be impossible to locate manually.

Strategies for Brand Growth with AI If you're looking to leverage AI to drive brand growth, here are some strategies to consider:

1. Understand Your Customers: AI can help you understand your clients better by analyzing their behavior, preferences, and interests. Use this information to create custom marketing campaigns that resonate with individual customers.

2. Optimize for Voice Search: With the rise of voice search, optimizing your content for this new medium is essential. Use natural language and long-tail keywords to ensure your content ranks well in voice search results.

3. Create Dynamic Content: AI can help you create dynamic content that changes based on the user's behavior and preferences. Use this technology to create personalized content that engages customers and drives conversions.

4. Use Predictive Analytics: Use AI-powered predictive analytics to identify trends and predict customer behavior. Use this information to create more effective campaigns that drive better results.

5. Embrace Chatbots: Use AI-powered chatbots to provide instant customer support and assistance. This can improve customer satisfaction and drive engagement.

Crafting Powerful AI-Enhanced Marketing Campaigns

To create powerful marketing campaigns that leverage AI, here are some tips to keep in mind:

1. Start with Clear Goals: Define clear goals and objectives before creating your campaign. Use these goals to guide your campaign and measure its success.

2. Use AI for Personalization to analyze customer data and create personalized campaigns that resonate with individual customers.

3. Create a Cohesive Customer Experience: Use AI to create a cohesive customer experience across all touchpoints. This can improve customer satisfaction and drive engagement.

4. Leverage Predictive Analytics: Use AI-powered predictive analytics to identify trends and predict customer behavior. Use this information to create more effective campaigns that drive better results.

5. Use Dynamic Content: Use AI to create dynamic content that changes based on the user's behavior and preferences. This can improve engagement and drive conversions.

6. Embrace Chatbots: Use AI-powered chatbots to provide instant customer support and assistance. This can improve customer satisfaction and drive engagement.

7. Measure and Optimize: Measure the success of your campaign and use the data to optimize your approach. Use A/B testing and other techniques to identify what's working and what's not. Conclusion AI is transforming the marketing world, providing businesses with new tools and capabilities that were previously unavailable. By leveraging AI, companies can create personalized, effective campaigns that drive growth and revenue. To succeed in AI-driven marketing, businesses must focus on understanding their customers, creating dynamic content, and embracing new technologies like chatbots and predictive analytics. With these strategies in mind, companies can create powerful AI-enhanced marketing campaigns that drive results and position them for success in the digital age.

CHAPTER 6

Maximizing Productivity with AI

Maximizing Productivity with AI The rise of artificial intelligence (AI) is transforming how we work and live. In the business world, AI is becoming an increasingly important tool for organizations looking to increase productivity and efficiency. From content creation to coding, AI is helping businesses and creators to work faster, smarter, and more effectively. In this chapter, we'll explore how AI is transforming productivity and providing creators with new tools and capabilities that were previously unavailable. Skyrocketing Your Content Creation Speed Content creation is a time-consuming task requiring much creativity and skill. However, with the help of AI, creators can now produce content faster and more efficiently than ever before.

Here are some ways in which AI is helping to skyrocket content creation speed:

1. **Automated Writing:** AI-powered writing tools can help creators generate high-quality content in minutes by analyzing data and developing text based on set parameters.

2. **Content Optimization:** AI can analyze content to identify areas for improvement, such as keyword optimization and readability. This can help creators produce content that is more effective and engaging.

3. **Video and Audio Editing:** AI-powered video and audio editing tools can help creators edit and enhance their content quickly and

efficiently. Coding Faster with AI Assistance Coding is a complex and time-consuming task requiring great skill and focus. However, with the help of AI, coders can now work faster and more efficiently than ever before.

Here are some ways in which AI is helping to speed up coding:

1. **Code Generation:** AI-powered tools can help coders generate code automatically, reducing the time and effort required to write code from scratch.

2. **Code Optimization:** AI can analyze code to identify areas for improvement, such as performance optimization and code refactoring. This can help coders produce code that is more efficient and effective.

3. **Debugging:** AI-powered debugging tools can help coders identify and fix code errors quickly and efficiently. Repurposing Social Media Content for Various Platforms social media is a powerful tool for creators looking to reach a wider audience and engage with their followers. However, creating content for multiple platforms can take time and effort. With the help of AI, creators can now repurpose their social media content for various platforms quickly and easily.

Here are some ways in which AI is helping creators repurpose their social media content:

1. **Automated Image and Video Resizing:** AI-powered tools can help creators resize images and videos automatically, making creating optimized content for different platforms easy.

2. **Content Optimization:** AI can analyze content to identify areas for improvement, such as caption optimization and hashtag selection. This can help creators produce content that is more effective and engaging.

3. **Automated Posting:** AI-powered tools can help creators schedule and post content automatically, reducing the time and effort required to

manage social media accounts. Five Reasons Creators Need AI Now As AI continues to evolve and become more accessible, it's becoming increasingly important for creators to embrace this new technology.

Here are five reasons why creators need AI now:

1. Increased Efficiency: AI can help creators work faster and more efficiently, allowing them to produce more content in less time.

2. Competitive Advantage: With the help of AI, creators can produce more effective and engaging content, giving them a competitive advantage in their field.

3. Unlocking New Revenue Streams: AI-powered tools can help creators monetize their content in new and innovative ways, such as through personalized recommendations and AI-generated content.

4. Improved Customer Experience: AI can help creators analyze customer information and provide personalized recommendations, improving customer experience and driving better relationships.

5. Access to Cutting-Edge Technologies: By embracing AI, creators can stay updated with the latest technologies and tools, giving them a competitive edge.

Case Study

AI in Film Editing: AI is already making a significant impact in the film industry, with AI-powered tools being used to enhance the editing process. One example of this is using AI-powered tools to analyze footage and identify key scenes, helping editors work more efficiently and produce better results. AI can also automate certain aspects of the editing process, such as color correction and sound editing, further improving efficiency and reducing costs.

Graphic Design Selections: Graphic design is another area where AI is making a significant impact, with AI-powered tools being used to assist with design selections. These tools can analyze data on user preferences and behavior to identify the most effective design choices, helping designers produce more engaging and compelling content.

Staying Ahead in the Market: As AI continues to evolve and become more widespread, it's becoming increasingly important for creators to stay ahead of the curve. By embracing AI and staying updated with the latest technologies and tools, creators can position themselves as leaders in their field and stay ahead of their competitors.

AI as a Differentiator: AI can also be used as a differentiator, helping creators to stand out from their competitors and provide unique value to their customers. By leveraging AI-powered tools and technologies, creators can produce content that is more engaging, more effective, and more personalized than ever before.

Personalized Customer Recommendations: One of the key benefits of AI is its ability to analyze customer data and provide customized recommendations. By leveraging this technology, creators can provide their customers with personalized content, products, and service recommendations, improving overall customer satisfaction and driving engagement.

Monetizing AI-Generated Content: AI-powered tools can generate content automatically, opening new opportunities for creators to monetize their work. From AI-generated articles to automated video editing, there are countless ways in which AI can be used to create high-quality and profitable content.

Analyzing Customer Data with AI: AI can analyze vast amounts of customer data, providing creators with valuable insights into customer behavior and preferences. By leveraging this data, creators can create compelling content and marketing campaigns, improving overall customer engagement and driving revenue.

Enhancing Customer Engagement and Loyalty: AI can also improve customer engagement and loyalty, providing customers with personalized recommendations and content that resonates with their interests and preferences. By leveraging AI, creators can build stronger customer relationships and increase customer loyalty.

Access to Cutting-Edge Technologies: Finally, by embracing AI, creators can access cutting-edge technologies and previously unavailable tools. From AI-powered writing tools to automated video editing, there are countless ways in which AI can be used to enhance creativity and productivity, opening new possibilities for creators in every industry.

The Rapid Evolution of AI Tools: As AI continues to evolve and become more accessible. Creators need to stay updated with the latest tools and technologies. From automated writing tools to AI-powered chatbots, there are numerous ways in which AI is transforming the creative process and providing creators with new tools and capabilities.

Staying Updated in the AI Landscape: Finally, creators need to stay updated in the rapidly evolving world of AI. By being updated with the latest trends, creators can position themselves as experts in their field and stay ahead of their competitors. From attending conferences and events to reading industry publications, there are countless ways in which creators can stay informed and up to date on the latest developments in AI.

AI is transforming the world of creativity and productivity, providing creators with new tools and capabilities that were previously unavailable. From content creation to coding, AI is helping creators work faster, smarter, and more efficiently than ever.

By embracing AI and staying updated with the latest technologies and tools, creators can position themselves as leaders in their field and stay ahead of their competitors. With these strategies in mind, creators can open new opportunities for success in the digital age.

CHAPTER 7

The Art of Mastering Prompt Engineering

The Art of Prompt Engineering. Master Prompt Engineering In AI-powered assistants, prompts are essential for engaging and communicating effectively with users. A well-crafted prompt can help users navigate complex tasks, provide valuable information, and elicit emotional responses. In this chapter, we will explore the art and science of crafting effective prompts, and in the first few pages of this book, we provide over 3000 ready-to-use prompts for immediate profits. We'll also guide you through custom prompt creation and introduce you to advanced techniques for maximizing ChatGPT interactions. Crafting Effective Prompts Effective prompts are clear, concise, and relevant to users' needs. They should be designed to elicit a specific response or action and tailored to the user's level of experience and understanding.

Check out this site https://gptprompttuner.com/. With this site, you can use AI to Generate ChatGPT prompt iterations and run conversations in parallel.

Here are some key elements to consider when crafting effective prompts:

1. **Clarity:** The prompt should be easy to understand and convey the intended message.

2. **Relevance:** The prompt should be relevant to the user's needs and

goals and provide valuable information or guidance.

3. Actionability: The prompt should be designed to elicit a specific action or response from the user and tailored to the user's level of experience and understanding.

4. Tone: The tone of the prompt should be appropriate to the situation and designed to elicit the desired emotional response from the user. These prompts cover various topics, from business operations to marketing and branding, and are designed to be clear, concise, and action-oriented.

Custom Prompt Creation

A Step-by-Step Guide While ready-to-use prompts can be helpful, custom prompt creation allows you to tailor your prompts to your users' needs. Here is a step-by-step guide to custom prompt creation:

1. Define the Goals: Determine the specific goals you want to achieve with your prompts and identify the key actions or responses you want to elicit from your users.

2. Identify the User Needs: Understand the needs and goals of your users and identify any pain points or areas of confusion that your prompts can help address.

3. Choose the Right Tone: Determine the appropriate tone for your prompts based on the context and the emotional response you want to elicit from your users.

4. Test and Refine: Test your prompts with users and refine them based on feedback and user behavior. The Art and Science of Crafting Prompts Crafting effective prompts is both an art and a science. Design prompts that engage and communicate with users effectively require creativity, empathy, and technical knowledge.

Here are some fundamental principles to keep in mind when designing prompts:

1. User-Centered Design: Design prompts with the user's needs and goals in mind and tailor them to their experience level and understanding.

2. Emotional Engagement: Design prompts that elicit emotional responses from users, such as curiosity, excitement, or a sense of accomplishment.

3. Contextual Relevance: Design prompts relevant to the user's context and providing valuable information or guidance. Maximizing ChatGPT Interactions ChatGPT is an AI-powered assistant that utilizes natural language processing (NLP) to communicate with users effectively. To maximize ChatGPT interactions, it's essential to design prompts that are clear, concise, and tailored to the user's needs and goals.

Here are some strategies for maximizing ChatGPT interactions:

1. Use Natural Language: Design prompts that use natural language and avoid technical jargon or complex terminology.

2. Provide Clear Guidance: Design prompts that provide clear guidance and instructions and avoid ambiguity or confusion.

3. Tailor to User Needs: Design prompts tailored to users' needs and goals and provide relevant information or guidance. Advanced Techniques for Effective Prompt Design Effective prompt design requires a deep understanding of user behavior and psychology and technical expertise in NLP and AI.

Here are some advanced techniques for effective, prompt design:

1. Personalization: Use data and insights about the user to personalize prompts and provide tailored recommendations or guidance.

2. **Emotional Intelligence:** Design prompts that demonstrate emotional intelligence, such as empathy or humor, to connect with users on a deeper level.

3. **Gamification:** Design prompts incorporating gamification elements, such as rewards or challenges, to increase engagement and motivation. Using prompts effectively requires a deep understanding of user behavior and psychology and technical expertise in NLP and AI.

Here's an introduction to using prompts effectively:

1. **Identify User Needs:** Understand the needs and goals of your users and identify any pain points or areas of confusion that your prompts can help address.

2. **Craft Effective Prompts:** Craft prompts that are clear, concise, action-oriented, and tailored to the user's level of experience and understanding.

3. **Test and Refine:** Test your prompts with users and refine them based on feedback and user behavior. Prompts for Business Operations Prompts can be used to streamline business operations and improve efficiency.

Here are some examples of prompts that can be used for business operations:

1. **Order Processing:** Use prompts to guide users through the order processing and fulfillment process and provide real-time updates on order status.

2. **Customer Support:** Use prompts to provide customers with quick and easy access to customer support and guide them through the troubleshooting process.

3. **Employee Training:** Use prompts to guide employees through the

onboarding and training and provide real-time feedback and guidance. Prompts for Marketing and Branding Prompts can be used to improve marketing and branding efforts by engaging users and providing relevant information or advice.

Here are some examples of prompts that can be used for marketing and branding:

1. **Product Recommendations:** Use prompts to provide users personalized product recommendations based on their preferences and behavior.

2. **Brand Awareness:** Use prompts to educate users about your brand and its values and foster a sense of connection and loyalty.

3. **Customer Feedback:** Use prompts to gather customer feedback and insights, and use this information to improve your marketing and branding efforts. Prompts for Product Development and Innovation Prompts can guide users through the product development and innovation process and provide real-time feedback and guidance.

Here are some examples of prompts that can be used for product development and innovation:

1. **Idea Generation:** Use prompts to facilitate idea generation and brainstorming sessions and provide real-time feedback and guidance.

2. **Product Testing:** Use prompts to guide users through the product testing and feedback process and gather valuable insights and feedback.

3. **Innovation Challenges:** Use prompts to initiate innovation challenges and competitions and foster a culture of creativity and innovation. Prompts for Ethical and Responsible AI Use Ethical and responsible AI use requires careful consideration of user privacy, security, and well-being.

Here are some examples of prompts that can be used to promote ethical and responsible AI use:

1. **Privacy and Security:** Use prompts to inform users about privacy and security measures and provide guidance on protecting their data and information.

2. **Bias and Fairness:** Use prompts to educate users about bias and fairness in AI systems and provide guidance on mitigating these issues.

3. **Transparency and Accountability:** Use prompts to promote transparency and accountability in AI systems and provide users with information about how their data is used. Conclusion Effective, prompt engineering is critical to AI-powered assistance and requires creativity, empathy, and technical expertise.

By crafting effective prompts that are clear, concise, and tailored to the user's needs and goals, you can engage and communicate with users effectively, streamline business operations, and promote ethical and responsible AI use. With these strategies in mind, you can unlock new opportunities for growth and success in the digital age.

CHAPTER 8

The Limitations of AI And Critical Mistakes to Avoid

The Limitations of ChatGPT and AI

Critical Mistakes to Avoid As AI-powered assistants like ChatGPT become more prevalent daily, it's essential to understand their limitations and potential pitfalls. In this chapter, we'll explore the constraints of ChatGPT and AI and guide how to avoid critical mistakes that can lead to business collapse. We'll also discuss the importance of ensuring sustainable and ethical AI use and provide strategies for promoting responsible AI practices. Understanding the Tool's Constraints While ChatGPT and other AI-powered assistants have proven compelling tools for engaging and communicating with users, they also have limitations. One of the most considerable constraints of ChatGPT is its reliance on data. ChatGPT relies on vast amounts of data to learn and generate responses, so if the data is biased or incomplete, the reactions caused by ChatGPT may be flawed or inaccurate. Another constraint of ChatGPT is its inability to understand context and nuance. ChatGPT operates based on patterns in data, so it may struggle to understand the subtle nuances of human communication or cultural differences. As a result, ChatGPT may generate inappropriate or offensive responses in specific contexts. An Honest Look at What AI Can and Can Not Do It's important to understand what AI can and cannot do. While AI-powered assistants like ChatGPT can be compelling tools, they are not magic solutions that can solve all problems.

Here are some key things to keep in mind when using AI:

1. AI can analyze vast amounts of data quickly and accurately, but it cannot understand context or nuance.

2. AI can generate responses based on patterns in data, but it cannot understand a user's emotional state or intentions.

3. AI can automate repetitive tasks and processes, but it cannot replace humans' creativity, intuition, and decision-making abilities.

The 4 Business Collapsing Mistakes When using AI-powered assistants like ChatGPT, it's crucial to avoid critical mistakes that can lead to business collapse.

Here are four common mistakes to avoid:

1. Overreliance on AI: While AI can be mighty, overreliance on AI can lead to a lack of creativity, innovation, and human connection.

2. Lack of Transparency: Lack of transparency in AI-powered systems can lead to mistrust and suspicion among users, ultimately leading to business collapse.

3. Neglecting Ethical Considerations: Neglecting ethical considerations in AI development and deployment can lead to unintended consequences and negative impacts on users and society.

4. Failure to Adapt: Failure to adapt to changing user needs and preferences can lead to user churn and, ultimately, business collapse. Ensuring Sustainable and Ethical AI Use To ensure sustainable and ethical AI use, it's vital to prioritize transparency, fairness, and accountability.

Here are some strategies for promoting responsible AI practices:

1. **Clear Communication:** Provide clear and transparent communication about how AI-powered systems work, what data is used, and how decisions are made.

2. **Fairness and Bias Mitigation:** Prioritize fairness and bias mitigation in AI development and deployment and actively work to identify and mitigate biases.

3. **Accountability and Oversight:** Establish clear lines of accountability and oversight for AI-powered systems and ensure that mechanisms are in place to address any negative impacts.

4. **User Education:** Educate users about AI-powered systems, their limitations, and their potential impacts, and encourage user feedback and engagement.

AI-powered assistants like ChatGPT have the potential to transform the way we live and work, but it's essential to understand their limitations and potential pitfalls. By avoiding critical mistakes and prioritizing sustainable and ethical AI use, we can unlock the full potential of these powerful tools while avoiding unintended consequences and negative impacts. With these strategies in mind, we can build a more inclusive, equitable, and responsible future powered by AI.

CHAPTER 9

Innovate with AI in Product Development

Innovate with AI in Product Development Innovation is the key to success in today's fast-paced business environment. With the rise of AI-powered technologies, product development has become faster, more efficient, and more creative. In this chapter, we'll explore the role of AI in modern product development and how it can foster creativity and innovation while streamlining the product development process. The Role of AI in Modern Product Development AI has revolutionized how we approach product development. It has enabled us to analyze vast amounts of data quickly and accurately, identify patterns and trends, and make informed decisions based on that data.

AI has enabled the automation of repetitive tasks and processes, freeing up time and resources for more strategic activities. One of the critical advantages of AI in product development is its ability to identify customer needs and preferences. By analyzing customer data, AI can identify patterns and trends in customer behavior, preferences, and feedback, allowing companies to develop products that better meet customer needs. AI can also help companies anticipate customer needs and respond to changing market trends, giving them a competitive edge. Another advantage of AI in product development is its ability to optimize the product development process. AI can automate tasks such as data analysis, prototyping, and testing, making the process faster and more efficient.

AI can help companies identify potential issues or roadblocks early in development, allowing them to address them before they become significant problems. Fostering Creativity and Innovation with AI One of the most exciting aspects of AI in product development is its potential to foster creativity and innovation. By automating repetitive tasks and processes, AI frees up time and resources for more strategic activities, such as brainstorming and creativity. Additionally, AI can help teams identify new ideas and opportunities by analyzing customer data and market trends. One way that AI can foster creativity and innovation is by using generative design. Generative design is an AI-powered approach to design that uses algorithms to generate multiple design options based on specific parameters and constraints. This approach can help teams explore new design possibilities and identify innovative solutions to complex problems. AI can also be used to facilitate collaboration and communication among team members. By automating tasks such as data analysis and documentation, AI can free up time for team members to collaborate and share ideas.

AI-powered collaboration tools can help teams work together more effectively, regardless of their physical location or time zone. Streamlining the Product Development Process Another significant advantage of AI in product development is its ability to simplify the process. By automating tasks and processes, AI can make the process faster, more efficient, and more cost-effective. Additionally, AI can help teams identify potential issues or roadblocks early in the development process, allowing them to address them before they become significant problems. One area where AI can be beneficial is product testing and validation. AI-powered testing tools can automate the testing process, making it faster and more efficient.

AI can help teams identify potential issues or defects early in the testing process, allowing them to address them before the product is released. AI can also be used to optimize the supply chain and inventory management. AI can help companies optimize inventory levels and reduce waste by analyzing customer demand, market trends, and supplier performance. Additionally, AI can help companies identify potential supply chain issues and respond to these issues quickly and effectively. Best Practices for AI-Powered Product Development While AI can revolutionize product development, using this technology responsibly and ethically is essential.

Here are some best practices for AI-powered product development:

1. **Prioritize data quality:** AI uses high-quality data to generate accurate insights and recommendations. Make sure that your data is clean, complete, and unbiased.

2. **Foster a culture of innovation:** AI can help teams generate new ideas and explore new possibilities. Encourage your team to experiment and take risks.

3. **Use AI to augment human decision-making, not replace it:** While AI can automate many tasks, it cannot replace the creativity, intuition, and decision-making abilities of humans. Use AI to augment human decision-making, not replace it.

4. **Prioritize transparency and accountability:** Be transparent about how AI is used in your product development process, and establish clear lines of accountability.

5. **Ensure ethical AI use:** Ensure that AI is being used ethically and responsibly, and actively work to identify and mitigate potential biases. Conclusion AI has the potential to transform the way we approach product development. AI can help companies develop products that better meet customer needs and respond to changing market trends by automating tasks and processes, fostering creativity and innovation, and streamlining the product development process.

However, it's important to use AI responsibly and ethically and to prioritize transparency, fairness, and accountability. By following these best practices, we can unlock the full potential of AI in product development while avoiding unintended consequences and negative impacts.

CHAPTER 10

Expanding Your Horizons with AI

ChatGPT is an AI-powered chatbot that can assist users with various tasks, from answering questions and providing recommendations to generating text and facilitating conversations. In this chapter, we'll explore ways other AI tools, beyond ChatGPT, can expand your horizons in fiction and non-fiction writing, job searching, and business networking. Using AI for Fiction and Non-Fiction Writing One of the most exciting applications of AI in the world of writing is in the realm of fiction and non-fiction writing. AI Tools can generate ideas, characters, plot lines, and stories.

AI Tools can help writers overcome writer's block, generate new ideas, and experiment with different writing styles and techniques. AI Tools can create outlines, summaries, and even articles on various topics for non-fiction writing. AI can also be used to conduct research and gather information, making writing faster and more efficient. However, it's important to note that AI-generated writing should be used to augment human creativity and not as a replacement for it. AI-generated writing is still in its infancy and may only sometimes produce the best results. Therefore, using AI-generated writing as a starting point and refining and editing the output to achieve the desired result is essential. The Wolfram Enthusiast's Guide to ChatGPT For those familiar with Wolfram Alpha, an AI-powered computational knowledge engine, AI can be used to extend the features of the Wolfram platform. AI can generate text-based results and answers to complex questions that traditional search engines cannot quickly answer.

AI can interact with the Wolfram Language and perform complex calculations and analyses. This can be particularly useful for mathematics, science, and engineering professionals. Job Searching and Business Networking with AI. Another exciting application of AI is job searching and business networking. AI can generate resumes, cover letters, and even interview responses.

AI can be used to identify job openings and opportunities that match your skills and interests. AI can also facilitate business networking by generating introductions, summaries, and pitches for potential clients and partners. Additionally, AI can be used to identify potential networking opportunities and events that match your interests and goals. However, it's important to note that AI-generated job applications and networking materials should be used as a starting point, not as a replacement for human interaction. While AI can help identify opportunities and generate materials, it's still important to tailor these materials to the specific needs and interests of the recipient. Best Practices for Using AI While ChatGPT has the potential to expand your horizons in a wide range of areas, it's essential to use this technology responsibly and ethically.

Here are some best practices for using AI:

1. Understand the limitations of AI: AI-generated output is still in its infancy and may not always produce the best results. Therefore, using AI-generated output as a starting point and refining and editing the output to achieve the desired result is essential.

2. Use AI to augment human creativity, not replace it: While AI can generate ideas and materials, it cannot replace human creativity and intuition. Use AI to boost human ingenuity and not replace it.

3. Be transparent about the use of AI-generated materials: If you are using AI-generated materials in a professional context, be transparent about the use of this technology and ensure that the recipient is aware of the source of the materials.

4. Prioritize quality over quantity: While AI can generate output quickly and efficiently, it's important to prioritize quality over quantity. Spend time refining and editing the creation to achieve the desired result.

AI is an exciting technology that has the potential to expand your horizons in a wide range of areas, from writing and research to job searching and business networking. However, it's essential to use this technology responsibly and ethically and to prioritize transparency, fairness, and accountability. By following these best practices, we can unlock the full potential of ChatGPT while avoiding unintended consequences and negative impacts.

Discover how AI revolutionizes the financial market, making money brighter like never before.

Unleash the power of data analysis with AI, the ultimate game-changer. The incredible world of financial markets as data flows ceaselessly creates a mesmerizing information tapestry. With such overwhelming data, comprehensive analysis becomes a Herculean feat for mortals. Experience the power of AI algorithms, meticulously crafted to effortlessly process and analyze vast amounts of data at lightning-fast speeds. With this remarkable capability, investors gain the advantage of swift responses to market changes, unlocking a world of opportunities that were once hidden.

Risk Mitigation: Discover the art of safeguarding your investments in the dynamic world of financial markets. With its remarkable capabilities, AI is revolutionizing how we navigate the unpredictable world of market trends and risks. By harnessing its unparalleled predictive abilities, AI enables us to foresee market trends accurately and confidently. Moreover, it acts as a vigilant guardian, swiftly identifying potential pitfalls that could hinder our success. With AI, we can boldly embrace the future, knowing we have the ultimate tool to mitigate risks and unlock new opportunities. Discover the incredible power of machine learning algorithms as they delve into the depths of historical market data, economic indicators, news sentiment, and the vast world of social media activity. Witness their unparalleled ability to forecast market movements and make astute investment decisions. Prepare to be amazed as these algorithms unlock the secrets hidden within the data, providing you with the knowledge and insights needed to thrive in the ever-evolving world of investments. Embrace the future of intelligent decision-making and let machine learning algorithms guide you toward financial success.

Introducing Algorithmic Trading: Prepare to be amazed by one of the most groundbreaking advancements in the financial market - the extraordinary rise of algorithmic trading! Let's talk about cutting-edge AI-powered trading systems that have revolutionized the trading world. With lightning-fast speed and unparalleled accuracy, these systems are designed to execute trades like never before. Advanced algorithms and real-time market analysis allow them to respond to predefined conditions and capture lucrative opportunities swiftly. Say goodbye to manual trading and hello to the future of trading with AI at your fingertips. Experience the power of technology and stay ahead of the market trends with our state-of-the-art trading systems—experience lightning-fast market reactions with our cutting-edge algorithms. In milliseconds, our advanced technology empowers investors to capitalize on market changes, unlocking unparalleled opportunities for profit. Harness the power of efficiency and stay one step ahead with our game-changing algorithms.

Introducing Personalized Financial Advice: Unlocking the Power of Tailored Guidance In the past, access to financial advice was a privilege reserved for the fortunate few who could afford exclusive, one-on-one services. But now, we're revolutionizing the industry by bringing personalized financial guidance to everyone. Gone are the days of feeling left out or overwhelmed by complex financial decisions. With our cutting-edge platform, you'll have the opportunity to receive tailored guidance that caters to your unique needs and goals. Imagine having a team of expert advisors at your fingertips, ready to provide personalized strategies that align with your financial aspirations. Whether you are planning for retirement, saving for a dream vacation, or looking to grow your wealth, our innovative approach ensures that your financial journey is tailored to you.

The revolutionary power of AI is making personalized financial advice more accessible than ever before! Introducing the incredible world of robo-advisors! These cutting-edge AI-powered algorithms can evaluate your unique financial goals, risk tolerance, and investment preferences. With their unparalleled expertise, they offer personalized advice and craft bespoke investment strategies just for you. Get ready to experience the future of financial guidance with robo-advisors! Experience the revolutionary shift in finance as financial advice democratizes individuals to transform how they invest and master their wealth management.

Introducing Fraud Detection: In an industry where, financial fraud has always been a pressing concern, we have developed a cutting-edge solution to safeguard your business. Discover the incredible potential of AI as an exceptional tool for detecting and preventing fraud. Discover the tremendous power of machine learning algorithms, capable of unraveling intricate patterns and detecting anomalies within financial transactions. With their unparalleled ability, these algorithms pave the way for early detection of fraudulent activities, safeguarding your economic well-being like never before. Experience the peace of mind that comes with cutting-edge technology, as it tirelessly works behind the scenes to protect your assets and secure your financial future. Experience peace of mind and safeguard your economic well-being with our exceptional solution. Say goodbye to potential financial losses and embrace a secure future. Rest assured, our cutting-edge technology protects businesses and individuals and upholds the integrity of the financial market. Trust in our expertise to keep your economic interests safe and sound.

Experience the next level of customer satisfaction with the remarkable advancements brought about by AI in the financial market. Prepare to be amazed as AI technology revolutionizes and enhances your overall customer experience like never before. Financial institutions are now harnessing the incredible capabilities of chatbots to deliver unparalleled customer support that never sleeps. These cutting-edge technologies swiftly address queries, ensuring prompt and efficient assistance. Experience the future of customer service today! AI virtual assistants are equipped with the power to handle a vast array of customer inquiries. From checking account balances to providing expert investment recommendations, these virtual marvels are revolutionizing how we interact with customers. Say goodbye to long wait times and hello to faster, more efficient interactions.

The remarkable advantages of embracing AI in the financial market while remaining mindful of the potential obstacles and drawbacks. Discover the undeniable power of the human touch and the extraordinary impact of emotional intelligence in prosperous investing. Discover the incredible power of AI algorithms, capable of effortlessly processing immense volumes of data and making accurate predictions. However, it's important to note that while these algorithms possess remarkable abilities, they have limitations. They may need to gain the innate intuition that humans possess, preventing them from accounting for unforeseen events or capturing the ever-changing market sentiment. Let us explore the fascinating world of AI algorithms, where their strengths and limitations intertwine to shape the future of technology.

The captivating realm of algorithmic bias, where AI algorithms can inadvertently perpetuate prevailing biases within the financial market.

Developers hold a pivotal role in shaping the future of technology. As they create algorithms, they are responsible for fostering fairness and impartiality. By crafting algorithms prioritizing equity, developers pave the way for unbiased decision-making that transcends biases or prejudices. The importance of creating fair and impartial algorithms cannot be overstated in this ever-evolving digital landscape. It is a crucial endeavor that empowers us to build a world where every individual is treated with the respect and equality they deserve.

The awe-inspiring impact of AI on the financial market, where it effortlessly transforms money into a more innovative force and propels investment decisions toward a realm of unparalleled data-driven precision. Discover the extraordinary power of AI - a game-changing tool that empowers investors with its exceptional ability to process colossal amounts of data, unravel market trends, and effortlessly navigate through risks. Experience the future of investment with AI, your indispensable ally in pursuing success. In the dynamic realm of finance, finding the perfect equilibrium between the power of AI and the irreplaceable human touch is of utmost importance. Recognizing the immense value that human judgment brings, it is crucial to strike a harmonious balance between these two forces. Harness the incredible potential of AI technology and the unparalleled wisdom of human expertise to revolutionize your investment decisions. Unlock the path to a more efficient future brimming with prosperity. Unlock the Power of AI Investments: Unleash Your Potential!

The remarkable allure of AI investments, where the power of data-driven analysis reigns supreme, transcending the limitations of human emotions and biases. Discover the secret to making sound investment decisions: free yourself from emotions. Unleash the power of rationality and watch your portfolio soar to new heights. Don't let fleeting emotions jeopardize your financial success. Embrace the wisdom of clear judgment and unlock a world of profitable opportunities. It's time to take control and make decisions that stand the test of time. Say goodbye to irrationality and hello to a future of intelligent investments. Discover the remarkable world of AI, where objectivity and logic converge to revolutionize the art of investing.

Experience the incredible speed and unparalleled efficiency of AI. Experience the tremendous power of AI as it effortlessly analyzes colossal amounts of data in mere seconds or minutes, a task that would leave even the most skilled human analyst in awe. Experience lightning-fast decision-making and seize investment opportunities before they vanish into thin air.

Humans, with all their brilliance and ingenuity, are not immune to the occasional slip-up. Yes, it's true! From time to time, we may find ourselves inadvertently overlooking crucial data points or, dare we say, misinterpreting information. But fear not, for recognizing our fallibility lies the opportunity for growth and improvement. After all, through these very mistakes, we pave the way for progress and innovation. So, let us embrace our imperfections and embark on a continuous learning journey, where each misstep becomes a stepping stone toward a brighter future. AI is the ultimate solution for processing information with unparalleled accuracy and unwavering consistency. Say goodbye to the risk of errors and embrace a new era of flawless data processing.

Unlock the Power of AI Investments: Your Ultimate Guide to Getting Started

Now that you have grasped the fundamental concepts of AI investments and recognized their numerous advantages, you may ponder how to embark on this exciting journey yourself. Embark on an extraordinary AI investment journey with these carefully crafted steps:

Ignite Your Knowledge: Begin your journey by immersing yourself in AI investments. Unlock the secrets of AI in the financial realm by immersing yourself in a captivating world of books, thought-provoking articles, and enlightening videos. Delve into the depths of knowledge and gain a profound understanding of the inner workings of this cutting-edge technology. Embark on a journey of discovery as you unravel the mysteries of AI's impact on the financial landscape. Expand your horizons and empower yourself with the knowledge that will shape the future of finance.

The perfect AI investment platform that aligns seamlessly with your unique needs and preferences. Selecting a trustworthy and dependable platform is paramount to your financial success. Discover the power of informed decision-making by embarking on a research journey, immersing yourself in the realm of reviews, and delving into platform comparisons. Unleash the full potential of your discerning mind as you navigate the vast sea of options, ensuring that your final choice is nothing short of extraordinary.

Achieve greatness with the power of goal setting. Take control of your destiny and unlock your full potential. Embrace the art of setting goals and watch your dreams become a reality. Discover your financial aspirations and set your investment goals. Discover the path to enduring prosperity or seize immediate advantages - the choice is yours. Unlock the power of informed decision-making by understanding your objectives. With a clear vision, you can confidently and precisely navigate the complex world of investments. Don't leave your financial future to chance - equip yourself with the knowledge and insight to make better investment decisions. Start today and pave the way to a prosperous tomorrow.

Begin your journey by taking small steps toward your goals. You can build momentum by starting small and gradually progressing to more considerable achievements. Embrace the power of small beginnings and discover the power of starting small as a beginner. Unlock your potential with a modest investment. Immerse yourself in the platform, embrace the challenges that lie ahead, and cultivate unwavering confidence in the process.

Monitor and Adjust: Unleash the power of vigilance as you meticulously observe the progress of your investments. Stay ahead of the game by regularly assessing the performance of your portfolio, ensuring it remains finely tuned to your financial aspirations. Revamp your investment strategy effortlessly, adapting it to the ever-changing market conditions and harnessing the power of cutting-edge AI-generated insights.

Unlock the power of diversification, the ultimate key to success, just like with any investment. Diversify your investment portfolio and unlock the power of risk management while maximizing your potential for lucrative returns.

Stay ahead of the game: Stay in the loop and stay informed about cutting-edge trends and groundbreaking developments in the exciting world of AI investment. Discover the power of informed decisions and unlock your ability to adapt to the ever-changing market landscape effortlessly.

Experience the groundbreaking transformation of earning money with AI investments. Discover a world where data-driven precision, unrivaled efficiency, and unwavering objectivity converge to unlock unparalleled investment opportunities. Embrace the future of wealth creation with AI at your side. Unleash the extraordinary capabilities of AI and unlock the boundless opportunities within the financial market. Experience the sheer brilliance of making astute investment choices guided by the unparalleled intelligence of artificial intelligence.

Begin your journey by starting small, allowing yourself to grow and learn. Arm yourself with knowledge, educating yourself on the intricacies of this exciting field. And most importantly, set realistic goals that will pave the way to your success. Embrace the possibilities and embark on your AI investment adventure today. Unlock the boundless potential of AI investments as you embark on a journey of growth and prosperity. With each passing moment and every valuable experience, you will effortlessly navigate the intricate landscape of AI investments, empowering yourself to witness your earnings soar to unprecedented heights.

Don't hesitate any longer! Experience the awe-inspiring future of investing and embark on a transformative journey to elevate your earnings with the power of AI investments. Embrace this groundbreaking opportunity now!

Unleash the Power of Artificial Intelligence to Skyrocket Your Earning Potential

In the dynamic and ever-changing landscape of today's world, the pursuit of maximizing our earning potential remains a perpetual aspiration for countless individuals. The remarkable technological strides, specifically the groundbreaking realm of artificial intelligence (AI), has graciously given us many possibilities to elevate our earnings and triumphantly attain financial prosperity. Discover AI's untapped power and unlock your earning potential in today's fiercely competitive job market. Join us as we delve into AI's transformative possibilities, propelling you to new heights of success.

The remarkable potential of AI to elevate your earning capacity by amplifying your skills and abilities. Discover the limitless possibilities of AI-powered platforms and applications! Unleash your potential with vast training and development opportunities that await you. Embrace the convenience and flexibility of acquiring new skills and knowledge at your own pace. It's time to embark on a transformative journey toward personal growth and success! Unlock your full potential with AI-powered learning! Whether you aspire to master coding, digital marketing, or project management, our cutting-edge technology offers personalized courses and resources to align with your unique learning style and goals perfectly. Experience a transformative educational journey like never before. Embrace the power of AI and elevate your skills to new heights. Elevate your professional profile and unlock endless possibilities in the job market by harnessing the power of AI to enhance your skill set. With this cutting-edge technology as your ally, you'll become an invaluable asset, increasing your chances of securing lucrative positions or advancing within your organization.

Increase your earning potential with the incredible power of AI. Say goodbye to mundane and repetitive tasks as AI takes charge, automating every step of the way. Experience a new level of efficiency and productivity, allowing you to focus on what truly matters - growing your success. Let AI be your secret weapon in the pursuit of financial prosperity. Experience the freedom and efficiency of AI, empowering you to unlock your true potential. With AI by your side, you can liberate your precious time and energy, enabling you to dedicate yourself to the activities that truly matter. Say goodbye to mundane tasks and embrace the opportunity to engage in high-impact endeavors directly contributing to your financial success. Let AI be your ally in maximizing your productivity and achieving your goals. Imagine the possibilities with AI-powered tools at your fingertips. Say goodbye to the tedious tasks of data analysis, report generation, and administrative duties. With these cutting-edge tools, you'll have more time to focus on what truly matters – making strategic decisions and engaging with your clients. Let AI be your secret weapon in streamlining your workflow and unlocking your full potential. Unlock your full earning potential by harnessing the power of AI. Seamlessly optimize your workflow, supercharge your productivity, and watch your client base and project load soar. With AI as your ally, you'll deliver exceptional results in record time, leaving you with more opportunities to thrive and succeed.

Discover the incredible potential of AI in revolutionizing your financial decision-making process. Experience the power of AI-driven financial planning tools that go beyond traditional methods. Our cutting-edge technology analyzes your spending patterns with precision and accuracy, unlocking a world of personalized savings strategies explicitly tailored to optimize your finances. Say goodbye to generic advice and hello to a new era of financial success. Let our innovative tools guide you toward a brighter future. Discover a world of possibilities with these incredible tools that provide valuable insights into investment opportunities and offer brilliant suggestions to help you trim unnecessary expenses. Unleash the power of financial intelligence and make informed decisions that will pave the way to a brighter future. Unlock the power of AI to revolutionize your finances! With cutting-edge technology at your fingertips, you'll gain the upper hand in making informed choices that pave the way for exponential wealth growth and skyrocketing earning potential. Embrace the future and take control of your financial destiny today!

Discover the extraordinary impact of AI on our quest for career prospects. Say goodbye to the tedious task of sifting through endless job listings or manually sending out resumes. Discover the incredible power of AI-driven job platforms that effortlessly streamline the job search. With their cutting-edge technology, these platforms expertly match your unique qualifications and preferences with the most relevant and exciting job openings.

Say goodbye to the tedious and time-consuming search and let AI revolutionize how you find your dream job. Discover the power of these cutting-edge platforms that harness the incredible potential of machine learning algorithms. Unleash the true potential of your skills, education, and experience as these platforms meticulously analyze every aspect of your professional journey. Brace yourself for a personalized experience as you receive tailor-made recommendations and timely notifications to propel your career to new heights. Get ready to witness these platforms' transformative power as they revolutionize how you navigate the professional landscape. Discover the power of AI-driven job platforms and unlock unparalleled opportunities. Stay in the know and seize the best chances to land lucrative positions. With cutting-edge technology at your fingertips, you can elevate your career to new heights.

The exciting possibilities AI has unlocked in the gig economy are expanding your horizons beyond the conventional job market. Experience the remarkable growth of platforms utilizing cutting-edge AI algorithms to connect freelancers with clients seamlessly. Unlock the power of your skills and expertise with these incredible platforms that will captivate and entice potential clients from every corner of the globe. Unleash the power of AI-driven gig platforms to unlock a world of opportunities and skyrocket your earning potential. Seamlessly connect with a vast global market and embark on projects that perfectly align with your passions and talents.

AI's boundless possibilities open a world of untapped earning potential. But remember, in this ever-evolving landscape, staying ahead means embracing change and the cutting-edge technologies driving it. Experience the ever-changing AI landscape and stay ahead by keeping yourself updated with the latest advancements and trends. It's not just important; it's crucial for maintaining your competitive edge in today's job market. Unlock the door to boundless possibilities by immersing yourself in cutting-edge AI tools and applications. Embrace the opportunity to expand your skillset and propel your career to new heights. Dedicate precious moments to unravel the mysteries of these innovative technologies and witness firsthand how they can revolutionize your professional journey. Seize the chance to explore, learn, and grow as you embark on an exhilarating adventure into the world of AI. Your future awaits, ready to be shaped by your unwavering dedication and thirst for knowledge.

Unlock your earning power's full potential with AI's remarkable capabilities. Experience a transformative journey as it amplifies your skills, liberates you from mundane tasks, empowers you to make smarter financial choices, revolutionizes your job search, and opens up exciting opportunities in the dynamic gig economy. Embrace the future of earning with AI by your side. Unlock your full potential in the job market by harnessing the power of cutting-edge AI technologies and platforms. Elevate yourself as an invaluable asset, supercharging your productivity and paving the way for long-term financial growth. Unlock the boundless potential of AI and embark on a transformative journey to conquer your economic aspirations.

The secrets of AI and embark on a lucrative journey with the power of machine learning. Delve into the fundamentals, equip yourself with essential skills, carve out a distinctive path, take those initial steps confidently, foster fruitful collaborations, expand your network, showcase your expertise with strategic marketing, and seize the abundant job prospects. Unlock the secrets to triumph in this extraordinary realm, where boundless possibilities await those who embrace the art of perpetual growth and unwavering commitment. Embrace your insatiable curiosity and remain at the forefront of cutting-edge innovations, for only then will you ascend to the pinnacle of achievement. Unlock the boundless potential of your passion for AI and pave the way to a future brimming with promise. With an unwavering mindset and commitment to hard work, you can transform your dreams into a thriving career. Experience the sheer joy of learning and embark on an extraordinary AI journey destined to lead you to unparalleled success!

CHAPTER 11

Structuring Your AI Business

Leverage AI for Your Business: Building a Business That Earns While You Sleep The goal of any business is to generate revenue while minimizing costs. However, achieving this goal can be challenging, especially in today's competitive business landscape. Fortunately, with the emergence of artificial intelligence (AI), businesses can now leverage the power of machine learning algorithms to create a company that earns while you sleep. The key to building a successful AI-powered business is identifying areas where AI can add value. This can include automating routine tasks, improving customer engagement, optimizing business processes, and enhancing decision-making capabilities. By leveraging AI in these areas, businesses can achieve significant cost savings, increase productivity, and boost profitability. Examples to Jumpstart Your Business Process One of the best ways to get started with AI is to look at successful businesses that have already leveraged the technology to their advantage. For example, Amazon has used AI to optimize its supply chain operations, reduce costs, and improve delivery times.

Similarly, Netflix uses AI to personalize its recommendations to each user, increasing customer engagement and retention. Another excellent example of AI in action is Tesla. The company has built an AI-powered autonomous driving system that has the potential to revolutionize the transportation industry. By leveraging machine learning algorithms, Tesla's autopilot system can learn from its mistakes, improving its performance over time. The Power of ChatGPT in Business Operations One of the most exciting developments in AI is the emergence of natural language processing (NLP) technologies. Chatbots powered by NLP algorithms can conversationally engage with customers, providing personalized support and assistance. This can be incredibly valuable for businesses that want to improve customer engagement while reducing the workload on their customer support teams.

One of the most advanced NLP technologies available today is ChatGPT. This AI-powered chatbot can understand and respond to natural language queries in real time, providing a seamless customer experience. By leveraging ChatGPT in business operations, companies can improve customer satisfaction while reducing costs. Enhancing Customer Engagement with AI One of the most significant benefits of AI is its ability to personalize customer experiences. By leveraging machine learning algorithms, businesses can analyze customer data to identify patterns and preferences, providing tailored recommendations and support. This can help to improve customer engagement, retention, and loyalty. For example, AI can analyze customer behavior on e-commerce platforms, identifying customers most likely to purchase products. By providing personalized product recommendations, businesses can increase sales and customer satisfaction.

AI can also be used to improve customer support.

AI-powered chatbots can provide customers instant approval and assistance, reducing the workload on customer support teams. This can help to improve response times, reduce wait times, and increase customer satisfaction. Boosting Profitability through AI Optimization Finally, AI can optimize business processes, reducing costs and boosting profitability. By analyzing data from various sources, machine learning algorithms can identify inefficiencies and areas for improvement. This can help to streamline operations, reduce waste, and increase productivity. For example, AI can optimize supply chain operations, identifying the most efficient routes for delivery and reducing transportation costs. AI can also optimize manufacturing processes, identifying the most efficient production methods and reducing waste.

AI has the potential to revolutionize the way businesses operate. By leveraging the power of machine learning algorithms, companies can create a business that earns while they sleep. Whether automating routine tasks, improving customer engagement, optimizing business processes, or enhancing decision-making capabilities, AI can add value to every aspect of a business. So, if you want to stay ahead of the competition, now is the time to leverage AI in your business operations.

CHAPTER 12

Navigate the Digital Frontier Responsibly

As artificial intelligence (AI) continues evolving, businesses must navigate the digital frontier responsibly. The ongoing evolution of AI and ChatGPT is opening new business possibilities. However, with these possibilities come new challenges. Businesses must prepare for the next wave of AI innovations, consider the ethical implications of AI in industry, and follow best practices for responsible AI use. This chapter will discuss these topics and guide addressing potential pitfalls and challenges.

The Ongoing Evolution of AI and ChatGPT AI is rapidly evolving, and new applications for the technology are being developed every day. One of the most exciting developments in AI is the recent emergence of natural language processing (NLP) technologies such as ChatGPT. ChatGPT is an AI-powered chatbot that can respond to natural language queries in real-time, providing a seamless customer experience. ChatGPT is constantly evolving, with new versions and updates being released regularly. Businesses that must stay ahead of the competition must keep up with these updates and incorporate the latest ChatGPT features into their operations. This will enable them to provide customers with the easiest possible experience and stay ahead of the competition.

Preparing for the Next Wave of AI Innovations As AI continues to evolve, businesses need to prepare for the next wave of AI innovations. This means staying current with the latest developments in the field and identifying opportunities to leverage AI to improve business operations. One area where AI is likely to have a significant impact soon is the field of predictive analytics. These analytics use machine learning algorithms to analyze data and identify repeating patterns that can be used to make predictions about future trends.

Businesses that can leverage predictive analytics to make better-informed decisions will be at a significant advantage over their competitors. Another area where AI is likely to have a substantial impact is in the field of autonomous systems. Autonomous systems are machines that can operate without human intervention. This includes self-driving cars, drones, and robots. As these technologies evolve, businesses leveraging them to improve operations and increase efficiency will be at a significant advantage over their competitors. The Ethical Implications of AI in Business As AI continues to evolve, businesses need to consider the ethical implications of AI in industry. While AI can potentially improve almost every business operation and increase efficiency, there are also potential ethical concerns that businesses need to address. One potential moral concern is the impact of AI on employment.

As AI becomes more advanced, it has the potential to automate jobs, leading to job losses and increased economic inequality. Businesses need to consider the impact of technology like AI on employment and take steps to mitigate these effects. Another potential ethical concern is bias in AI algorithms. If the data used to educate an AI algorithm is biased, the algorithm will also be slanted. This can lead to discrimination and unfair treatment of certain people. Businesses need to ensure that their AI algorithms are free from bias and take steps to address any identified bias.

Best Practices for Responsible

AI Use To navigate the digital frontier responsibly, businesses need to follow best practices for responsible AI use.

This includes:

Transparency: Businesses need to be transparent about using AI and what data they are collecting.

Privacy: Businesses need to ensure that they are protecting the privacy of their customers and employees.

Security: Businesses must ensure their AI systems are secure and protected from cyber threats.

Accountability: Businesses need to take responsibility for the actions of their AI systems and ensure that they are not causing harm.

Human oversight: Businesses must ensure human oversight of their AI systems to prevent unintended consequences.

Addressing Potential Pitfalls and Challenges

As businesses navigate the digital frontier, they inevitably encounter pitfalls and challenges. Companies must be prepared to address these challenges and take steps to mitigate their impact. One potential pitfall is the reliance on AI for decision-making. While AI can be beneficial for making predictions and identifying patterns, it should not be the sole basis for decision-making. Businesses need to ensure that there is human oversight of AI systems and that decisions are based on a combination of AI and human input. Another potential challenge is the risk of cyber threats.

AI systems can be vulnerable to cyber-attacks, and businesses must ensure their AI systems are secure and protected. This includes regularly implementing robust security protocols and monitoring AI systems for potential threats. As AI continues evolving, businesses must navigate the digital frontier responsibly. This means preparing for the next wave of AI innovations, considering the ethical implications of AI in the industry, following best practices for responsible AI use, and addressing potential pitfalls and challenges. By doing so, businesses can leverage the power of AI to improve operations, increase efficiency, and stay ahead of the competition.

Chapter 13

Over 100 Ways to Make Money With AI

Here is a graphical representation of some of the newest AI Tools, separated by job function. In this chapter, we will discuss some of these and other new AI tools that go way beyond ChatGPT.

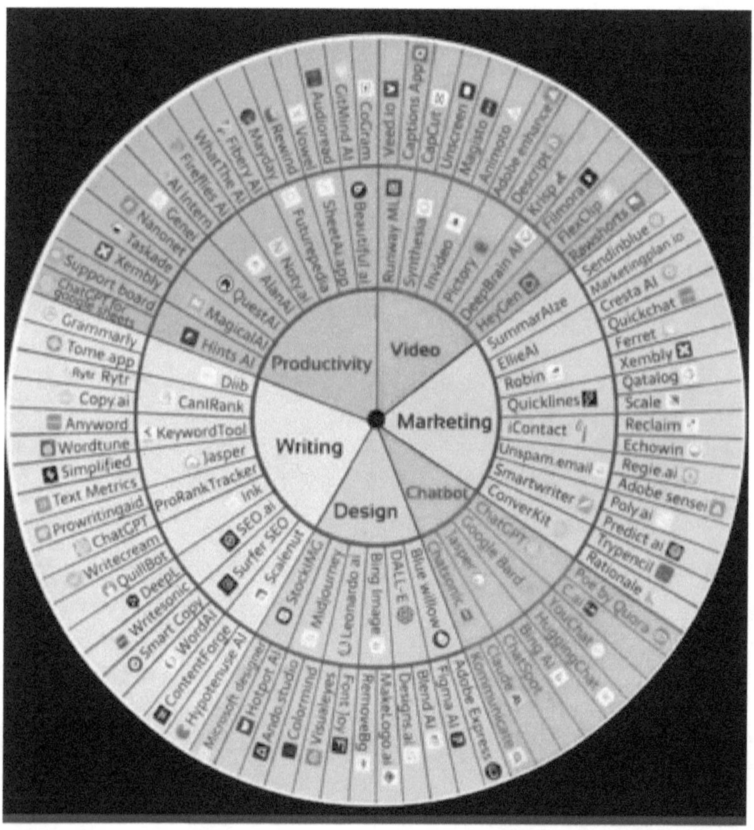

One of AI's best sites for finding new AI Tools is https://theresanaiforthat.com. Discover the latest and newest tools to captivate your interest. Bookmark this site for future searches, as it's a treasure trove of invaluable resources.

Content Creation Tools

- Write Sonic
- Beautiful AI
- Tome AI
- Murf AI
- Steve AI

Writing AI Tools

- Copy AI
- AISEO
- Jasper AI
- Quill Bot
- Rytr

Sales AI Tools

- Lavender
- Regie
- Warmer
- Twain

- Octane

Research Ai Tools

- Paperpal
- Consensus
- Writesonic
- Scholarcy
- Trinka

Marketing Tools

- Contentedge
- Copysmith
- Pepper type
- Mutiny
- Sinplified

Chatbot AI Tools

- Yatterplus
- Typewize
- Quickchat
- Cohere
- Kaizen

Copywriting Tools

- Write Sonic
- Adcreatvie
- Betha AI
- Simplified
- Articleforge

Design AI Tools

- Flair AI
- Booth AI
- Stock IMG
- Autodraw
- Clipdrop

Daily Life AI

- Taskade
- Notion AI
- Bardeen AI
- Vandy AI
- TLVR

Even more, ways to Make Money with AI

Find Unclaimed Money.

Discover the extraordinary power of cutting-edge artificial intelligence (AI) technology as it unveils a remarkable tale of individuals reclaiming their long-lost fortunes from the government's clutches. Witness the awe-inspiring impact of this viral claim as the AI tool emerges as a beacon of hope, guiding numerous individuals toward recovering their unclaimed wealth. Prepare to be captivated by this extraordinary journey of rediscovery and triumph! Discover the awe-inspiring tales of countless individuals who have harnessed the power of AI to effortlessly reclaim their hard-earned funds from none other than their State or the illustrious US government. Prepare to be captivated as these remarkable stories unfold, showcasing the potential of artificial intelligence in financial restitution.

Get Business Ideas From AI

https://topai.tools/t/validatorai. Validator AI is a cutting-edge web-based tool revolutionizing feedback and business idea analysis. With Validator AI, you can unlock the true potential of your ideas and take your business to new heights. Say adios to uncertainty and hello to success with the power of Validator AI at your fingertips. Introducing a revolutionary tool meticulously crafted to empower entrepreneurs in their quest to validate their business ideas and receive invaluable, objective feedback. Say goodbye to uncertainty and hello to a world of constructive criticism that will propel your venture to new heights. Unlock the power of foresight and gain invaluable knowledge about the viability of your business idea. Let our expert analysis guide you toward informed decisions that may shape the destiny of your entrepreneurial journey.

Turn into a Prompt Expert.

We talked about it in Chapter 6, but find your potential and embark on a lucrative career as a Prompt Engineer with the help of this exceptional website. Join the ranks of highly skilled professionals who are earning a staggering annual income of over 200k USD. Don't miss out and take advantage of this incredible opportunity to elevate your earning potential and achieve financial success. Start your journey today with https://promptify.prohttps:/or check out this site https://gptprompttuner.com/ Use AI to Generate ChatGPT prompt iterations and run conversations in parallel.

Text to Image

Go to https://www.midjourney.com/. Discover the extraordinary capabilities of this exceptional AI Tool, designed to transform text into captivating images. With an extensive collection of samples and examples at your fingertips, unleash your creativity like never before. Explore the vast realm of digital images people buy and sell on Etsy, and witness the endless possibilities that await you.

Create AI Audio Content

Unlock the power of AI and revolutionize your audio content creation with cutting-edge text-to-speech technology. Experience the seamless transformation of written words into captivating audio masterpieces, opening up a world of possibilities for your creative endeavors. Let AI be your trusted companion in crafting various types of audio content that will captivate and engage your audience like never before. Embrace the future of audio creation and unleash your imagination with the limitless potential of AI-driven text-to-speech functions. Unlock the power of your vision and effortlessly craft captivating scripts for audiobooks using the brilliance of AI prompts. With this groundbreaking technology, you can transform your ideas into mesmerizing narratives that leave listeners spellbound. And that's not all! Elevate your audiobook to new heights by harnessing the magic of a text-to-speech creator, which will breathe life into your words, infusing them with emotion and authenticity. Prepare to embark on this journey as you bring your stories to life with the perfect blend of innovation and creativity. The possibilities are endless, and the world of audiobooks is yours to conquer.

Unlock the power of AI tools to effortlessly translate videos or written content into any language you desire. Experience the seamless transformation of language barriers into global communication and understanding opportunities. With AI at your side, the world becomes your playground, where linguistic boundaries are effortlessly transcended. Embrace the future of translation and open up a world of possibilities with AI tools.

Nova A.I. software

Just may be the ultimate solution for translating and seamlessly adding captivating subtitles to your videos. With Nova A.I., https://wearenova.ai/, unlock a world of possibilities as you effortlessly bridge language barriers and captivate your audience like never before. Experience the power of Nova A.I. and take your videos to new heights of global appeal and engagement. Unlock the full potential of video creators by offering them top-notch translation services! With the power of freelance platforms like Upwork and Fiverr, you can seamlessly connect with these talented individuals and help them reach a global audience. Take advantage of this fantastic opportunity to elevate their content and expand their reach. Start providing translation services today and be the catalyst for their international success! Experience the power of text-to-speech tools, where written content effortlessly transforms into captivating audio. Immerse yourself in a world where words come alive as written text gracefully converts into an auditory masterpiece. Unlock a realm of possibilities, from translating written content into an enchanting audio format to providing a lifeline for the visually impaired. Let the magic of technology elevate your communication to new heights.

Affiliate Marketing.

Discover the incredible potential of joining an AI product affiliate program and unlock a world of limitless earning possibilities. Experience the thrill of turning your passion for cutting-edge technology into a lucrative source of income. Embrace the opportunity to monetize your expertise and seize the chance to embark on a rewarding journey towards financial success. Take advantage of the chance to transform your economic landscape - join an AI product affiliate program today! Unlock the potential of AI technology and pave your way to success by offering an array of cutting-edge products and services. Delve into machine learning software, harness the power of data analytics, and embrace the limitless possibilities of cloud-based infrastructure solutions. Elevate your business to new heights and captivate your audience with the transformative capabilities of AI. It's time to seize the opportunity and thrive in the ever-evolving world of technology.

Unlock your earning potential by harnessing the power of current market trends through the incredible opportunity of joining an exclusive affiliate program. Unlock a treasure trove of invaluable resources at your fingertips! Immerse yourself in a world of marketing materials backed by the unwavering support of our exceptional customer service team. And that's not all - brace yourself for exclusive product discounts that will leave you in awe. Prepare to be amazed by the endless possibilities that await you! Discover the tools to revolutionize your promotional efforts and propel your message to new heights. Unleash the power of optimization and unlock a world of untapped audiences. Discover the simplicity and ease of affiliate marketing, a powerful way to generate income online. Unlike the complexities of selling goods or services, with affiliate marketing, all you need to do is strategically place a link. Watch as the magic unfolds, and you earn money effortlessly when people purchase the brand's exceptional products through your link. It's time to unlock the potential of affiliate product marketing and embark on this journey toward financial abundance.

However, more than simply grasping the mechanics of affiliate marketing is required. Unlock the secret to building a thriving affiliate website with the power of meticulous preparation and strategic prowess.

Create Short Form Videos

Go to vidyo.ai/ set up a free account. Then, find a video on YouTube with 1m views. Import the video, and the AI will turn it into several short-form videos you can sell to the Youtuber, make $25-$50 per video, and do several every hour.

Generate AI Content

Let's dive into the revolutionary power of ChatGPT and other cutting-edge generative AI algorithms! Now, anyone can effortlessly produce high-quality written content in no time. Unlock the power of captivating blog post content, irresistible website copy, persuasive sales text for businesses, engaging sponsored social media posts, and more. Unlock the boundless potential of AI to craft your content effortlessly. With its remarkable capabilities, AI becomes your trusted ally in creating captivating outlines, crafting eloquent paragraphs, igniting the fires of inspiration during brainstorming sessions, and even composing entire articles with unparalleled finesse. Embrace the power of AI and witness your words come alive in ways you never thought possible. Unlock your full writing potential with our revolutionary tool for freelance writers. Say goodbye to the dreaded writer's block and hello to a seamless writing experience that will have you producing content at lightning speed. Our innovative solution is here to empower you, helping you break through barriers and unleash your creativity like never before. Get ready to take your writing game to new heights and effortlessly churn out captivating content with our game-changing support system. Say hello to productivity and bid farewell to sluggishness - it's time to write faster, write better, and conquer the freelance writing world.

Learn the art of turning your content into a lucrative money-making machine! Monetizing your valuable creations has become a widely embraced strategy for generating substantial income. Discover the tried-and-true methods that will take your blog to new heights! Unlock the power of strategic advertising by seamlessly integrating eye-catching adverts into your captivating blog content. And that's not all! Elevate your online presence with sponsored social media postings that captivate your audience and leave them craving more. Unleash the potential of these standard techniques and watch your blog soar to unprecedented success!

Unlock the secret to a steady and reliable income stream by consistently crafting captivating and one-of-a-kind content.

Discover the transformative power of AI-driven tools that will revolutionize your creativity, research, and writing processes, enhancing their efficiency to unprecedented levels. Jasper is the ultimate solution that effortlessly generates captivating content for all your needs. Whether you're looking to create a compelling blog post, a beautiful Instagram caption, or a mesmerizing YouTube script, Jasper has got you covered. With its unparalleled versatility, Jasper is your go-to tool for crafting engaging material across various platforms. Say goodbye to writer's block and hello to limitless creativity with Jasper by your side.

Unlock the power of creativity with a simple yet effective solution. Step into a world of possibilities by providing a descriptive prompt, and let our program work its magic to generate the perfect wording for you. Say goodbye to the hassle of crafting compelling content and let our innovative tool do the heavy lifting. Embrace efficiency and watch as your ideas come to life with ease. Experience the convenience of automated creativity and unlock a whole new level of productivity. Refrain from settling for the ordinary when you can have the extraordinary. Try it now and witness the transformative power of our program. Jasper is the ultimate solution to tailor your preferences and bring your vision to life. Suppose the current offering doesn't quite hit the mark, fear not! Jasper is here to revamp and renew it, ensuring it perfectly aligns with your unique taste and style. Say goodbye to settling for less and let Jasper transform it into something extraordinary.

Enhance the visual allure of your blog entries by incorporating AI-generated art from cutting-edge platforms like DALL-E, An exceptional solution tailored for those seeking a cost-effective alternative to hiring a professional artist yet still requiring a swift and captivating illustration.

Discover the remarkable potential of AI-generated content, but remember the essential role of human editing and moderation. Ensure the utmost credibility and trustworthiness of your content by diligently fact-checking every piece of information. Your audiences deserve nothing less than accurate and reliable insights.

Provide AI Integration Services

Unlock the untapped potential of your industry with the revolutionary power of machine learning and AI automation services. These cutting-edge technologies are poised to revolutionize your business from finance to healthcare, retail, and beyond. Discover the limitless possibilities and gain a competitive edge by harnessing the transformative capabilities of machine learning and AI automation. Embrace the future today and watch your industry soar to new heights of success. Are you a tech-savvy individual who possesses a deep understanding of cutting-edge technology? If so, we have an incredible opportunity for you to capitalize on your expertise and generate substantial income. You can unlock a world of financial success by providing top-notch AI integration services to companies. Take advantage of this lucrative venture that perfectly aligns with your profound technological knowledge.

Discover the incredible potential of artificial intelligence in revolutionizing your company's business intelligence. Discover the power of understanding your customers' behavior - a crucial element for brands running impactful online marketing campaigns.

Experience the power of AI's cutting-edge predictive analytics integrated seamlessly into your system. Elevate your business by unlocking the ability to identify customer behaviors, market patterns, and emerging trends like never before. With AI at your fingertips, you'll gain invaluable insights that will revolutionize your decision-making process and give you the competitive edge you need to stay ahead in today's dynamic market. Take advantage of this game-changing opportunity to optimize your business strategy and drive unprecedented growth. Embrace the future of analytics with AI's predictive capabilities.

Unlock the power of NLP models to effortlessly analyze customer reviews and feedback, allowing your agency to uncover prevailing themes and sentiments quickly. This strategy will enable individuals to craft compelling ad copy that resonates with their target audience's unique desires and challenges.

Discover the incredible potential of machine learning for retail businesses as they unlock the power of AI chatbots to revolutionize their customer service channels. Unlock the full potential of your AI by empowering it to recognize crucial keywords within customer messages effortlessly. With this cutting-edge capability, your AI will seamlessly retrieve answers from a meticulously curated database of frequently asked questions. Say goodbye to manual searches and hello to an unparalleled level of efficiency and customer satisfaction.

Enhance your business strategy by seamlessly incorporating cutting-edge recommendation algorithms. These advanced algorithms leverage valuable customer data, including purchase history, search history, and personal preferences, to provide tailored product suggestions. Elevate the shopping experience for your customers and boost sales by offering them precisely what they desire.

Offer AI Consulting

Now that I am a best-selling author in the ChatGPT / AI, people have reached out asking me if I will consult with them as they look to use AI and earn even more money online. Unlock the door to boundless financial opportunities as an esteemed artificial intelligence expert. Elevate your income potential by offering unparalleled consulting services to prestigious corporations. Unlock the potential of AI for your business! In this ever-evolving technological landscape, where AI reigns supreme, it's not uncommon for companies to feel a bit lost. But fear not! We're here to guide you towards optimal utilization of this groundbreaking technology. Let us show you the way to AI success!

Learn the potential for growth and success by pinpointing the areas your esteemed client desires to enhance. Discover the untapped potential within their existing systems, processes, and obstacles, and unlock the transformative power of AI integration.

The limitless possibilities as you embark on integrating cutting-edge AI technology into your business. Craft a compelling proposal that captures the essence of your visionary ideas and outlines the comprehensive range of AI integration services that will revolutionize your operations. Unleash the power of artificial intelligence and pave the way for unparalleled growth and success. Let your proposal be the catalyst that propels your business into a future where innovation knows no bounds. Discover the remarkable potential of outlining the specific technologies and tools you will skillfully employ, unveiling a meticulously crafted timeline for seamless implementation while envisioning extraordinary results.

The potential of your business with the unparalleled expertise, strategic prowess, and innovative approach of AI consultation services. Discover the lucrative possibilities that await as you harness the power of artificial intelligence to generate substantial revenue.

Create online courses

Learn the remarkable potential of this exceptional strategy that solidifies your status as a proper authority in your field and presents an unparalleled opportunity to generate substantial financial gains. Unlock the power of AI software to effortlessly craft and curate captivating online courses that captivate your audience and generate lucrative sales. Seamlessly delve into the realm of AI education as you empower others to harness the potential of this cutting-edge technology. Unlock the boundless potential of your creativity with advanced artificial intelligence tools like ChatGPT. Seamlessly navigate the vast landscape of ideas and topics as you craft engaging course materials. Let the power of AI be your guiding light, igniting your imagination and propelling your educational endeavors to new heights. Embrace the future of innovation and watch as your ideas flourish with the assistance of ChatGPT. Unlock the power of AI tools to revolutionize your content creation process! With cutting-edge technology, you can effortlessly craft captivating videos, generate compelling scripts, and transform text into fascinating voiceover lessons. Elevate your course materials to new heights with the help of AI, making your content creation journey a breeze. The incredible power of AI in crafting compelling marketing materials that will captivate your audience and drive sales for your online courses. With AI by your side, you'll effortlessly create irresistible content that resonates with customers, propelling your systems to new heights of success. Unleash the potential of AI and watch as your marketing efforts soar to unprecedented levels, attracting and converting customers like never before.

AI software's power to revolutionize how you showcase and promote your lessons, captivating a wider audience and attracting a surge of eager customers. Unlock the power of AI technology to revolutionize your market research phase. Are you looking to create an exceptional coding course? Look no further! With the incredible power of ChatGPT, you can unlock invaluable insights into the world of programming languages. Discover the secret to captivating your target audience and crafting a course that leaves a lasting impact. Let ChatGPT be your guide on this exciting journey of educational excellence.

Create an AI Chatbot.

Maybe you have heard about this one, but you had no idea what it even means. Well, let's unlock the boundless potential of your expertise in natural language programming and machine learning! With your remarkable skills, you have the power to craft an extraordinary chatbot that will captivate companies worldwide. Imagine the thrill of creating a cutting-edge solution that seamlessly interacts with users, revolutionizing the way businesses engage with their customers. Embrace this incredible opportunity to showcase your talent and reap the rewards of selling your innovative creation to eager companies seeking to enhance their customer experience. The possibilities are limitless when you combine your expertise with the lucrative world of chatbot development. Seize this moment and embark on a journey that will redefine the future of communication! Unlock the potential of AI-driven wealth creation! Embarking on this exciting journey may require a modest investment of time and a solid educational foundation, such as a college degree or specialized courses in AI programming.

Generate Art

Unleash your creativity with cutting-edge AI tools like DALL-E, Stable

Diffusion, and Midjourney. These powerful tools empower you to create prompts that bring captivating images to life. With their help, anyone can tap into limitless imagination and unlock a world of visual possibilities. Let your ideas take flight as you harness the incredible potential of these remarkable AI companions. The power to generate stunning images is now at your fingertips. Unlock the full potential of AI-generated ideas by providing exquisitely detailed prompts. Delve into the depths of specificity and witness the awe-inspiring results that await. With each additional morsel of information, the AI's creative prowess flourishes, conjuring images that transcend the ordinary. So, embrace the power of precision and witness the extraordinary unfold. Discover the incredible possibilities that await you on platforms like PromptBase. Unleash your creativity and unlock your potential by effortlessly listing and selling your captivating prompts. But that's not all – immerse yourself in a world of inspiration as you effortlessly find and craft unique prompts that will leave your audience in awe. With PromptBase, the power to create, share, and monetize your ideas has never been more accessible. Join us today and embark on a journey of limitless imagination.

Unlock the boundless potential of your artistic creations! Transform your art into captivating NFTs, allowing you to showcase and sell your masterpieces like never before. And why stop there? Seamlessly convert your AI-generated art into delightful memes that entertain and serve as a lucrative source of income. Embrace the power of innovation and monetize your artistic genius today! Unlock the full potential of your AI-generated art by transforming it into captivating physical products that will leave a lasting impression. Imagine the sheer delight of owning a one-of-a-kind masterpiece meticulously crafted from your very own creative algorithms. The possibilities are endless, from stylish t-shirts that exude artistic brilliance to mesmerizing wall art that transforms any space into a gallery and enchanting decorations that breathe life into your surroundings. Embrace the power of your AI-generated art and let it transcend the digital realm, captivating hearts and minds in the tangible world.

Discover the incredible world of AI art generators, where your imagination comes to life with the stroke of a keyboard. Like ChatGPT's ability to craft captivating written content and mesmerizing melodies, these cutting-edge tools empower you to unleash your creativity and bring visually stunning masterpieces into existence. By simply inputting specific parameters, you'll embark on a journey where artistry knows no bounds. Prepare to be amazed as the realm of visual art becomes your canvas, waiting to be transformed into breathtaking creations. Introducing the extraordinary world of AI art generators! Prepare to be amazed by the brilliance of products like DALL-E, DeepDream, and NeuralStyle. These cutting-edge technologies are now pushing the boundaries of artistic expression, harnessing the power of artificial intelligence to produce mind-blowing masterpieces. Immerse yourself in a realm where imagination meets innovation, and witness the awe-inspiring results that these remarkable tools can achieve. Step into the future of artistry and let your creativity soar with these incredible.

Unlock the boundless potential of AI art and embark on a lucrative journey toward financial prosperity. Discover the captivating realm where creativity meets cutting-edge technology and witness the extraordinary possibilities that await you. Delve into the realm of AI art and uncover the secrets to transforming your passion into a profitable venture. Explore the myriad avenues for monetizing AI art and let your imagination soar.

Unlock the potential of your artistic genius by transforming your creations into captivating prints or mesmerizing digital copies. Elevate your artistry to new heights by venturing into the world of NFTs, where your designs can be transformed into unique digital assets that are highly sought after. And why stop there? Let your AI art transcend the digital realm and come to life on a stunning merchandise line featuring trendy t-shirts, stylish mugs, and fashionable tote bags. Embrace the power of your creativity and unleash its full potential in commerce.

Build Websites

Unlock the limitless potential of AI and revolutionize your web development journey. Harness the power of artificial intelligence to construct stunning websites that captivate and engage your audience effortlessly. Experience the seamless fusion of cutting-edge technology and unparalleled creativity as you embark on a transformative digital experience. Embrace the future of web development with AI as your trusted ally, and watch Unlock the potential of your websites and watch the income flow in! With our expert guidance, you'll discover the lucrative opportunities of selling or utilizing these sites to generate income through the power of affiliate product marketing, Google AdWords, or subscriptions. Take the chance to turn your websites into money-making machines! Experience the seamless wonders of platforms like WIX, Site123, and Webador. These innovative tools harness the power of artificial intelligence to bring your website dreams to life. Say goodbye to the complexities of traditional website creation and embrace the future of effortless design. Building an amazing and stunning website has never been easier with these remarkable platforms at your fingertips. Discover the possibilities and unlock your online potential with AI-powered website builders like WIX and Site123, and Discover the incredible potential of https://www.framer.com/ - the ultimate platform that empowers you to effortlessly create stunning websites, whether it's for your personal use or to showcase and sell to others. Unleash your creativity and bring your visions to reality with Framer, the game-changing tool that will revolutionize your web design experience. Take advantage of this opportunity to elevate your online presence and unlock endless possibilities. Visit https://www.framer.com/ today and embark on a journey of limitless web design mastery.

Unlock a world of limitless possibilities by launching your very own website. Experience the boundless potential to generate income and take control of your financial future. Discover the incredible power of AI tools in revolutionizing website creation. Unleash your creativity and watch these cutting-edge technologies effortlessly transform your vision into stunning, professional websites. Experience the future of web development today with AI at your fingertips. Unlock the power of web development and tap into a world of endless possibilities. You can craft stunning websites catering to small business clients' needs with your skills. But why stop there? Imagine the potential for generating revenue through affiliate marketing, captivating ads, and lucrative subscription sales. The digital realm is your canvas, and with your expertise, you can transform it into a thriving source of income. Embrace the art of web creation and watch your entrepreneurial dreams come to life.

Discover the incredible power of website-building tools like Wix and other innovative platforms that empower individuals to create stunning, professional-grade websites effortlessly. With an array of captivating templates and the revolutionary Wix Artificial Design Intelligence (ADI) at your fingertips, you can now bring your online presence to life easily. Unleash your creativity and watch your website transform into a visually captivating masterpiece that leaves a lasting impression on your audience. Experience the power of creating stunning websites in a flash! Our platform covers you whether you're looking to impress clients with professional designs or boost your sales through captivating product showcases and affiliate marketing. Say goodbye to time-consuming website development and hello to effortless success!

Unlock the potential of your online presence with a stunning website that captivates audiences and drives results. Whether you're looking to sell products, monetize your content through online advertising, or join a lucrative affiliate program, a visually appealing website is the key to expanding your reach and attracting more customers than ever before.

Experience the incredible possibilities of the digital age with the rapid advancement of artificial intelligence. Now, effortlessly bring your website to life and unlock the potential to generate substantial income, regardless of your technical expertise. Discover the incredible world of website builders, where cutting-edge AI-powered tools seamlessly transform the art of building a website into an accessible and awe-inspiring experience.

Discover the incredible power of Hostinger Website Builder, where innovation meets simplicity. Our cutting-edge AI Heatmap feature will unlock the secrets of your website's success. Unleash the potential of your online presence as you effortlessly identify the captivating elements that draw visitors in. Experience the thrill of understanding what captures your audience's attention with Hostinger Website Builder.

Create YouTube Videos

Unlock the power of AI tools and unleash your creative potential! With these cutting-edge technologies at your fingertips, you can effortlessly craft captivating videos for YouTube that will captivate your audience and drive your promotional or sales efforts to new heights. Say goodbye to the days of complex video editing and hello to a world of limitless possibilities. It's time to take control of your destiny and make your mark in the digital realm. Let AI be your trusted ally in the pursuit of success! ChatGPT - your ultimate creative companion for video production! With its remarkable ability to generate captivating video ideas and craft compelling scripts, ChatGPT is here to revolutionize your content creation process. Say goodbye to writer's block and hello to an endless stream of innovative concepts and engaging narratives. Let ChatGPT be your trusted ally.

An incredible feature that will take your videos to the next level - the program's remarkable text-to-speech capability! With this cutting-edge functionality, you can effortlessly transform your written content into captivating voiceovers that will captivate and engage your audience like never before. Say goodbye to the limitations of traditional narration and let your words come alive with the power of our state-of-the-art technology. Elevate your videos to new heights with the program's exceptional text-to-speech feature.

The power of evergreen videos - the ultimate source of recurring passive income! Picture this: videos that stand the test of time, captivating audiences with their timeless content. And here's the best part - these videos can effortlessly generate revenue through ad placements or strategically embedded affiliate links. Say goodbye to fleeting trends and hello to a sustainable income stream that keeps on giving. Get ready to unlock the potential of evergreen videos and watch your earnings grow!

YouTube Automation

https://invideo.io simplifies video creation with ready-made templates that you can quickly customize even if you've never done it before. To make money, create a niche, make 1 video per day, and spend some money on ads to get traffic.

Write e-Books or Articles and blogs.

Discover the incredible earning potential of freelance writing! ZipRecruiter reports that the average freelance writer brings in an impressive $68,690 annually. Unleash your creativity and passion for words while enjoying a lucrative career in freelance writing. Join the ranks of successful writers reaping the rewards of their talent and hard work. Embrace the freedom and flexibility of being a freelance writer, all while earning a substantial income. Take advantage of this incredible opportunity to turn your experience into a weekly windfall of over $1,000! Imagine a world where your writing prowess knows no bounds. Picture yourself effortlessly crafting masterpieces at lightning speed, all thanks to the ingenious assistance of ChatGPT. With its remarkable ability to outline and conduct research, your writing process will be elevated to unprecedented levels of efficiency and productivity. Say goodbye to the days of struggling to find inspiration or spending countless hours on tedious research. Embrace the power of ChatGPT and unlock your true potential as a writer. The possibilities are endless, and the future of your writing journey is brighter than ever. Unlock your earning potential and maximize your time efficiency.

Unlock the full potential of your affiliate marketing website with the incredible assistance of ChatGPT. Seamlessly enhance your article writing process and captivate your audience like never before. Experience the power of ChatGPT as it effortlessly crafts compelling content that drives conversions and boosts your online presence. Elevate your affiliate marketing game and watch your website soar to new heights with ChatGPT by your side. Unlock the incredible potential to generate income by showcasing and endorsing exceptional products on your website. Experience the thrill of earning money through the power of sales. Discover the excellent potential of ChatGPT, your ultimate ally in uncovering highly profitable affiliate programs for you to join.

Social Media Management

Unlock the power of ChatGPT to craft captivating and persuasive social media content that will effortlessly elevate your affiliate website's promotional efforts. Unlock the untapped potential of social media earnings with ChatGPT - the ultimate tool for influencers. Elevate your content creation game and maximize your profits like never before. With ChatGPT, influencers can craft captivating and highly engaging content in record time. Say goodbye to the mundane and hello to a world of limitless possibilities. Supercharge your social media presence and watch your earnings soar to new heights with ChatGPT.

Unlock the full potential of your business with ChatGPT, your ultimate assistant. But that's not all - leverage your expertise as a social media manager and watch your services soar to new heights. With ChatGPT by your side, you'll effortlessly captivate other companies with unparalleled skills in managing their social media presence. It's time to seize the opportunity and become the go-to social media guru in the industry. Let ChatGPT empower your entrepreneurial journey and propel your success as a sought-after social media manager. Unlock the power of ChatGPT and master the art of crafting captivating content. Harness the specialized skill of utilizing ChatGPT to create the perfect type of content that leaves a lasting impression. Unlock the full potential of your skillset as the program's capabilities soar to new heights. Embrace the rising demand for your expertise and watch your value skyrocket.

FIVVER / Upwork

Online platforms like Upwork and Fiverr are crucial in today's interconnected digital world. These platforms connect freelancers and clients, offering several opportunities in various fields. You have more options with AI skills. You must explore these platforms to determine how to use them to capitalize on your AI skills. AI has spread to healthcare, marketing, data analytics, visual design, and content development. Many Upwork and Fiverr job ads are automated or augmented with AI. Machine learning techniques for predictive analytics and Natural Language Processing (NLP) for chatbots can make these jobs more efficient and productive. Select your AI interests or expertise first. Are you passionate about machine learning algorithms? Are you an NLP practitioner?

You may be an AI data analyst or picture recognition expert. After choosing your specialty, create compelling Upwork and Fiverr profiles to showcase your skills. Show your AI expertise with a complete portfolio and past work. However, creating a profile is not enough. You must act. Browse job and gig listings to find tasks that interest and match your skills. Make personalized proposals to potential clients. Explain how AI can help their project and why you're the best choice. Your AI talents can set you apart from competitors that use traditional methods. Look for long-term or recurring tasks. Sometimes, long-term customer ties are necessary for freelance success. If you show that your AI skills can regularly create high-quality results, you'll get more work and predictable revenue. Not to mention financial benefits. Specialized skills like AI are often paid more. Thus, you will like your work and make an excellent livelihood. The global AI market will multiply in the coming years, increasing the need for AI specialists. Now is a great moment to get engaged.

Finally, Upwork and Fiverr offer the best chance to sell your AI skills. Establishing AI expertise, creating an attractive profile, and aggressively pursuing and responding to suitable jobs will boost your online revenue. Don't delay—immerse yourself in these platforms and use AI to grow your freelance career.

Create a Meme

Would you like to learn to turn any Meme into an NFT and sell it repeatedly? Go to https://memechat.app/blogs/the-meme-club.html and discover the untapped potential of memes - a lucrative realm of endless possibilities! Unleash the power of these digital sensations and witness the incredible financial rewards that await. Be amazed as memes become your gateway to substantial wealth and success. Embrace the meme revolution and seize the opportunity to turn your creativity into big money! Unleash your creativity and tap into the power of MemeChat, the ultimate app for meme enthusiasts! With MemeChat, you can craft and share memes while earning serious cash.

Join the MemeChat revolution today and let your memes take the world by storm! Unlock the power of earning money effortlessly with our revolutionary app! Picture this: You have the incredible opportunity to share hilarious memes with someone who has yet to experience the wonders of our app. And the best part? You'll be rewarded handsomely for your efforts, even if they need to download or register. Get ready to embark on a journey of meme-sharing and financial gain like never before!

Discover the transformative power of AI prompting with our comprehensive learning program. Unlock your potential and become a master in this cutting-edge technology. Embrace the future and embark on a journey of knowledge and skill development.

Let us guide you toward success in the exciting world of AI prompting. Say goodbye to mundane and uninspiring text and say hello to captivating and engaging content that will leave your audience wanting more. The revolutionary world of prompting frameworks! Experience the power of seamless guidance and effortless navigation. Unleash your potential with cutting-edge tools to enhance productivity and streamline your workflow. Unlock the full potential of your language model with the art of fine-tuning. Elevate your LLMs to new heights by harnessing the power of prompts. Experience the magic of tailored text generation as you guide your model towards unparalleled performance. With fine-tuning,

Unlock the power of communication with AI by mastering the 2nd step: Discover the art of conversing with artificial intelligence. Discover a world of individuals yearning to harness the power of AI for unparalleled excellence. Discover your true potential. Unleash the extraordinary within you. Explore the endless possibilities of who you can become. Unlock your potential with our cutting-edge office solutions. Whether you're a thriving business, a budding entrepreneur, or a dedicated student, we have the tools and resources to elevate your success. Experience the power of efficiency and productivity with our innovative office products. Maximize your potential, seize opportunities, and conquer your goals with our tailored solutions. Join the Unlock the secret to a lucrative income stream by directing your attention towards businesses.

Unleash the power of AI to revolutionize your service and embark on a growth journey, starting with a small but mighty step. The all-new, revolutionary text rewriting service! Experience the power of captivating copywriting as we transform. Unlock the full potential of your workforce with our cutting-edge training program tailored specifically to empower your employees in harnessing the remarkable capabilities of ChatGPT.

Elevate your business to new heights as your team becomes proficient in leveraging this game-changing technology. Experience the transformative power of ChatGPT training and witness the seamless integration of innovation into your daily operations. Unlock the extraordinary potential of your business with our expertly crafted design prompts that work like pure magic.

Discover the transformative power of ChatGPT and unlock its full potential by equipping your esteemed workforce with the essential knowledge and skills to harness its capabilities. Elevate your team's expertise and efficiency through our comprehensive employee training program, meticulously designed to empower them with the proficiency to navigate and utilize ChatGPT's remarkable features seamlessly. Witness a new era of productivity and seamless communication as your employees become adept at leveraging the immense benefits of Unlocking the power of ChatGPT and joining the ranks of countless individuals who have already experienced its incredible benefits.

Discover a more innovative way to obtain your ChatGPT account and embark on a journey of enhanced communication and limitless possibilities. Take advantage of this opportunity to connect with the future - seize it now!

Discover the ultimate tool for unleashing your creativity - a prompt generator that will ignite your imagination like never before! Whether you are a writer, artist, or simply seeking inspiration, this remarkable tool will guide you to limitless ideas. Unleash your creative genius and embark on a journey. Unlock the power of effective communication by simply asking questions in plain and straightforward language. With the help of AI, your queries can be seamlessly transformed into well-structured and organized prompts.

Experience the ease and efficiency of this innovative solution today! Revolutionize your business with the cutting-edge prompt generator! Experience a game-changing transformation as you deploy this powerful tool into your operations. Unlock a world of endless possibilities and ignite creativity like never before. Seamlessly integrate the prompt generator into your business and witness its remarkable impact on your team's productivity and innovation. Take advantage of this game-changing solution: Say goodbye to the pressure of being a pro at prompting all employees!

Unlock your creativity with the extraordinary power of our prompt generator. Experience the exhilarating rush of inspiration as you delve into a world of endless possibilities. No longer will you be plagued by the dreaded writer's block - our prompt generator will ignite your imagination and propel you toward unparalleled success. Don't Experience the convenience and simplicity of a one-time contract. This is an incredible opportunity to own this remarkable item, priced at an unbeatable range of $3000 - $5000. This is your chance to acquire an exceptional piece that will elevate your lifestyle and bring unparalleled satisfaction. Take advantage of this extraordinary offer - act now and make it. Unlock the potential of your business with our exclusive subscription package, priced at an unbeatable $300+ per month.

Experience the transformative power of AI Agents as they revolutionize your operations and propel your business to new heights. Take advantage of this incredible opportunity to build, deploy, and harness the full potential of cutting-edge artificial intelligence technology. Introducing our revolutionary AI Agent, the ultimate solution for effortlessly managing your business emails! Say goodbye to the tedious task of composing replies, and let our cutting-edge technology do the work for you. With our AI Agent, you'll experience unparalleled efficiency and professionalism, ensuring that every email response is crafted to perfection. Streamline your communication process and elevate your business to new heights with our game-changing AI Agent.

Agent, equipped with the remarkable ability to analyze data like never before. With advanced algorithms and unparalleled processing power, this revolutionary tool effortlessly transforms raw information into comprehensive weekly and monthly reports. Say adios to tedious manual data analysis and hello to efficiency and accuracy. Let our AI Agent take the reins and unlock the true potential of your data-driven decision-making.

Experience the future of reporting today. AI Agent, the ultimate solution for resolving customer complaints! Say goodbye to frustrating interactions and hello to seamless problem-solving. Our cutting-edge Chatbots are designed to provide unparalleled assistance, ensuring customer satisfaction every step of the way. Our AI Agents are ready to tackle any challenge with their advanced capabilities, delivering prompt and efficient resolutions.

Experience the future of customer service with our Unlock the potential of these exceptional agents by offering them as an irresistible subscription and introducing our exquisite collection of high-ticket products. Unlock the secret to skyrocketing your income. Revolutionize your workflow with the power of automation. Streamline your processes and maximize efficiency like never before. Say goodbye to tedious tasks, and hello. Discover the hidden gems within your business by identifying all those repetitive and mundane tasks just begging for innovation. Uncover the true potential of your operations by pinpointing the areas where efficiency and excitement can be injected, transforming the ordinary into the extraordinary. Let us help you break free from the chains of monotony and unlock a world of endless possibilities.

Say goodbye to the mundane and hello to a future filled with Unlock the power of automation with the dynamic duo of Zapier and Make. Transform your workforce into ChatGPT experts with our comprehensive employee training program. Unlock the full potential of your team by equipping them with the knowledge and skills needed to harness the power of ChatGPT. Empower your peers and coworkers to deliver exceptional customer experiences and drive business success through our cutting-edge training curriculum. The revolutionary "Prompt Generator" - your ultimate shortcut to bypass extensive training! With this advanced tool, you can effortlessly fast-track your progress and achieve remarkable results in no time. Say goodbye to the tedious hours spent on traditional training methods and embrace the power of innovation.

Unlock your full potential with the Prompt Generator and witness your teams' skills soar to new heights. Get ready to revolutionize your learning journey like never before! Introducing our revolutionary solution: the ability to construct and implement cutting-edge AI agents seamlessly within any business environment. With our expertise, your company can harness the power of artificial intelligence to drive unprecedented growth and efficiency.

Say goodbye to outdated practices and hello to a new era of innovation. Let us help you build and deploy AI agents to revolutionize your business operations. Embrace the future. Design and embed AI automation. Revolutionize your workflow with the power of artificial intelligence. Seamlessly integrate intelligent automation into your processes and watch your productivity soar. Say adios to manual tasks and hello to efficiency like never before. With our expertly crafted designs and seamless embedding, Unlock the power of training, AI agents, and automation to secure a lucrative $20,000 contract for your esteemed company. Alternatively, revel in the exceptional opportunity to receive a generous monthly compensation of $5000. Embrace the future of business with cutting-edge technology and elevate your success to unprecedented heights. The all-new and improved version of AI - now, that's what we call a game-changer!

50 of the newest, most popular AI Tools.

1. https://godmode.space AI-powered formula generation, data preparation & and data analysis combined into one tool.

2. http://Formulabot.com Supercharge Excel and Google Sheets

3. https://promptchan.ai Create Your Dream Girl with AI.

4. http://Cohesive.so Next-generation AI editor

5. https://learningstudioai.com the next-gen online course creation tool

6. http://Tldv.io Advanced meeting assistant

7. https://www.uimagic.io/ Unlock the future of website design with the power of AI-driven User Interface technology.

8. http://Swimm.io Generate codebase docs in IDE.

9. https://venturusai.com/ Turn your business idea into reality!

10. http://Kaiber.ai Captivating visuals from image or text

11. https://text-to-video.vercel.app Create videos from text with Artificial Intelligence

12. http://Airops.com/sidekick AI data sidekick

13. https://www.magicslides.app Say bye-bye to boring, laborious presentations making.

14. http://Tripnotes.ai AI travel assistant

15. https://www.tutorai.me/ An AI-driven platform that allows users to quickly and easily learn about any topic of their choosing.

16. http://Meetcody.ai AI assistant trained on your biz

17. https://agentgpt.reworkd.ai AgentGPT is a browser-based AI tool used for creating, configuring, and deploying autonomous AI agents. Using its intuitive interface, users can easily assemble agents for various tasks and objectives.

18. https://scisummary.com Use AI to summarize scientific data in seconds.

19. https://jobhuntmode.com/ Whether seeking advancement or a fresh start, this AI career service platform holds the key.

20. https://www.imagetocaption.ai Unlock the Power of Your Images for Social Media

21. https://stratup.ai/ AI-Powered Startup Ideas and Tools to Fuel Your Entrepreneurial Journey

22. https://simplerlist.com/ A productivity assistant that helps you get things done.

23. https://gptprompttuner.com/ Use AI to Generate ChatGPT prompt iterations and run conversations in parallel.

24. https://photoai.com Create beautiful AI photos with different lighting and outfits without a camera.

25. https://gptexcel.uk/ An ideal solution for individuals and businesses looking to streamline their spreadsheet processes.

26. https://codeamigo.dev/ An AI-powered assistant that helps you learn to code like a developer.

27. https://vcai.mpi-inf.mpg.de/projects/DragGAN Drag Your GAN is an AI tool developed for controlling generative adversarial networks (GANs) with increased flexibility, precision, and generality.

28. https://ultrabrainstomer.com/ An AI-powered productivity tool that helps create social media posts, product campaigns, speeches, and emails.

29. https://www.scholarcy.com/ An online summarizing tool that provides a convenient way to quickly assess and evaluate the importance of documents such as articles, reports, and book chapters.

30. https://business-generator.vercel.app/ An AI-based tool that helps users generate business ideas by answering questions.

31. https://www.smexy.ai/ The easiest, fastest, and best platform to develop and share your fantasies. Create, tune, and enjoy your art in minutes.

32. https://eightify.app Extract insights from YouTube videos in seconds.

33. https://www.gptinf.com Bypass AI content detection.

34. https://stockimg.ai/ Create images with artificial intelligence.

35. https://stunning.so/ Website generator that allows users to generate websites, including copy and images, in seconds.

36. https://appintro.io/ai-story-generator-novel-writer AI-powered application that enables users to create their own unique stories and novels with ease.

37. https://generated.photos/humans AI tool designed to generate realistic whole-body images.

38. https://autogpt.thesamur.ai/ Chatbots site with GPT models, prompts, and chat history.

39. https://www.d-id.com Transform photos into video presenters at scale.

40. https://ailawyer.pro/ Personal AI lawyer at your fingertips.

41. https://kaiber.ai/ An AI creative lab on a mission to unlock creativity through robust and intuitive generative audio and video.

42. https://audioread.com/ Use AI to listen to articles, PDFs, emails, etc. in, your audio player. Read while walking, driving, cleaning.

43. https://mytales.io/ Creative writing and image visualization assistant.

44. https://www.voicify.ai An AI-based music platform that allows users to create custom songs with the voices of their favorite artists.

45. https://ess.ai/ An AI-powered no-code platform that lets users build websites 10X faster.

46. https://www.openread.academy/ An AI-powered platform that provides users with a comprehensive way of organizing, interacting with, and analyzing various literature.

47. https://www.fineshare.com/finecam/ An AI virtual camera specially designed for video recording and video conferencing.

48. https://chatmind.tech/ AI Mind Mapping & Brainstorming by GPT-4.

49. https://www.save.day/ A bot that allows users to quickly capture and save various content, such as web pages, blogs, articles, and PDFs.

50. https://tethered.ai/ Research, Write, and share. Search the web to compile notes, so you can edit & share.

Thank You

You could have picked from hundreds of other books, but you bought mine, and I appreciate it. Thank you so much for purchasing my book.

Not that you enjoyed (I hope) my book, can I ask you for a tiny favor? Can you please post a review on the platform? You posting a review is the best way to support the work of independent authors like me.

Your feedback will help me keep writing the books that will help you get the desired results. It means a lot to me to hear from you.

I am happy for anyone to reach out to me for help, comments, collaboration ideas, or feedback at brian@brianscottfitzgerald.com

Visit my author page with this link or Scan this QR code

https://www.amazon.com/author/brianscottfitzgerald.

www.ingramcontent.com/pod-product-compliance
Lightning Source LLC
LaVergne TN
LVHW100259210926
848480LV00003B/965
* 9 7 9 8 3 4 9 5 3 4 5 0 8 *